SEYMOUR ?

CAMPAIGNING

ON THE

UPPER NILE AND NIGER

Elibron Classics
www.elibron.com

Elibron Classics series.

© 2005 Adamant Media Corporation.

ISBN 1-4021-8975-3 (paperback)
ISBN 1-4021-1088-X (hardcover)

This Elibron Classics Replica Edition is an unabridged facsimile
of the edition published in 1898 by Methuen & Co.,
London.

CAMPAIGNING

ON THE

UPPER NILE AND NIGER

LIEUTENANT SEYMOUR VANDELEUR, D.S.O.

From a Photograph by the Stereoscopic Co.

CAMPAIGNING

ON THE

UPPER NILE AND NIGER

BY

SEYMOUR VANDELEUR, D.S.O.
LIEUTENANT, SCOTS GUARDS

WITH AN INTRODUCTION BY

Sir GEORGE T. GOLDIE, K.C.M.G., D.C.L., LL.D.

WITH MAPS, ILLUSTRATIONS, AND PLANS

METHUEN & CO.
36 ESSEX STREET, W.C.
LONDON
1898

PREFACE

I MUST plead as an excuse for writing this book the interest now being taken in the countries about the source of the Nile, to which a railway is hastening from the East Coast, and in the valuable Niger territories which recent events have brought so prominently before the public. My grateful thanks are due to Sir George Goldie for having honoured me by writing an Introduction.

I am much indebted to Lieutenant A. H. Festing for allowing me to make use of his drawings for the *Graphic* during the Niger Sudan Campaign, which, by the courtesy of the Editor, I have been able to reproduce.

I have also to thank the Manager of the *Times* for kind permission to make use of letters which I wrote for the *Times* on the Niger, and Major Pulteney, D.S.O., Mr. Edward Heawood, M.A., and Dr. Scott Keltie, for their kind assistance in looking over the proofs.

I have done my best to eliminate the dull record of latitudes and longitudes, and of the geographical work, which is embodied in the maps at the end of the book,

b

but which gave me an absorbing interest in these countries, an interest to which I feel I owe my comparative immunity from fever.

I cannot conclude without paying a tribute to those brave native troops—Sudanese and Hausas—who help to keep up the prestige of the British Empire at her farthest African outposts, where in East or West Africa hardly a day passes without a shot being fired in its defence.

SEYMOUR VANDELEUR, D.S.O.,
Lieut., Scots Guards.

BERBER, SUDAN,
19*th January* 1898.

CONTENTS

LIST OF ILLUSTRATIONS

MAPS

INTRODUCTION[1]

IF, in the year of grace when Her Majesty was born, a traveller had combined in a single volume his experiences on the Nile and Niger, the incongruity of the subjects would have then appeared almost as great as though the rivers had been the Ganges and St. Lawrence. We now know that the vast regions between the Nile and the Niger are so closely connected by unity of religious faith and by internal commerce, that political events on the one stream react upon the other; we recognise that the Nile and Niger questions

[1] Some months ago I promised Lieutenant Vandeleur, who has since gone to the Upper Nile, to write an Introduction to his book dealing with the Nupe War. I could do no less for one of the thirty-four officers whose high qualities carried us successfully through perhaps as hazardous an enterprise as any in which so small a force has ever been engaged. It did not at that time seem possible that the negotiations in Paris would not have come to a close before the book appeared. I have no reason to suppose that the author has inserted anything that could give offence in France or prejudice the negotiations; but in view of my quasi-official position, I feel bound to take the precaution of saying that I have not yet read the book, and must not be considered as endorsing anything contained in it.   G. T. G.

are not disconnected, but are two sides of a single question—that of the Sudan.

In treating this subject it is well to remind the general reader of the geographical position of the Sudan; as, since the British occupation of Egypt and the military operations in the Egyptian Sudan, a slipshod habit has crept into some English newspapers of applying to the latter alone a name which belongs properly to the whole of Negroland under Mohammedan influence or visited by Mohammedan trading caravans. *Chambers's Encyclopædia*, in 1860, defined the Sudan as " bounded on the north by the Sahara, on the west by Senegambia, on the south by Upper Guinea, and on the east by Kordofan "; but it would be inconvenient to treat the Sudan to-day as ending on the western frontier of Kordofan, for the regions between it and the Red Sea, north of Abyssinia, are now habitually included in the term. With this amendment the definition above given will serve all practical purposes. The French, who during the last seven years have become far more fully informed than our compatriots about Africa north of the Equator, are strictly correct in naming their vast sphere to the east of Senegambia the French Sudan. The question is not one of geographical accuracy alone. It involves a recognition of the essential homogeneity of this great belt of Africa, on which important point I propose to touch presently.

In 1819, only those interested in geographical research were familiar even with the name of the Niger, or knew that its upper waters, down to Bussa, had been traced fourteen years before by a Scotchman, Mungo Park, the father of African exploration in modern times. It was only in 1831 that the lower waters of the Niger and their path from Bussa to the ocean were discovered by an equally great Englishman, Richard Lander. A like mystery veiled the sources and upper waters of the Nile until Speke, Baker, and other explorers, during the sixties, connected them geographically with the Nile of Nubia and Egypt.

Between these great rivers of East and West Africa lie regions of the breadth of the entire continent of Europe, regions which were, in 1819, altogether unknown and believed to be but sparsely inhabited. It was not until Major Denham and Captain Clapperton, in 1823–25, and Dr. Barth, in 1849–55, explored this vast area on behalf of the British Government, that the civilised world recognised that this heart of Africa was no barren desert. They found that it was filled with populous and organised States, .

that it possessed a fertile soil and intelligent and industrious inhabitants; but they did not sufficiently recognise — and this discovery was reserved for our days — that the considerable civilisation of the Sudan could make no further progress, that this lost thirtieth of the human race could have no adequate connection through commerce with the outer world, until a sound basis was substituted for that on which the social system in those regions has hitherto rested.

No student of history can, indeed, assert that the institution of slavery in its customary forms is an absolute barrier to intellectual progress and the creation of wealth. Greece, Rome, and the United States of America have afforded a sufficient answer to that extreme view. Nor can the slave *trade* be such a barrier, if the word be confined to its usual and proper meaning of buying and selling of slaves; for this has been the natural course in all ages in all slave-holding countries; while the capture of slaves in war has proved, at anyrate, preferable to the more ancient practice of killing all prisoners.

The radical vice of the Sudan, the disease which, until cured, must arrest all intellectual and material progress, is the general, constant, and intense prevalence of slave-*raiding*. It is not

possible, in a brief preface, to present any
adequate picture of a system under which considerable towns disappear in a night and whole
tracts of country are depopulated in a single dry
season—not as a result of war, but as the normal
method of the rulers for collecting their human
cattle for payment of tribute to their suzerains or
for sale to distant parts of the continent. Much
has been written on this extraordinary subject.
It may suffice to refer the reader to Canon
Robinson's *Hausa Land*, and to Sir Harry
Johnson's *Autobiography of a Slave*, which,
though presented in the form of fiction, is an
understatement of the facts. But perhaps a more
vivid picture is given in *The Life and Travels
of Dorugu*, dictated by himself, a translation of
which appears in Dr. Schoen's *Magana Hausa*,
published by the Society for Promoting Christian
Knowledge. Dorugu was a native of the Niger
Sudan, who was ultimately brought to London
by Dr. Barth. The merit of his story lies in its
artlessness and brevity. His childhood is largely
filled with sudden flights into the forest or hills
to escape the slave-raiders. His family rebuild
their burnt farmhouses, or change their homes
with philosophic equanimity like that of vine
cultivators on the slopes of a volcano. The

simplicity with which Dorugu relates the fears and dangers of his boyhood shows that to him they seemed as inevitable as measles and school to an English boy. At last he is caught in his turn ; his parents, brothers, and sisters, for whom he evidently had a strong affection, vanish suddenly and entirely out of his life, and he himself becomes one of the millions of pieces of human currency which pass from one Sudanese State to another.

At first sight it seems impossible to reconcile this universal and continual slave-raiding in times of peace with the considerable civilisation and complex political organisation of the Sudanese States. The system probably originated from the great demand for negro slaves that has existed from time immemorial amongst the lighter coloured races of mankind. The docility of the negro, combined with his intelligence and capacity for work, must have given him a special value in the slave markets of antiquity, as in those of modern days. The growth of Mohammedanism, with its polygamous institutions, during the eight centuries after the Hegira, gave an immense impulse to the export slave trade of the Sudan to Asia, Europe, and North Africa. At the commencement of the sixteenth century the philanthropic efforts of Bishop Las Casas laid the foundations of the negro slave trade to the New World. Three centuries of this export trade on a large scale must have contributed to confirm and develop the old slave-raiding habits of the Sudan, though it seems unjust of certain writers to lay the entire blame on Christendom for a social canker which had existed in Africa for many hundreds of years, before Charles v., out of pure benevolence, permitted the import into St. Domingo of slaves from the Portuguese Guinea Coast. But although the qualities of the negro and the demand for his services by lighter coloured races in all ages account for the inception of the remarkable system of slave-raiding, the number of slaves exported has probably been insignificant compared with the number dealt with in the internal traffic of Negroland.

To understand this question properly, it must be remembered that the value of a slave is extremely small near his place of capture. His initial price is often lower than that of a sheep, which has less tendency to escape. As the slave is taken farther away from his home, his value rises rapidly ; so that it is commercially a sound transaction to send a hundred slaves, say, from Bornu to Darfur, while bringing a hundred others from Darfur to Bornu. No doubt they have also a value as transport animals, but I venture to assert that this feature of the traffic has been over-estimated, especially as camels are plentiful in the northern regions, while horses and donkeys are largely used and might be cheaply bred to any extent throughout the Sudan. While, there-fore, a well-planned system of Sudanese railways would have a considerable indirect effect on the internal slave trade, and consequently on slave-raiding, it would not, as generally believed, directly touch the root of the evil. This can only be eradicated by the same vigorous means which we employ in Europe for the prevention of crime and violence. It is, I fear, useless to hope that commerce with Europe will, by itself, suffice to alter a social system so deeply ingrained in the Sudanese mind; for the creation of com-merce on a large scale is impossible until slave-raiding is abated.

Let me not be misunderstood as preaching a crusade of liberty against the Sudanese States. To this policy I am most strenuously opposed. Force must indeed underlie all social action, whether in Africa or Europe, whether in public life or in the more intimate relations of parent and child, schoolmaster and pupil. But there is a wide difference between its necessary and constant display and its unnecessary use. The policemen of our towns have not their batons habitually drawn, though they do not hesitate to use them on occasions. There is probably no part of the world where diplomacy is more effective than Negroland, provided it is known that behind diplomacy is military power. There is certainly no part of the world where the maxim *Festina lente* is more applicable.

It was the just perception of this principle which led France, at the Berlin Conference, to induce the civilised States to agree that, except on the *coasts* of the continent, effective occupation—or, in other words, forcible occupation—should not be a necessary condition of political influence. The French Ambassador at Berlin pointed out very clearly the distinction in this respect between the coasts and the interior of Africa, and the disadvantages of requiring early effective occupation inland. The adoption of his view by the fourteen States represented at Berlin has consecrated this important principle as a recognised rule of international law until otherwise decided by the signatory nations. International rivalry is thus reduced to reasonable limits, and time is given for the gradual and natural growth of European influence in those regions.

When, however, the application of force becomes absolutely necessary, it ought surely to be thorough and rapid. Yet last spring, after the completion of the operations described by Lieutenant Vandeleur in the latter half of this book, one of the most able and respected organs of public opinion in this country questioned the morality of "mowing down natives with artillery and Maxim guns." Now, these "natives" were the fighting organisation of great regions which they—though in a comparatively small minority —held down with a hand of iron, treating the less warlike inhabitants as cattle to be raided when wanted. The death of each Fulah killed at Bida secured the lives and liberty of scores of peaceful and defenceless natives. If Europe had no material interests to protect and develop in Africa, it would still have the same right, the same duty to extirpate slave-raiding that a man has to knock down a ruffian whom he sees maltreating a woman or child in the street.

While, however, this consideration should satisfy the consciences of persons interested in the welfare of the oppressed millions of Africa, the material importance of opening up the Sudan cannot be overlooked by any European State which subsists largely on its manufacturing and shipping interests. On this point it will be well for me to confine my remarks to the region lying between Lake Chad and the Niger, to which my studies of the last twenty years have been mainly directed. This region has been known of late under the name of the Niger Sudan. It comprises Bornu and the Fulah or Sokoto-Gando Empire, the greater and more valuable portion of which is mainly peopled by the civilised, commerce-loving, and industrious Hausas, who form about one-hundredth of mankind, and whose intellectual capacity H. M. Stanley has aptly emphasised by describing them as the "only Central African people who value a book."

In dealing with the value of the markets to be developed in the Niger Sudan, it is difficult to decide on how much must be said and what may be assumed as known. On the one hand, all geographers and many publicists are familiar with the fact that the region in question possesses populous towns and a fertile soil, and, most important of all, races whose industry is untiring, notwithstanding the discouraging and paralysing effects of insecurity of life, liberty, and property. They know that these races are possessed of high intelligence and considerable artistic skill, as displayed in their fine brass and leather work.

They know that the early marriages in those latitudes, and the fecundity and vitality of the negro races, have, through countless generations, largely counteracted the appalling destruction of life resulting from slave-raiding, and that under reasonable conditions of security the existing population might soon be trebled and yet live in far greater material comfort than at present. They know, in short, that all that is needed to convert the Niger Sudan into an African India is the strong hand of a European protector. But, on the other hand, the general public and a considerable section of the press seem still inclined to confuse the Niger Sudan with the very different regions which border the Guinea Coast. The well-clad, intelligent, and fairly civilised races of the interior are constantly referred to as half-naked and indolent savages ; the fine country which forms three-fourths of the Niger Sudan is confounded with the swamps of the Niger Delta. It is not difficult to recognise how this delusion originated and is maintained. The Niger Sudan is separated from the civilisation of the Mediterranean regions by a thousand miles of the Sahara, which the Tuareg and other wandering tribes render well-nigh impassable. It is separated from the Guinea coast-line by a maritime belt,

malarious in climate, and inhabited by lower races
who have, perhaps, been gradually pushed sea-
wards by the successive waves of higher races
coming from the North. The vast majority of
Englishmen—whether soldiers, officials, missionaries, or traders—who have visited West Africa
have seen only the coast-line or, at most, the
maritime belt, and their impressions of this small
section of the continent have very naturally been
accepted by uninformed readers as applicable to
the vast *Hinterlands*. The difficulty of access
to the Niger Sudan regions accounts amply for
this important and valuable portion of the earth's
surface having been cut off from outside intercourse for all practical purposes until the last
quarter of the nineteenth century. The barriers
which from time immemorial have separated the
Sudanese races from the remainder of the human
family have at last been effectually broken down,
and it may be safely prophesied that within twenty
years the union will be complete, provided vital
errors of policy are avoided. The two principal
dangers can hardly be too often urged, and I propose to deal with them briefly in turn.

Central African races and tribes have, broadly
speaking, no sentiment of patriotism, as understood in Europe. There is therefore little

c

difficulty in inducing them to accept what German jurisconsults term *Ober-Hoheit*, which corresponds with one interpretation of our vague term " Protectorate." But when complete sovereignty, or *Landes-Hoheit*, is conceded, they invariably stipulate that their local customs and system of government shall be respected. On this point they are, perhaps, more tenacious than most subject races with whom the British Empire has had to deal; while their views and ideals of life are extremely difficult for an Englishman to understand. It is therefore certain that even an imperfect and tyrannical native African administration, if its extreme excesses were controlled by European supervision, would be, in the early stages, productive of far less discomfort to its subjects than well-intentioned but ill-directed efforts of European magistrates, often young and headstrong, and not invariably gifted with sympathy and introspective powers. If the welfare of the native races is to be considered, if dangerous revolts are to be obviated, the general policy of ruling on African principles through native rulers must be followed for the present. Yet it is desirable that considerable districts in suitable localities should be administered on European principles by European officials, partly to serve as types to which the native governments may gradually approximate, but principally as cities of refuge in which individuals of more advanced views may find a living, if native government presses unduly upon them; just as, in Europe of the Middle Ages, men whose love of freedom found the iron-bound system of feudalism intolerable, sought eagerly the comparative liberty of cities.

The second danger to be apprehended—a war of religions—will probably present itself to every thoughtful European. Fortunately for the Niger Sudan, Moslem fanaticism in this region has not the intensity of that now existing farther East—in Wadai, Darfur, and the Nile provinces. Yet ill-advised legislation, a careless administrative system, or a bad selection of officials, might well create an entirely different state of things. Twenty-five to thirty years ago one was able to travel in the Egyptian Sudan without escort, and without even keeping watch at night. With what incredulity would one have then received a prophecy that only ten or fifteen years later that district would become a hotbed of Mohammedan fanaticism, and would be absolutely closed to Christendom for a long period of years! The danger in the Sudanese States is accentuated by the close connection between them, due not only

to a common faith and similar modes of life, but
also to the constant communications kept up by
the Hausa trading caravans which radiate from
Hausa-land into distant parts of the continent.
Prior to the Mahdist conquests, the pilgrim
caravans from Central and Western Africa used
to pass through Darfur to the Red Sea. I
have travelled with no less than eight hundred
Hausa pilgrims in a single caravan between
Khartum and Suakin. The rise of Mahdism
has temporarily diverted these pilgrim travellers
northward from Lake Chad to the Mediterranean;
but every part of the Sudan is still permeated by
trading caravans constantly passing to and fro,
and carrying news, almost always distorted and
exaggerated, from one part of this vast region to
another. About twelve years ago a placard
issued by the late Mahdi was found posted in a
street of Bida, no less than two thousand miles
distant across country from Khartum; while one
of the incidents that precipitated our war last
year was the receipt of letters from the Khalifa
at Omdurman by the Sultan of Sokoto and the
Emirs of Nupe and other provinces of the Sokoto
Empire, urging them to drive the Christians out
of their country.

The similarity of the Sudan regions from east

to west may be further illustrated by a striking fact of no little importance to the British Empire, and in which personally I take more interest than in the commercial development of the Sudan. Its entire northern belt, from Senegambia to the Red Sea, is inhabited by races at once capable of fighting and amenable to discipline. The value of the Sudanese regiments of the Egyptian army is widely known. Less has been heard, as yet, of the splendid qualities of the Hausa as a soldier when well officered. In the campaign described by Lieutenant Vandeleur, these qualities were fully proved. On the rapid and arduous march of seventeen days from Lokoja to Kabba, and thence to Egbon, and again on the march to Ilorin, with serious scarcity of water, and at times shortness of rations, our troops were always good-tempered and cheerful; and, although in heavy marching order, would pick up and carry the seventy-pound loads of the porters who fell by the way. In camp their conduct was exemplary, while pillaging and ill-treatment of the natives were unknown. As to their fighting qualities, it is enough to say that, little over 500 strong, they withstood for two days 25,000 to 30,000 of the enemy; that, former slaves of the Fulahs, they defeated their dreaded masters; that, Mohammedans, they fought for

their salt against their brethren of the faith ; and
finally, that though they had never before faced
cavalry, they stood firm under charges *home* on to
the faces of their squares, maintained perfect fire-
discipline, and delivered their volleys as steadily
as if on parade. Great Britain has had to rely
too much of recent years on Indian troops for
tropical climates. This is not a healthy condition
of things, for many reasons. She may well find
an independent source of military strength in the
regions bordering the southern limits of the Great
Sahara.

I have necessarily touched very briefly on the
main features of the Nile and Niger question,—
one which must inevitably become better known
in the early future. When the history of the
Victorian age is written from a standpoint
sufficiently removed to allow a just perception of
proportion, the opening up of Tropical Africa will
probably stand out as a prominent feature of the
latter half of that era. The fifty years that
followed 1492 formed by no means the least
interesting period in the domestic and international history of England, France, Germany, or
Spain, or in the history of freedom of human
thought and action ; yet no events of that half
century appear to us now more important than the

discoveries of Columbus and the conquests of Cortes and Pizarro. The results of opening up Tropical Africa cannot, of course, be on a similar scale; yet it seems to me that they must be so great as to dwarf many contemporaneous questions which now occupy the public mind in a far higher degree.

The share that Great Britain may take in this movement depends on the condition of the national fibre. A statesman of the early Stuart period would have deemed it impossible that these little islands could control an empire such as that of the days of Chatham; while the Great Commoner himself might have felt misgivings could he have foreseen the Greater Britain of the Diamond Jubilee year. Yet the growing burden of empire has brought with it a more than equivalent accession of wealth, vigour, and strength to maintain it; and although it may be that the British Empire has now reached its zenith, and must gradually decline to the position of a second-rate power, we are not bound to accept such assertions without the production of more valid evidence than has yet been adduced in their support.

GEORGE TAUBMAN GOLDIE.

NAVAL AND MILITARY CLUB,
    16th February 1898.

CAMPAIGNING ON THE
UPPER NILE AND NIGER

I

FROM LONDON TO THE VICTORIA NYANZA

I HAD only been home three months after a most successful shooting expedition into Somaliland, and along the high range of hills which forms the Abyssinian frontier, when I received an appointment under the Foreign Office in Uganda, to which country they were sending out more officers.

On the 10th August 1894, Mr. Jackson,—so well known in East Africa, and the writer of that excellent account of big-game shooting in those parts, which forms one of the volumes of the Badminton Library,—Captain Ashburnham of the 60th Rifles, and I, left London for Marseilles, where we embarked on the Messageries Maritimes steamer *Iraouaddy* for Zanzibar. Poor "Roddy" Owen, who had just returned from Uganda himself, and who afterwards died of cholera in Egypt, came to see me off, and I little thought I should never see him again.

On hearing of my appointment I had written at once to Messrs. Cowasjee at Aden to procure me a good Somali pony from Berbera, and to send it on for me to

Zanzibar.   There had been very rough weather in the
Indian Ocean, and the captain of the ship then sailing
refused to take it.   On my arrival at Aden I found
the pony still there, and was obliged to take it with
me on the French steamer, of course at a much higher
rate.   At Aden I found several Somalis who had been
with me before, some of whom were anxious to come
again, but I eventually engaged a man called Nur
Fabil, who had already been to East Africa, and had
journeyed up to and beyond Lake Victoria through
German territory.   He was invaluable to me, as, besides
speaking Arabic and a little English, he knew Ki-Swahili,
the language of the East Coast, as well.   He had
already had charge of ponies in German East Africa,
and knew well how to look after them.

After rounding Cape Guardafui the sea became very
rough, owing to the south-west monsoon.   On our ship
was a French bishop, with some priests and nuns, on
their way to Nyasaland and Lake Tanganyika, where a
mission had been started.   Every morning the bishop
held a class in the saloon to teach Swahili, and we
could hear his pupils repeating the words which were
to become so familiar to us afterwards.

We arrived at Zanzibar on the 30th August, and
went off to the consulate, where we found Mr.
Hardinge.   After a very pleasant week spent at the
residence, we embarked on H.M.S. *Sparrow*, and were
taken across to Mombasa, anchoring opposite the picturesque old Portuguese fort which commands the
entrance to the harbour.   The porters and loads had
been collected a few days previously, and were
encamped at a place called the Banderini, about 10
miles up the river, which we reached in a steam-launch
the following day.   There were just over 400 men,

and these had to be divided up into companies of fifteen, each in charge of an askari. Loads had also to be checked, and porters told off for them, so there was little time to be lost if we wanted to start as arranged on the next day, Saturday, 8th September. The loads consisted principally of military stores and equipment for the Sudanese force in Uganda, such as Martini-Henry rifles and bayonets, ammunition, and six Maxim guns, some of the loads formed by the latter being very heavy.

However, at last, with Mr. Martin's help, everything was arranged, and we started on our long march to Uganda on the 8th, along a narrow well-beaten track. A Union-Jack was carried at the head of the column, and at the halts a native drum was beaten to encourage the laggards and stragglers in the rear. It was now the middle of the dry season, and the great difficulty during the first few days' march from the coast was with regard to water. There was nearly a full moon, so we were fortunately able to march at night, and crossed the Taru Desert (54 miles) in two and a half days, carrying water with us. The only white men with the caravan were Jackson, Ashburnham, and myself. The first named was a great naturalist, and fired Ashburnham with his own zeal, so that in the pursuit of a rare butterfly he fell into a thorn bush—not such as one sees in England, but an African thorn bush, from which he had to be extricated, and subsequently had to ride a donkey.

My pony had endured the sea-journey to Zanzibar and the march to the Tsavo River very well, but had now to pass through the dangerous tsetse-fly country. In the hope of keeping the flies away I covered him all over with a greasy concoction formed by boiling the fat of a sheep and mixing it with Keating's powder. It certainly had the desired effect, and the pony got through without being bitten.

On the 25th the caravan reached Kibwezi, the station of the Scotch Industrial Mission, a delightful spot 3070 feet above the sea. It is here one sees what can be done with a swamp in Africa. By artificial means the swamp close to the station has been transformed into a lovely clear stream of water, on each side of which is laid out a garden growing all kinds of plants and vegetables. We stayed one day to give the men a rest, and on the 27th Dr. Charters, the head of the mission, and Mr. Colquhoun, who was staying with him, accompanied us on our way to Mikinduni—very bad going for the first 2 miles, over lava rocks and stones. Dr. Charters and Mr. Colquhoun had sent their servants the day before to prepare a camp in what Dr. Charters said was a good country for game, which lay to the westward of our route, and after going 6 miles with us they said good-bye and branched off in a westerly direction.

Since that time they have never been seen or heard of again, dead or alive, and I suppose it is the most extraordinary disappearance that has ever occurred in Africa or anywhere else. Numerous have been the causes assigned for it—lions, want of water, and Masai.

It seems most probable that they were killed by a raiding party of Masai from the German territory, but even then one would think some trace of them would have been left. Dr. Charters knew the country perfectly, and had often been there before, so it is hardly likely they could have lost themselves. They had a boy with them when they left us, and, according to his story, he was left to skin a hartebeest which they had killed, and then missed them. Several search-parties were afterwards sent out, without success. It was on our march from Kibwezi that we first viewed the deliciously cool-looking snow-peaks of Kilimanjaro, peeping over the wreaths of cloud and mist which concealed the base ; and on the following day, at sunrise, the whole mass of the mountain appeared delicately outlined against the sky, the two snow-peaks, like the large and small horns of a rhinoceros, being now tinged with red by the rapidly rising sun.

It is wonderful, in Africa, to watch the great orb of fire—which becomes so unpleasant later in the day—suddenly shooting up above the horizon as it starts on its long journey across the heavens. An eclipse of the sun, such as occurred at sunrise on the 29th September 1894, had indeed a curious effect, and, though not quite total, the heavens were obscured, and the birds and antelopes had not realised that the night was past. It was on this morning I shot my first water-buck, a very fine buck, with horns just over 27 inches in length, almost a record in East Africa. We reached our first important point—Machako's—on 5th October, meeting there Mr. Ainsworth, who was in charge of the post, and through his hospitality we enjoyed all sorts of luxuries again. The whole of the country, from the coast to Lake Victoria, was still in the hands of the East African Company, and had not yet been taken over by the Government. Major Smith, Captain Arthur of the Rifle Brigade, and Captain Gibbs met us here on their way down to the coast. The latter was being carried down in a hammock, and looked very ill. As may be imagined, he did not give us an inspiriting account of Uganda, and his only advice was to turn back and go the other way.

The Wa-Kamba, among whom we now were, were the funniest-looking people I have ever seen, the fashion being to cover themselves and the little toga which they wear over the shoulders with red grease, to put vermilion round the eyes, and fix between them a sort of brass two-shilling-piece, which was fastened by a band round the head. The " mashers " also wore spats made of strings of white and red beads round the ankles, and a profusion of brass wire bands round their arms and legs. The whole effect was admirable, especially when the men were standing together with bows and arrows. Their costume was scanty, to say the least of it, and the women only wore girdles of blue beads.

We had already risen 5400 feet since leaving the coast, and were now in the highlands of East Africa, where the days were often cool and cloudy, and it was a pleasure to live.

We stayed five days at Machako's, and then continued our march to Kikuyu across the Athi plains, a great sea of gentle grass-covered u_dulations, intersected by watercourses, and in places teeming with game—a perfect sportsman's paradise. After my expedition in Somaliland, at the beginning of the year, I was naturally very keen about the shooting, and was fortunate to get a good deal during the next few days. Captain Montgomerie, R.N., and Mr. Charrington, were encamped on the Athi River, having come to East Africa on a shooting-trip two months before. They were kind enough to ask Ashburnham and myself to go with them for two days to the westward, a little away from the caravan road, where there was more chance of finding game. On the very first day I was lucky enough to shoot a big male lion soon after leaving camp. He came out towards me from some bushes in which he was lying, and received a shot from my 10-bore close to the eye, which stopped him; but it required two more shots to finish him.

One day three lions were marked down in some grass in the morning, and a lion-drive was organised after lunch. After the guns had taken up their position the grass was fired, and the beaters advanced behind the line of flame and smoke, mingling their shouts and yells with the crackling of the burning grass and dried-up wood, and the dull roar of the fire. It was an exciting moment as they drew near. Now and then a frightened antelope would dash past, but, sad to relate, the lions had already moved away, and a male lion was seen at the same time just out of shot on the other side of the Athi River, near to which the left gun was posted.

Ashburnham and I had to strike across country to reach the caravan road to Kikuyu, and on our way passed a valley where the fresh green grass was just sprouting. This was literally covered with game of all sorts; thousands of zebra were placidly feeding with innumerable herds of antelope of different species— wildebeest, hartebeest, a few mpala, and many gazelles (*G. thomsonii* and *G. grantii*), whilst away in the distance there were a few stately giraffe. Secure in their numbers, they seemed to scorn the presence of three lions which were eagerly watching them from one flank, whilst in the middle of the moving mass stood two great unwieldy rhinoceros, which contrasted strangely with the diminutive gazelles.

As the caravan went along, the zebra, followed by the rhinoceros, galloped off in a cloud of dust, and, as they so often do, swung past the head of the caravan. One of the rhinoceros took up a position almost directly in front of us, and, crawling to within 60 yards of him, I had an easy shot, but unfortunately only wounded him.

We rejoined Mr. Jackson at Kikuyu on the 15th, and found that fifteen askaris (soldiers) had been sent to reinforce us for the march through the forest, owing to the still uncertain temper of the natives.   Here arrangements had to be made for a twenty-four days' march across a foodless district, and the loads were curtailed as much as possible so that more food could be carried. The boxes of Martini-Henry rifles were opened, and seven rifles were packed together in sacking so as to form one load, instead of three in a case as before. Some extra porters and donkeys were engaged, and each man had to carry twelve days' food besides his load.

Making our way through what is known as the meridional trough or rift, which has been so thoroughly described by previous travellers,—a series of valleys with three lakes, Naivasha, Elmenteita, and Nakuro, bounded by high ranges on each side,—we reached the Eldoma Ravine on 27th October, and the next day commenced the ascent of the Mau escarpment.   One unfortunate porter who had lagged behind, and had hidden himself away in the grass at the side of the road, was devoured by hyænas during the night.   These animals were voracious and daring; and the camp was aroused by a fearful commotion one night—a hyæna having seized a porter by the foot as he was lying asleep near the fire; another got inside the circle of fires, and went off with a man's food and part of his tent.

It   rained   usually   every   day   now,   commencing about 2 p.m., and the road was in consequence in very bad condition. The crossing of the Eldoma Ravine took a long time, as, after the first few men had passed, the path down to the stream became frightfully slippery owing to the mud, and porters and loads frequently tumbled down the steep slope. The track beyond through the Subugo Forest had become a sort of torrent in places, and it was with a sense of relief that we emerged from the blackness of the forest and the sea of mud under foot to find ourselves on the top of the mountains at a height of 8700 feet above the sea. This may be said to be a part of the main watershed of Africa, as, after leaving the Mau escarpment all the rivers and streams flow into the Victoria Nyanza, thus helping to form the source of the Nile.

A great charm in the march to Uganda is the variety and utter dissimilarity of country through which one passes. Here, at the top of the escarpment, the ground was not flat as one would imagine, but the path led over one hill after another, covered with long grass and studded with bamboo thickets, the home of a few buffalo which have survived the rinderpest, and whose tracks can sometimes be seen. We were glad, however, to leave this cold and cheerless place and to descend into warmer climes.

Game was not so numerous on the north side of the mountains; the ungainly looking Jackson's harte-beest had replaced Cooke's hartebeest, and besides these only a few zebra, with some giraffe and small antelope, were seen. When out shooting I used often to wish that I could have some of the Somalis with me again. The natives of the East Coast, including one's own gun-bearers, are, with very few exceptions, the most utter idiots as regards sport of any kind, and only think of one thing, namely, ugama (in Ki-Swahili = meat), a word

which in their language applies to every kind of animal
without distinction. Many a time was my chance of a
shot spoilt by the behaviour of the men with me.

An unpleasant incident, common in African travel,
was the attack on the caravan by a swarm of bees.
Luckily their sting is not so venomous as that of an
English bee.

At last, on the 6th November, we came to Kabras
and Kavirondo, an inhabited country again, though
not exactly a civilised one, to judge from the appearance of the natives, who dispense with clothing altogether. On the 9th inst. we reached Mumia's, which
had just been taken over by Colonel Colvile under the
Uganda administration, and where a station was then
being established, though there was still some dispute
about it with the East African Company. Dr. Moffat
was here on his way down to the coast, and we also
met the German naturalist, Herr Neumann, who was
on his way home after two years' travelling in East
Africa.

The caravan road made a great detour to the
northward, and it had taken us thirteen days, including
one day's halt, to reach Mumia's from the Eldoma
Ravine. It had become much warmer as we descended
towards Lake Victoria. Owing to the heavy rain
there was a great deal of water in the Nzoia River,
which flows close to Mumia's, and the crossing had to
be effected in native canoes, which took only three
men and their loads across at a time, so that it was a
lengthy process. The march being continued across
the Samia Hills and down to Sio Bay, on the first day
after leaving the Nzoia River, our guide, Mwanga, mistook
the way, and led us across two very bad swamps. He
was a well-known character in East Africa, where he held

CAMP AT USOGA

the position of strongest porter, having been known to carry a tusk of ivory weighing 140 lb. down to the coast from Uganda with the greatest ease. He had been made a headman in our caravan, but had few qualifications for the post except his physical strength, and was reduced to the grade of porter again soon after reaching Uganda.

We saw the Victoria Nyanza for the first time on the 15th November,—the day we crossed the Sio River,—and it was a great joy to me to view the blue waters of this great inland sea, which it had long been my ambition some day to reach. From here we marched a distance of 12 miles to an old market-place, a sudden transition from Kavirondo to Usoga occurring during the latter part of the march, which was through banana plantations. Here the people were all clothed in bark cloth; they were much more intelligent-looking, and very different from the naked savages of Kavirondo.

It was a delightful change to march through Usoga after the barren and deserted country we had passed through on the way to Kavirondo. Sometimes the track led through shady banana plantations, sometimes through woods with lovely trees, and the whole country seemed like a great garden. Overhead flew innumerable grey parrots, large numbers of which are caught and offered for sale. The rains had only just ceased, and in the hollows between the hills there were nasty swampy streams which delayed us very much. There were occasionally heavy thunderstorms in the afternoon, and to a new-comer in the region of the Equatorial Lakes the thunder is indeed a revelation. Whilst the lightning seemed to come down almost between our tents, the claps of thunder shook the very ground, and sounded just like a battery of artillery firing from the camp itself.

The villages, composed of houses like enormous bee-hives, are surrounded by a high wall of reeds neatly plaited together, and outside the gateway there is usually a large open space, which we often used as a camping-place. Instead of crossing the Victoria Nile just above the Ripon Falls we went to Lubwa's, so called after the chief of that name, and thence crossed Berkeley Bay. After a stuffy march through woods and banana plantations we reached a line of hills, and after ascending this ridge were well repaid by a most lovely view of the lake, or at least of a large bay of a turquoise colour, studded with little picturesque islets, and reminding one much of the Italian lakes. A large station had been established at Lubwa's under Mr. Grant, whom we met here, and settled round about were 1200 Sudanese, formerly on the Nile with Emin Pasha.

All our caravan crossed to the Uganda side of the bay, a distance of 7 miles, on Thursday, November 20th, and camped close to the lake. We were taken over by a fleet of the picturesque-looking canoes, with long prows ornamented by antelope horns, which are used by the Wasoga and the Waganda on the Victoria Ny-anza, the paddlers making a great noise and singing all the time. My pony could not be induced to enter a canoe, and had to be sent round *vià* Jinja, where animals are able to swim across above the Ripon Falls, and consequently did not arrive at Kampala till some days later.

Although I have lingered for a while over the beauties of Usoga, there is no necessity for me to continue to describe a journey which has already become so familiar, and about which so much has been written.

Our first impression of travelling in Uganda was that it was like going along a switchback railway with immensely high grass threatening to overwhelm us on each side, and we were at once struck by the luxuriance of the tropical vegetation.

Our journey of 800 miles came to an end on the 28th November, when we reached Port Alice, the headquarters of the Uganda administration, after a most successful march under the leadership of Mr. Jackson, and all the loads were safely deposited at their destination. We reported ourselves that afternoon to Colonel Colvile, the Commissioner, who had built a charming house on a cliff overhanging the lake. Our arrival was unfortunately signalised by the destruction of his kitchen by fire, and the rest of the house narrowly escaped the same fate.

I had been suffering for some time from a sore throat—a common complaint in Uganda—and, as it had now become worse, it was fortunate for me that I found Dr. Ansorge at Kampala, into which place I managed to struggle the next day. I was laid up there for several days.

II

UGANDA TO THE ALBERT NYANZA

EVENTS move with such rapidity in Central Africa that it is difficult to keep pace with them, and although so much has been written about Uganda it may be as well to give a brief account of the various transformation scenes through which this distressful country has passed. Until the arrival of Speke and Grant in 1862, Uganda was an unknown country, except to a few Arab traders who had penetrated thither from the East Coast, but after that time European visitors became more frequent, both from the East Coast and from Egypt.

In 1884 King Mtesa died, and was succeeded by his son, Mwanga, who outvied him in cruelty and bloodshed, until in 1888 he was driven out of the country. A year later, however, he was reinstated on the throne. Commencing as a pagan, he has tried every religion in turn. After attempting to raise a rebellion against the English in the present year (1897), his forces have been defeated, and he has fled from the country to take refuge in German territory.

To anyone who has visited Uganda lately, it seems almost incredible that only ten years ago a horrible massacre of Christian converts took place, and that the country was given over to such complete barbarism.

It is true, one still sometimes meets horrible objects in the streets without hands, noses, ears, or lips—awful proofs of the old barbarities.

It was not until the 24th December 1890 that Captain Lugard made a treaty with Mwanga, establishing the East African Company's Protectorate over Uganda. Little thanks have the Company received for thus securing for the British Empire this fertile land with its great lakes, the sources of the Nile, and with it the key to Central Africa.

From henceforth starts a new era, and how Captain Lugard maintained his position here, in spite of strife and religious wars by which the country was torn and rent, has been set forth in his admirable book, *The Rise of Our East African Empire*. The strain on the Company's resources was too much, and at the end of 1892 it intimated to the Government that it would be obliged to withdraw from the country owing to financial difficulties. The Government demurred to taking it over, and for some time the fate of Uganda hung in the balance, until at last it was decided to send out, as Her Majesty's Commissioner, Sir Gerald Portal, K.C.B., who left the coast with a staff of officers and an escort of Zanzibari troops on 1st January 1893.

The date of the Company's final evacuation of Uganda had been fixed for the 31st March, so there was little time to be lost.

However, Sir Gerald Portal arrived at Kampala on the 17th, and the retention of Uganda was ultimately decided on. On his departure, Major Macdonald was left as Assistant Commissioner, and in the summer of that year a war again broke out between the Protestants and the Mohammedans, who had arranged to drive the

Christians out of the country and establish their own government. They were defeated on 17th June, some of the Sudanese soldiers who were thought to be implicated having been disarmed ; their leader, Selim Bey, was afterwards sentenced to transportation to the coast.

Major Owen, who was at this time in Southern Unyoro enlisting soldiers from the Sudanese left by Captain Lugard (it being now intended to evacuate the forts in which he had settled them), fought an action with another body of Mohammedans, completely routing them.

It was not until August 1894 that a British Protectorate was formally established, and then only over Uganda proper, bounded by the countries of Unyoro and Toru to the west and Usoga to the east.

In November 1893 Colonel Colvile, C.B., arrived to take over the duties of Commissioner, bringing with him two officers, Captains Gibbs and Thruston, to reinforce the small staff then serving with the Sudanese troops. Soon after his arrival he declared war against Kabarega, king of Unyoro, the *bête noir* of Uganda, who had lately resumed his old practice of raiding the surrounding countries, and had sent armies into Toru on the west and Usoga on the east. He is a thorough scoundrel, as anyone may see by looking at Sir Samuel Baker's book, *Ismailia*, and his life has been one of continual hostility and treachery to Europeans. After a successful campaign a line of forts was formed commanding the road through Unyoro to Kibero on the Albert Nyanza, and a steel boat was placed on the lake. Thruston was left in command with 300 men, and the road to the Nile was thus assured. The inhabitants, however, remained hostile, and until Kabarega made peace or was driven right out of his country, and his power of retaliating on them ceased, it was impossible for them to be otherwise.

In a despatch from the Foreign Office, dated June 1894, it is stated: "Any temporary and partial occupation of Unyoro must be for purely defensive purposes, with the object of protecting Uganda against aggression. Every effort to be made with a view to establish friendly relations with Kabarega, and to prevent him from entering into an alliance with adherents of the Mahdi."

Unyoro is a large and important country which extends along the eastern shore of Lake Albert from the Victoria Nile to the Ruwenzori Mountains, and is inhabited by a race closely allied to that of Uganda, though lower in the scale of civilisation. There is no doubt that Kabarega, and his father Kamrasi before him, possessed immense power and influence over distant tribes west of Lake Albert and down the Nile, mainly owing to his mercenaries—the Warasura, and the supplies of guns and gunpowder which he obtained from the Arabs.

The history of the Sudanese colony in Uganda, expatriated from their own country, is indeed a romantic one. Driven step by step up the Nile by the dervishes, the army under Emin Pasha was the only Egyptian force to hold out after the rise of Mahdiism. Cut off from all civilisation, they were finally obliged to retire to Wadelai, where, it will be remembered, Mr. H. M. Stanley relieved Emin Pasha in 1888. The discipline of the troops had become very lax, and, owing to the dissension caused among them by envoys from Omar Saleh, general of the Mahdi's forces, a mutiny broke out, and a large section of mutineers established themselves under the leadership of Fadi

2

Mula at Wadelai, whilst Emin Pasha and Mr. Stanley were waiting at Kavalli's. After the departure of the latter we hear no more of them until, in August 1891, Captain Lugard found Selim Bey, and a number of the loyal Sudanese who had been left behind, on the west side of Lake Albert. Wisely foreseeing the use that might be made of them as an armed force to garrison the Protectorate, he enlisted a small number as soldiers, and, taking the rest back with him from Lake Albert, he placed them in forts through Southern Unyoro to act as a buffer against Kabarega's Warasura, and to ward off raids on Toru, King Kasagama's country.

It is from the old officers and men of this remnant of Emin Pasha's army, and their sons and followers, that the present force of over 1000 men, now known as the "Uganda Rifles," has been recruited and organised by English officers. They belong to many different tribes in the Sudan, and many come from the Makraka tribe west of Dufile, a fact which supplies an incentive to push on to this place, where we can find a recruiting ground, as, of course, the supply of Sudanese in Uganda is very limited. Some of the soldiers serving now are very old, and many of them are scarred with wounds received in old days when fighting the dervishes.

It was with great delight that I heard that Colonel Colvile had arranged for me to go with Major Cunningham, D.S.O., to Unyoro, and to accompany him on a reconnaisance down the Nile from Lake Albert.

It had been Colvile's intention to go to Unyoro again himself, but malarial fever decided otherwise, and he became so ill soon after our departure from Port Alice that he was invalided home, and was carried all the way to the coast in charge of Dr. Ansorge. Mr. Jackson became Acting Commissioner in his place, and held this post until the arrival of Mr. Berkeley in August 1895.

There was a good deal of fever among the Europeans at this time, and Major Cunningham was ill also, so that I began to think I should have to start for Unyoro by myself; however, he pluckily determined to march on the appointed day, 19th December, although ill at the time, and, in spite of wading through swamps under a tropical sun, became better and stronger each day. At the start a broad creek had to be crossed in canoes. The road then used led by Singo, and across the river Kafu at Baranwa, and was a very bad one, crossing many large and deep swamps. Cunningham and I both determined to try and get our ponies through to Unyoro, though none had ever reached the country from the East Coast. His was an Arab pony purchased at Zanzibar, and had, like mine, reached Uganda in good condition. The bottoms of some of the swamps were very bad, and full of roots of trees and holes, in which the ponies ran great danger of spraining their legs. There was great difficulty in leading them across these, and they very often collapsed into the papyrus at the side of the passage, and had to be put on their legs again by the Sudanese soldiers with us. My pony was the worse of the two, and when passing through a river swamp would lose his head, and plunge madly into the reeds, soon sinking up to his neck in the water before we could stop him.

The Kola River was the worst obstacle we had to pass, and although the breadth was not much more than 400 yards it took us over two hours to get across, hampered as we were by the Sudanese women and followers in front of us. All our sheep and goats for the journey were drowned, which was a great misfortune.

The worst of moving about with the Sudanese soldiers is the crowd of women and followers who accompany them, and in our case the number was augmented by a number of women and children belonging to the soldiers stationed in Unyoro, and going out to rejoin them.

Passing through one of these swamps is a most tiring experience. Now clutching hold of the papyrus at the side, now stepping from one bit of floating vegetation to another, one tries in vain to save oneself from sinking deeper than necessary, until at last a treacherous root gives way, and down one goes into a quagmire of evil-smelling mud and water, only to recommence the whole process again. Except where the papyrus and weeds have been beaten down in form-ing a passage across them, there is no water to be seen, and from a distance one of these sluggish river swamps appears like a beautiful green lawn of varying shades. This appearance is in reality caused by the great heads of the papyrus with their innumerable little delicate spikes, supported 4 or 5 feet above the level of the marsh by the long thin stems growing out of the tangled mass of floating vegetation. In three days we reached Fort Raymond, so named after poor Raymond Portal, who died in Uganda in 1893. It consists of a large palisaded enclosure, situated on a hill, round which lie the houses of the Sudanese colony. Near to the fort is Muquenda's, the capital of the province of Singo, where there is a mission station. Two roads branch off here, one leading to the fort in southern Unyoro, called Nakabimba, and then on to our fort at Kasagama's in Toru, under the Ruwenzori Mountains, and the other to Kibero on Lake Albert.

Captain Dunning, D.S.O., who had only arrived in Uganda a short time before us, was then in command of this station. One would think that, near an important place like this, the inhabitants would have bridged the swamps over which the main roads passed, but this was not the case, and only an hour after our start on the following day we had to plunge into another dismal morass, which delayed us very much.

After leaving Muquenda's the country altered entirely, and on Christmas Day we marched for eight hours along a ridge over an open grass country, the road at one point attaining a height of 4900 feet above the sea; hence we looked down upon an enormous plain, which stretched away to the east towards the Victoria Nile. We camped close to the village of Nsali, a curious place in which to spend Christmas Day, and, after our long march, were glad of a good dinner to celebrate the occasion. An old Sudanese soldier had accompanied us from Fort Raymond as far as this, and was going to try to shoot some elephant. He was, curiously enough, armed with an old 4-bore gun, which originally belonged to Sir Samuel Baker, and is now held together by pieces of hide sewn round it. It must require some nerve to shoot with it in its present condition, but the man had already successfully killed several elephants.

For the next three days we passed through a fertile and inhabited country, until, on reaching the village of Ntuti, we approached the barren and deserted plain drained by the Kafu River, which forms the boundary between Uganda and Unyoro, and, like most frontiers in savage lands, has been the scene of much strife and bloodshed. The descent of 640 feet to the plain is made through a steep and picturesque gorge, from which the track, winding in all directions, leads through some very thick jungle, and across some swampy ground to the frontier post, Fort Kaduma, garrisoned by a

Sudanese officer and twenty-five men. We met with the first Wanyoro at Kaduma, and there was a marked difference between them and the Waganda, the former having much sharper features, and being of a slighter build than the Waganda. Between this and the Kafu River there is dense tropical vegetation, and there are belts of thick forest, many of the trees being covered with a curious kind of growth like enormous cabbages with yellow and green leaves.

This was evidently a playground for elephants, and the track was scored by great holes made by them as they had floundered about in the mud during the rainy season.

We took the loads across the Kafu at Baranwa by means of a berthon boat and small canoe, the Sudanese followers and men crossing by a ford lower down the river, which was very swampy on either side. An old crocodile tried to make a meal off some of the Sudanese who were having a bathe, and soon cleared them out of the water. At Baranwa there was another fort on some rising ground overlooking the crossing, garrisoned by a small force of soldiers, but this has now been withdrawn, as the road is no longer used. A good road leads from here to the lake connecting the forts. There are high ranges of hills to the north-east, and between the road and Misriandura lie some curious steep and high hills, the biggest of which is Msaga Nkuro, an old stronghold of the Wanyoro, which had been recently stormed by Captain Thruston.

The country is covered for the most part with grass and bush about 10 feet high, through which it is impossible to penetrate except by the native tracks, although in the dry season, when fires are to be seen all over the country, a great deal of the grass is burnt down. The country, therefore, is well adapted for ambushes, a method of fighting which the natives prefer above all others, and only in September last, on this same road, Mr. Forster, a civilian official, was suddenly attacked by the Wanyoro, losing five or six men killed and wounded, including his cook, who was close beside him.

On the 1st January 1895 we arrived at the head-quarters, Fort Hoima, which had, with the other forts on the road to the Albert Nyanza, been established by Colonel Colvile at the close of his expedition in February 1894. It was a pretty place, facing a valley which led to the north through lofty and broken ranges of hills. Protected on two sides by river swamps, which joined together about 200 yards from the fort, and flowed to the eastward in a sluggish stream bordered with papyrus, the post was surrounded by fields of cultivation—sweet potatoes, Indian corn, and rice, so necessary for the support of the garrison.

Captain Thruston was awaiting our arrival here with interest, as on Major Cunningham taking over the command in Unyoro from him he was to return home at once.

After a year of strife and unrest in Unyoro, affairs seemed to have assumed a more peaceful aspect. In consequence of the attacks on convoys and detach-ments marching along the road between the forts, Captain Thruston had, in the beginning of November, made a forced march to Machudi, where Kabarega was living, and, covering the distance in a very short space of time, had effected a most successful surprise, rushing the town at night, whereupon in an instant all was confusion. His hopes of capturing the king him-self were, however, dashed to the ground, as on the

first alarm the latter fled into the darkness and succeeded in evading the soldiers who were surrounding
the enclosure.   A severe blow had, however, been
dealt, and much of the king's property and cattle was
captured.   After the return of the expedition to Fort
Hoima two emissaries had arrived from Kabarega to
treat for peace, and an armistice had been agreed
upon.   A message had been sent to Kabarega, and
one of the envoys was still waiting at the fort.

Thruston looked very thin and worn after his hard
work, and was ill whilst we were at Hoima.   He left
for Uganda on 5th January.   The garrison, increased
by the reinforcements brought by us, now consisted of
three companies,—No. 3 commanded by Yuzbashi
Abdullah; No. 4, by Yuzbashi Mabruk; No. 9, by
Yuzbashi Bilal.   The last named had been formerly
in the Egyptian army.

Mabruk, the senior of the black officers here, was
an excellent man, and besides being chief staff-officer
was also the great authority on agriculture and archi-
tecture.   The Sudanese method of building a house
was of the simplest kind, and consisted in making the
roof first, which was then hoisted on to a number of
poles, forked at the top, and planted in the ground
in the shape required.   Long thin laths of wood were
then lashed on each side of the poles parallel to the
ground, and the space between was tightly filled with
dry grass, the whole being then plastered over with
mud, forming an excellent wall.   Room had, of course,
to be left for the door and the windows, and a verandah
could be made by prolonging the roof to another series
of poles placed about 3 feet from the wall of the house.
It is essential that the roof should be made slanting
enough to carry off the heavy tropical rain.

My house was constructed in this fashion, and more than a year after my return home I heard that the house was still in good order, though rather draughty; that the poles of the verandah were sprouting and were covered with little branches and green leaves, so that the house may be said to have been actually growing, such is the extraordinary power of vegetation in this country.

Stables had also to be constructed for our two ponies, which had safely surmounted all the obstacles *en route*, and had arrived in the country fit and well, a great triumph, as they were the first animals of their kind to reach Unyoro from the east coast of Africa. It was ludicrous to see the way in which the natives used to run away from them at first, and, if suddenly confronted round a corner by this strange unknown quadruped they would drop whatever they were carrying in the pathway and dive into the high grass at the side.

Sir Samuel Baker took horses with him in his expedition up the Nile from Egypt to Unyoro in 1872, but of these only two reached Unyoro, and one died and another was speared in the disastrous return march from Masindi to the Victoria Nile, when Kabarega behaved with such treachery.

On my return afterwards from the Nile I made some polo sticks and balls, and we used to amuse ourselves of an evening practising on the parade-ground round the fort, rather a dangerous pastime owing to the deep holes made in the ground by the red ants, into which one used occasionally to subside. Polo may thus be said to have found its way even to Equatorial Africa.

The men of the three companies forming the garri-

son were now all armed with the Martini-Henry rifles
which we had brought up from the coast, and were
especially pleased with their new sword-bayonets. It
is surprising how well a black soldier will look after
his rifle and accoutrements, and after the hardest
marching and rough work I used to find these clean
and in good order.

Our stay at Hoima was as short as possible, as
Cunningham was anxious to start off for the Nile, and
on the 7th January we set out for Kibero, leaving
Mr. Forster in charge of the post.

The country becomes more open on nearing the
Albert Nyanza, and is rocky in places, until all of a
sudden one reaches the edge of an enormous escarpment, 1200 feet below which the great sheet of water,
bordered by a strip of yellow sand, unfolds itself to the
traveller's astonished gaze. The Sudanese fort, and
the few wretched huts comprising the village of Kibero,
down to which a steep and stony path leads from the
edge of the plateau, appear mere specks close to the
water's edge, and in the distance the calm clear waters
vanish in the white haze which obscures the western
shore and seems to continually overhang this great rift
in the earth's surface.

Sometimes, even from Fort Hoima, we could, after
rain, distinctly see the blue peaks of the mountains on
the western shore, below which a dense white cloud
revealed the line of the water.

We pitched our tents on the sandy shore of the
lake, and soon realised the wretchedness of the place.
All the burning rays of the sun seemed concentrated
on this depression, and there was not a particle of
shade.

The natives live by the salt which they make and

sell for food; and the few other articles which repre-
sent their scanty wants, and everything, including firewood, has to be brought down from the plateau above.
A few dug-out canoes were lying on the shore, and I
have seen the largest of these returning from a voyage
to the opposite shore laden with fish, chickens, and
eggs. It is rather a dangerous voyage for them, and
takes about twelve hours. There are several varieties
of fish, which run up to a very large size.

III

In the Steel Boat to Dufile

OUR home for the next three weeks was to be a steel boat about 20 feet long, which had been brought in sections from Lake Victoria by Colonel Colvile, and had been put together by Mr. Purkiss, who unfortunately died at Kibwezi, on his way home, from hæmaturic fever. After several trials a crew of sixteen was selected, consisting of eight Sudanese—most of whom had been on Emin Pasha's old steamers—and eight Zanzibaris, including our own servants. Two or three of the latter had learnt to row at Zanzibar, but the remainder were the worst rowers I have ever seen, and it required continual curses and exhortations to keep them in time. They had little idea where they were going to, and, imagining it was only for a pleasant cruise across the lake, several men clambered into the boat, in addition to the appointed crew, but these were promptly deposited in the water by Cunningham. With us also came a friendly Wanyoro chief, called Keyser, who spoke the Lure language. He had been at Wadelai in Emin Pasha's time, his father having been killed by Kabarega. We were packed pretty tightly, what with men, luggage, two goats, chickens, etc., and Cunningham and I sat on our tents and bags in the stern, with the Maxim gun between us. There

were two reliefs of eight men, who rowed for an hour
at a time, and we took it in turn to steer. We sailed
all the first day with a good breeze, and camped on the
western shore at Mahagi after dark. It was quite
rough in the middle of the lake, and several of the
crew succumbed to the unaccustomed motion. There
was difficulty in finding a landing-place, owing to the
reeds and swampy nature of the shore, and we coasted
along in the darkness until a welcome strip of sand
glimmered in the dim moonlight, and we were able to
pitch our tents on *terra firma*. There happened to be
a village near at hand, the inhabitants of which brought
down torches and assisted us in landing our loads in
the darkness. When daylight came we could see that
the high mountains were close to us, and that the lofty
peak of Nelia dominated its companions.

The next day we coasted along the west shore. Here
the mountains gradually recede from the coast and
become a low range of hills, whilst some villages inhabited
by the Lure, or Alure, tribe are scattered along the
shore. The lake gradually narrows to the point where
the Nile starts on its long journey to Egypt, and
almost imperceptibly one finds oneself on the great
river, the left bank being thickly wooded and covered
with magnificent trees, whose luxuriant foliage is the
home of many monkeys and baboons. There are a
few clearings close to the water's edge, where some
wretched huts have been erected by the native fisher-
men, whose primitive - looking dug - out canoes lie
fastened to the bank. At the village of Amat, where
we camped, the river is about 600 yards broad, but on
leaving this, and until reaching the bend, the river is
only 150 yards broad in places, and the country on
both sides appeared very barren and dried-up after the

green verdure and lovely banana groves of Uganda and Unyoro.

In the early morning we stopped to speak to Aiyara, an important chief on the left bank; he was a very fine-looking man, clothed in skins, and wearing some ivory ornaments, and his people all seemed very friendly. Soon after this the river opened out into a small lake, papyrus and floating vegetation on either side making it difficult to judge the size of it. On nearing Wadelai the river narrows considerably, and there is a very strong stream, against which it was as much as we could do to make way on our return journey.

We passed Fachora, a very large village on the right bank, situated on some rising ground overlooking the rapid, and camped a mile farther on at Emin Pasha's old fort of Wadelai, which was then completely overgrown. We set fire to all the grass round, just as much to diminish, in a measure, the myriads of mosquitoes as to give us a clear field of fire in case of surprise, the natives appearing very hostile, and having evidently thrown in their lot with Kabarega. Just under a year before, "Roddy" Owen had reached the same place, where he made a treaty with Ali, Sheikh of Wadelai, and hoisted the British flag on both sides of the Nile. There were no villages near the old fort, and Cunningham went up to Fachora in the afternoon to buy some food, which he did with difficulty. The mosquitoes here, and afterwards throughout the journey, were dreadful both at night and in the early morning, and it was only by using a mosquito head-net, waterproof coat, and gloves that I was able to take observations for latitude and longitude at night. Even the blacks themselves could not sleep, and it used to be a relief to push out into the middle of the river in the lovely cool mornings and watch the sun gradually rising over the green banks of papyrus.

Nothing was known at this time of the river beyond Wadelai, and the Maxim gun was got ready for eventualities when we continued our journey down stream on the 12th. There was a very strong current in places, and we glided rapidly past narrow channels formed by the floating vegetation, stopping sometimes near the villages on the banks to ask for news. At all of these they informed us that the dervishes were advancing from Dufile by both banks. Though we doubted the truth of their statements, it was exciting work as we proceeded, and we had no wish to fall into the arms of the dervishes and be transported to Khartum. Our guide did not at all like coming on, and relapsed into silence; crouching down in the bows of the boat with his chin resting on his knees, he frequently, after this, invoked Allah, and comforted himself with a long pipe. Our soldiers also were alarmed at the idea of meeting their old opponents; and the corporal, a rather faint-hearted Egyptian, declared on one occasion that he could hear the dervish noggara beating.

The first Madi village was met with at Towara; it differed from the Lure villages in being surrounded by a thorn zariba.

The farther we went from Wadelai the more friendly the natives seemed to become. They are continually fighting among themselves, and lead a precarious existence. Several poor wretches came to us to have their wounds dressed, and at Mgerenin, a village on the left bank, the chief had lately been raided at night by some people on the opposite bank, and had lost all his women and possessions, besides receiving a bad spear wound in a place which showed he was ignominiously flying from the enemy. The fame of our medicine spread rapidly, and on our return journey a canoe suddenly shot out from the bank bringing another chief suffering from several old spear wounds, and evidently in the last stages of decay. His head was supported by his wife, who was fanning him with a bunch of green leaves to keep the flies off, and it was altogether quite a touching scene, but, alas! we could do little for him.

We camped on the high bank overhanging the river near Mgerenin, and I was reading in my tent in the evening when my servant suddenly rushed up to say a big animal had emerged from some swampy ground near the river and could be seen from the camp. Taking my 10-bore rifle, I started out after him, and soon made out it was a huge rhinoceros. When about 200 yards from him a shot rang out from the opposite side, and I made the unpleasant discovery that I was exactly in the line of fire, so, thinking prudence the better part of valour, I retired on all-fours as I had come. Cunningham had seen the rhinoceros as he was returning to camp from shooting, and was, curiously enough, stalking the animal at the same time from the other side, but unfortunately did not kill him.

An enormous amount of floating vegetation passes down the Nile in this part of its course. It is gradually broken off from the sides of the river by the force of the current, and floats down until it attaches itself to the sides again, or reaches the cataracts below Dufile, where it is broken up into little pieces. The size of the floating islands or rafts, principally composed of papyrus rushes, and little green plants (*Pistia Stratiotes*), is quite extraordinary, and I have seen one fully 100 yards long with a small hut ensconced in the papyrus.

Care has to be taken in a strong stream not to be carried away by one of these islands, or to be jammed between two of them. They are to be met with in the middle of the Albert Nyanza making their way towards the Nile, having, I suppose, drifted from the *sudd* at the mouth of the Semliki.

There is a great deal of floating vegetation also on the Victoria Nile between Lake Kioja and the Karuma Falls. During one expedition a Waganda chief informed us that Kabarega was having a march-past of his army on the opposite bank, about 1100 yards off. One could apparently see the soldiers, or Warasura, as they are called, passing through the trees in their white cloths; and the deception was perfect until, on looking through the glasses, it was discovered that they were really a flock of white birds sitting on the top of a large papyrus raft floating rapidly past under the far bank.

After passing Bora, an old Egyptian fort on the right bank, the river is very broad — about 1½ miles—though the actual channel through the *sudd* is only about 500 yards in breadth. A place was pointed out to us close to Bora where the last of Emin Pasha's steamers had sunk, simply from old age and want of repair.

A Sudanese soldier had been pilot on board one of the steamers, and it was to him we trusted for directions as to the right channel, and it was wonderful how seldom he was at fault. He was able to talk the Madi language, and was consequently of the greatest value to us. When passing a village he used to stand up in the bows and shout out, *ana Murgan*—I am Murgan;

and to our astonishment the natives all seemed to know him, and were delighted to see him again. The line of hills which runs from Wadelai down the right bank of the river, and about 2 miles distant from it, ends about 12 miles before Unigwe, and the country to the east becomes open and flat.

There is such a quantity of *sudd* about this reach that it is for miles and miles impossible to land, and not until late in the afternoon of the 13th did we find a passage to the bank, where there was a landing-place used by hippopotami. From the noise made by them after dark they were evidently indignant at the presence of trespassers, and at being disturbed in their evening walk. We named this place Mosquito Camp, on account of the clouds of mosquitoes which assailed us during the night, and we were only too glad to leave early the next morning. We stopped at the village of Unigwe about 8 a.m., and obtained grain and some chickens. The chief's name is Abu Suma, and his people complained much of being raided by a chief from the interior called Abu Kra.

The banks between this and Dufile seemed well populated, though the country did not look very inviting. A few trees were scattered about, and villages were hidden away among high rocks and boulders on small hills close to the river. There was a certain amount of mtama and dhurra cultivated, but very few sheep and goats, and we had to subsist entirely on very skinny chickens, when we were lucky enough to buy them. It was impossible to obtain any accurate information, but everything pointed to the dervishes not being at Dufile itself, and about 5 p.m. on the 14th January we reached the old fort situated close to the water's edge on the left bank at a

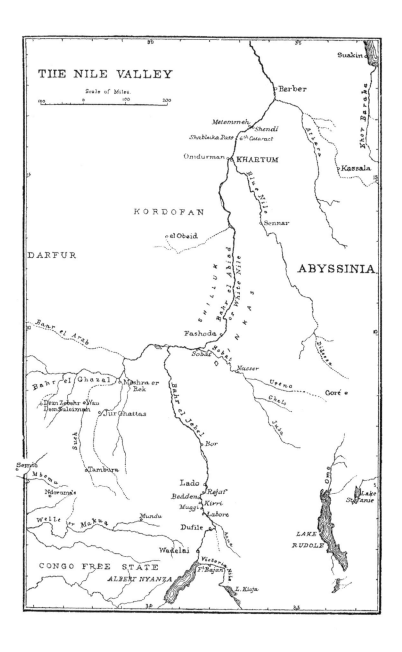

THE NILE VALLEY

Scale of Miles.

100   0   100   200

Suakin

Berber

Metemmeh   Shendi
Shabluka Pass   6th Cataract

Omdurman   KHARTUM

Kassala

KORDOFAN

el Obeid

Sennar

DARFUR

ABYSSINIA

SHILLUK

Bahr el Abiad or White Nile

NUKAS

Bahr el Arab

Fashoda

Sobat

Nasser

Ugeno

Goré

Chelo

Bahr el Ghazal   Meshra er Rek

Dem Zebehr   Wau
Dem Suleiman

Jur Ghattas

Juba

Bahr el Jebel

Bor

Such

Tambura

Semio

Mbomu

Ndoruma's

Lado   Rejaf
Beddens   Kirri
Muggi   Labore

Welle or Makua   Mundu

Dufile

Wadelai

Ome

Lake Stefanie

LAKE RUDOLF

CONGO FREE STATE   Victoria
ALBERT NYANZA   Ft Bajan

L. Kioja

bend of the river. As at Wadelai, we had to burn down all the grass and reeds, which rose up here to a height of 10 feet. The parapet and ditch were very distinct, and the mud-brick walls of the houses still remained, whilst behind these, in what had evidently been the garden, were some lemon and cotton trees, the only signs remaining of the Egyptian occupation.

It was a relief to get on shore after sitting cramped up in the stern on one's tent and luggage, together with a Maxim gun, for no less than ten or eleven hours. We also felt the heat very much after the climate of the lake districts.

I believe we were the first white men to reach Dufile since the abandonment of the place in November 1888.

There was then very severe fighting here for three days, and Casati says in his book that—

"During the night of the 27th the Mahdists succeeded in penetrating into the station and attacking the steamers, killed the captain of the *Nyanza*, the engineer, the pilot, and the stoker ; all these died on the *Khedive*. The fight lasted till 8 a.m., when the enemy shortly afterwards retreated. Owing, however, to the almost complete exhaustion of ammunition, the abandonment of Dufile and the mustering of the troops at Wadelai was decided upon. Fear lends wings, therefore the evacuation of Dufile was speedily effected, quite an unknown thing with the people of the province."

We were shown the site of the old dervish camp on the high ground about 1½ miles off, and behind this again there are some high rugged peaks.

Major Cunningham concluded a treaty with the chief, Wador, at Dufile, who received us in a friendly manner, and the British flag was duly hoisted on both banks. The chief told us that the dervishes were then at Rejaf, at the lower end of the rapids.

On the following day we rowed down to the head of the rapids, above which there appeared to be a number of black rocks projecting out of the water, and seemingly immovable. As we approached, however, all the rocks began to move, and were soon transformed into a school of hippos, snorting and splashing in the water. The river Unyama joins the Nile at this point.

We walked across from a village called Karas to a bend of the river below the head of the rapids. Here the Nile was a seething torrent, only about 50 yards wide, and the banks were strewn with enormous boulders of rock.

Coming from the south, navigation ends at the mouth of the river Unyama, and between Dufile and Labore foaming rapids succeed each other at short intervals ; and the Fola cataracts (enclosed within the walls of a narrow gorge), at the confluence of the Nile with the Asua, make navigation quite impossible. About 2½ miles south of Fola the river is, however, free from obstacles, and between Kiri and Bedden navigation is easy. At Bedden transhipment has again to take place, owing to the rapids.

Forty miles farther on, and 120 miles from Dufile, is Lado, whence steamers can journey to Khartum, a distance of 900 miles, in sixteen days or less, and can ascend even to Bedden, except in the dry season.

Below Lado, as far as Fashoda, is an unpleasant, swampy, malarious region, where during part of its course the Nile splits up into two channels, and is sometimes so choked with the *sudd*, or vegetable débris, that navigation is impossible until the obstruction has been cut through. Other causes also combine to render navigation on this stretch of the Nile difficult.

In 1870 Sir Samuel Baker found the White Nile entirely blocked by an immense number of floating islands, which had converted the river-bed into a solid marsh, so that he was obliged to try another route, *viâ* the second channel, called the Bahr Giraffe. Here, however, his crews found themselves entrapped in a sea of apparently boundless marsh and water-grass, from which, in spite of all their labour, they did not emerge for forty-six days. Making another attempt on 12th January 1871, he succeeded in cutting a way through, and arrived in open water again on 19th March.

In 1875 Colonel Gordon wrote: "Navigation from Lado to Khartum is almost impossible; firewood is scarce and becomes more so every year; there are numerous sand-banks."

Again, in 1878, an unusual rise of the Nile bore off so much débris from the flooded banks that it was not until 1880 that communication between the upper and lower reaches of the river was re-established.

Near the 9th parallel of latitude—here, as in West Africa, a line of much importance at the present time—the Nile makes a bend to the eastward for about 100 miles, and is joined first by the Bahr-el-Ghazal from the west, and farther on by the Sobat River from the east; from the latter down to Khartum navigation is fairly easy.

Baker tells us that the Bahr-el-Ghazal, though navigable for 200 miles, and the receiver of a multitude of rivers some 3 to 400 miles long, is in the dry season nearly empty of water, being at that period only a line of stagnant pools and marshes. It seems probable, however, that by cutting through the obstructions with great labour navigation is feasible even in some dry seasons, as Junker one year ascended to Meshra-er-Rek in February, or about the middle of the dry season. A lake called the Magren-el-Bahur, or Meeting of the Waters, is formed during the rainy season by the junction of the Bahr-el-Jebel (White Nile) and Bahr-el-Ghazal, but at low water it is divided into two sections, which communicate through a channel a little over half a mile long. On leaving the lake and ascending the Bahr-el-Ghazal the channel narrows to about 50 yards, and Junker describes how "on both sides extensive tracts of country are permanently flooded, and only an occasional fishing hamlet is visible on a dry patch of ground in this submerged region."

This account reminds one very much of the Delta of the Niger, except that here the mangrove swamps are replaced by miles and miles of floating grass and vegetation.

Junker took eight days to ascend the river to Meshra-er-Rek in a steamer, and on the afternoon of the first day met with the first real grass barrier, which was surmounted in twenty minutes. Later followed other loose accumulations, which though easily removed still caused much delay, one obstacle taking an hour to cut away. On the second day a few scattered trees denoted the presence of dry ground, but the same difficulties were met with, although once or twice the river opened out into a good broad waterway. On the third day, after getting through some smaller masses, the steamer was blocked for several hours by a huge barrier of a felt-like consistency, and

nearly a third of a mile in extent; whilst the whole of
the fourth day was occupied in forcing a way through
sudd 1¼ miles in length. On the fifth day the main
stream—shortly before it is joined by the Bahr-el-
Arab, 90 miles from its mouth—was found to be 350
yards wide and 20 to 30 feet deep, with the banks
wooded on either side.

The Bahr-el-Arab, rising on the borders of Wadai
and Darfur, is a fine river over 400 miles in length,
and is joined by numerous streams from the south.
Little is known of the country lying immediately to
the north of it, and on the left bank.

After passing the junction of the two rivers, Junker
says, " there was another expanse of stagnant water,
beyond which the open channel contracts at first to
fifty, then a little over twenty yards. Here the woods
become thinner, and at last again give place to boundless flooded grass plains, with patches here and there
of tall ambatch. Beyond the mouth of the Jur, coming
from the south-west, there was little to suggest a river,
—there being apparently a boundless sea of grass and
sedge, with an open expanse winding away to the head
of the steam navigation at Meshra-er-Rek."

After struggling through more obstacles he reached
this place, a journey of 130 miles, in eight days, and
cast anchor off the little island dignified by the name
of Meshra-er-Rek, on which there were only a few
Government huts, and which is surrounded by a dreary
marsh through which carriers have to wade waist-
deep to reach *terra firma* 3 or 4 miles to the southward. This, then, is the way of reaching the harbour
of the rich and fertile Bahr-el-Ghazal province from
the Nile, and a precarious way too, judging from the
disaster which occurred to Gessi Pasha when leaving

the province with 400 Arabs and officials after the
war with Soliman. Hopelessly hemmed in by *sudd*,
all their efforts to get disentangled were in vain, and
half of them died of starvation and typhus before a
steamer appeared from Khartum and rescued the survivors. Amongst these was Gessi Pasha, who, however, never recovered from the horrible experience, and
died shortly afterwards.

It will be seen what an immense difficulty the *sudd*
offers to navigation on the reaches of the middle Nile
and Bahr-el-Ghazal. Steamers are being built with a
special view to their ability to cut through it, the screw
working in a jacket to protect it from the weeds, and
it will be interesting to see how these succeed.

All accounts agree as to the value and abund-
ance of natural resources of the Bahr-el-Ghazal
province, which Slatin Pasha describes as a most
fertile district, extending over an enormous area,
watered by a labyrinth of streams and covered with
mountains and forests, the soil being exceptionally
good and producing quantities of cotton and india-
rubber. About 60 miles south of Meshra-er-Rek,
and connected with it by water navigable for flat-
bottomed boats, is a place called Wau, which Gessi
Pasha had intended to make the chief station of
the province, with a view to sending down thence to
Khartum many products which could not bear the
cost of transport by carriers all the way to Meshra-
er-Rek. The other great tributary which joins the
White Nile near the 9th parallel, and 60 miles above
Fashoda, is the Sobat, which is known to be navigable
for 180 miles, and from its numerous sources near
Lake Rudolf and in the highlands of Abyssinia to the
eastward brings down an immense volume of muddy

water. In 1874 Gordon established a post called Nasser on its banks at the head of the navigable portion, and there was also an Egyptian post at the mouth of the river.

In a straight line east of Dufile, and about 220 miles off, lies Lake Rudolf. By drawing lines from these two places to the north for 450 miles—at which distance the line from Dufile will strike Fashoda—we enclose a tract of country entirely unexplored, with the exception of a small area east of Lado and Dufile traversed and occupied by Emin Pasha's troops, and another to the west traversed by Captain Bòttego's route; it is, in fact, the only large portion of Africa left whose mysteries still remain to be revealed. To the south of this line for 100 miles the country inhabited by the Langos is also almost unknown. There are reports as to the richness and importance of the tracts lying to the north-east, which are probably watered by tributaries of the Sobat, and it may be from here the Egyptians obtained gold in old days.

To the east of Fashoda a great plain, inhabited by the warlike tribe of the Shilluks, stretches away until it reaches the mountain spurs of the Abyssinian highlands. Captain Bòttego, who, like so many other brave Italian officers, has given his life in the cause of geography, has by his recent wonderful journey explored a portion of the country lying north-west of Lake Rudolf, and discovered the principal source of the Sobat. Leaving Brava on the east coast in October 1895 with four white companions, 250 soldiers, 121 camels, etc., he reached Lake Rudolf and explored the western shore. A few days' march in a north-westerly direction from that lake, and slightly to the north of the 6th degree of latitude, he found a great valley

running from east to west which he at once conjectured to contain one of the affluents of the Nile;
this proved to be the Juba, a name given to the
principal upper branch of the Sobat.

It is curious that in 1872 Baker alludes to this river
rising in the Lobbohr country, beyond the Langgos, east
of Dufile, and confuses it with the other Juba River
which flows into the Indian Ocean.

Bòttego followed the course of the river for several
days, at first through a sparsely inhabited country,
until he arrived among the Jambos. On his way
he came across two affluents on the right bank, the
Ghelo and the Upeno, and altering his direction made
his way along the latter river, nearly 300 yards broad
in the dry season, towards the lofty plateau of Abyssinia.

At Saio he came into contact with the Abyssinians,
and was killed by them, his companions Vanutelli and
Citerni being captured, and the whole expedition
broken up.

In view of the recent ridiculous claims of the
Emperor Menelik to all the country extending from
his dominions to the banks of the Nile, it is worthy of
note that no Abyssinian was met with until approaching Saio or Lega in longitude 35° 10′ east of Greenwich.

It is towards Fashoda that French expeditions are
now hurrying, both from the French Congo on the
west, a journey of nearly 2000 miles *viâ* the Ubangi
and Mbomu Rivers, and from Abyssinia on the
east. Two years ago Semio, an advanced post on the
Mbomu River, was occupied; and latterly a further
advance has been made across the watershed between
the Congo and the Nile, to Dem Zibehr or Dem

Suliman, a distance of 180 miles, and a small post established at Tambura, on the Sue River, 170 miles to the east, without opposition on the part of the natives. The post is, of course, isolated, and necessary supplies have to be transported all this long distance from the base, but the fact remains that the French are now on the watershed of the Nile, and they need find no difficulty—except in the matter of transport and food—in establishing themselves at Meshra-er-Rek, even if they have not reached that place already. Junker journeyed from the latter place to Dem Suliman by Jur Ghattas in nineteen days, through the country inhabited by the Dinkas. It is reported that a large and well-armed expedition, composed of men of the Foreign Legion, tirailleurs Sénégalais, all starting from Semio under Captain Marchand,—supported by four other officers,—is to co-operate with that under M. Liotard at Dem Zibehr, and is carrying a small steel gunboat with it. The difficulties in the way of transporting such a vessel a distance of over 300 miles are very great, as we have seen in trying to transport a steamer in sections to the Victoria Nyanza from the East Coast. Although the Bahr-el-Ghazal province is peopled by some of the most warlike races in the Sudan, and supplies the best recruits for the Sudanese battalions, there is no cohesion among them, and they recognise no single ruler or head. This fact will make the French advance easier, as no organised opposition on a large scale will be met with. The majority of the natives are also pagans, and not fanatical Mohammedans (see *Fire and Sword in the Sudan*, by Slatin Pasha).

The other expedition from the east, under the Marquis de Bonchamps, who is taking with him an escort of armed Abyssinians, had, in July 1897, reached Goré, close to the place where Captain Bòttego was killed four months before, joining here an expedition under another Frenchman, Captain Clochette, who has since died. They went on from here to the Didessa River, which flows into the Blue Nile. Besides experiencing transport difficulties they were beginning to suffer from desertions on the part of their men.

Whether the Abyssinians will care to descend from their homes in the highlands to the swampy plains and heated wastes near Fashoda, with the probability of fighting the Shilluks, is a matter of opinion. The unhealthy nature of the country below the Ethiopian highlands induced Captain Bòttego to make for the mountains, where he was to meet his death at the hands of the Abyssinians.

One can but admire the enterprise of these French officers in leading their perilous expeditions; but what does it all mean, and why should the French be pushing on with such speed into what is clearly regarded as the Anglo-Egyptian sphere of influence in the Nile valley, remote as it is from their own territories in Africa?

Speaking on this subject in the House of Commons in 1895, Sir Edward Grey stated that "any advance into the Nile valley on the part of the French would be an unfriendly act, and it was well known to the French Government that we should so regard it."

In April 1897, in answer to a question relating to M. Liotard's expedition, Mr. Curzon stated: "The Egyptian Government has not relinquished any of its claims to territory in the basin of the Upper Nile."

The Bahr-el-Ghazal province must be surely looked upon as the most important of its old possessions, and it seems ridiculous, and contrary to all geographical conditions, that this region lying in the Nile valley should be developed and opened up by way of the Congo.

By the agreement of the 12th May 1894, between Great Britain and King Leopold as sovereign of the Congo Free State, all the territory between the 30th meridian east of Greenwich and the Nile up to the 10th parallel of latitude was leased to King Leopold for his lifetime, and the situation is summed up in a form easily understood in the following telegram sent at the time by Lord Kimberley to Mr. Cracknall at Zanzibar (*Uganda Blue Book*, April 1895):—

" Write to Colonel Colvile that we have made a friendly arrangement under which Belgians will hold left bank of Nile from Lake Albert to Fashoda as leaseholders under Great Britain. If he comes into contact with them, he should maintain perfectly amicable relations. They will eventually fly a slightly altered British flag."

France, claiming her right of preemption over the Congo Free State, objected strongly to this arrangement, and any attempt to annex the Bahr-el-Ghazal province; and only three months afterwards an agreement was signed at Paris, 14th August 1894, between France and the Congo Free State, which rendered the previous one virtually nugatory. In this the Congo Free State renounced all occupation or political influence in the future in the territory leased to it by Great Britain north of 5° 30′ north latitude. In return for this renunciation, France agreed to move the boundary of the Congo Free State considerably to the north of the 4th parallel north, which had been laid down as a limit according to the Berlin Act; and the boundary between France and the Congo Free State is now formed by the Ubangi and Mbomu Rivers, and the northern boundary of the latter is continued eastward from the source of the Mbomu, eventually touching the Nile a short distance north of Lado.

After Gordon was appointed Governor of Equatoria in 1874, he established his headquarters at Lado, with a series of military stations for the protection of the Nile route, and placed steamers on the Upper Nile. Rejaf and Bedden at first, then Kirri, Muggi, Labore, Dufile, and Magungo secured the way to the Albert Nyanza. The road to Unyoro and Uganda was opened up later by the stations Paniatoli, Foweira, Kerota, and Mruli.

It is sad to think how, in consequence of the rise of Mahdiism, the whole of the Upper Sudan has relapsed into savagery, and that, where steamers were regularly running, now our only means of communication is a small steel boat. The forces of the Congo Free State have made numerous attempts to push on to the Nile, which met with little success, owing to reverses sustained in fights with the dervishes and mutinies amongst their own troops, until, towards the middle of February 1897, Commandant Chaltin, marching from the Upper Welle, occupied Rejaf.

His force consisted of 700 soldiers and 500 lancers under A-Zandeh chiefs, and after two days' hard fighting defeated the so-called dervishes, who were driven towards Bor, 100 miles north of Rejaf. A Belgian officer was killed during the engagement. In the report of the affair it is stated that the enemy's killed included several Egyptians, Abyssinians, and people of Darfur. Although some of the leaders were dervishes of note, it may be assumed that these were banished from Omdurman for some reason or other, and there could have been little connection between the riff-raff at Lado and the Khalifa in the north.

Two brass cannons, 700 rifles, two magazines filled with arms and ammunition, drums and other musical instruments, were found at Rejaf. On pushing forward to the old site of Lado the place was found quite deserted, and surrounded by swamps. The Belgians have now established a small post at Muggi farther south.

The Madi tribe extend to a distance of about three days' journey to the east of Dufile; then come the Umiro, a tribe of the Lango; then the real light-coloured Lango (Galla), who breed donkeys and camels (*Emin Pasha in Central Africa*, edited by Felkin and Schweinfurth). The natives are a fine strong-looking race, and we tried to persuade two of them to enlist, but they were afraid of leaving their homes for the unknown. They were very friendly, and helped to take our loads out of the boat. They wear little or no clothes, and have no wants except beads and iron wire.

At Umia's village at the bend of the river we met a representative of Abu Sulla, an important chief living one day's march below Dufile on the right bank. He wore a fez, and was dressed in white cloth, probably obtained from the Arabs or Mahdists to the north. Most of the villages are reached by narrow channels cut through the *sudd*, and almost impossible to find. We attempted to pay the chief of the village at Dufile a visit in the boat, and he had the channel enlarged for us, but after hard work for half an hour we found we had only advanced a few yards, and gave it up as hopeless.

Our return journey to the Albert Nyanza was rather tedious owing to the strong stream, and the wind was often against us. If there was time I used to go out shooting in the evening, and saw plenty of game, though the dried-up grass with which the country was covered to a height of 4 or 5 feet made shooting difficult. One day I killed two water-buck, which came in very useful, as provisions were running short. A species of hartebeest and a smaller antelope with short curved horns were seen, but to my great regret I never succeeded in killing any.

Curiously enough, on our return to Mgerenin, where Cunningham had a bad attack of fever, I walked about 2 miles inland, and suddenly came upon what I am convinced was the very same rhinoceros which had emerged from the marsh the last time we camped at Mgerenin. He seemed to bear a charmed life, and again got away wounded into the bush, where it was impossible to follow him.

Just before reaching Wadelai the body of a wretched woman floated past us, with her hands tied above her head and a spear wound in her abdomen.

On inquiry afterwards it appeared that the chief, Wadelai, had charged her with witchcraft and poisoning his daughter, who had died a few days before, and she was then speared and thrown into the river. As the chief knew we were returning at that time, it may also have been meant as a defiance to us.

The people of these countries, as also the Sudanese soldiers, have the most implicit belief in witchcraft, and it was a common occurrence for a soldier to be put under arrest by the black officers and brought up on a charge of bewitching and causing the death of others. They do not seem to be able to take in the idea of a natural death.

We met with a hostile demonstration at Wadelai

on our return, the natives assembling along the banks armed with spears, bows and arrows, and a few guns. They seemed great cowards, and dared not do anything except shout. We were obliged to camp on the right bank, and our guide, Keyser, tried to parley with them here, but in vain. They kept a respectful 300 yards away, but held their positions round us during the remainder of the afternoon. It would have been easy to rush us during the night, but they did not attempt to do so. We slept close to the boat, and the Maxim gun was placed ready for action.

The friendly chief Iyara told us the next day that Wadelai had sent messengers to incite him also against us.

On reaching Lake Albert we coasted along the east shore, which was swampy and bordered with *sudd*, but beyond this we could see a fine open grass plain with scattered bushes in the distance, over which some stately giraffe were walking along, also some Senegal hartebeest and other antelope. To our great disappointment, it was impossible to find a landing-place through the *sudd*, and at a late hour we had to sail across to the other side of the lake, camping a little north of Boki.

It was a very dark night, and a large herd of elephants came down to drink on both sides of our small camp. Cunningham and I were sitting together after dinner listening to the trumpeting which resounded from all sides, but we had not realised that they were so close until two of our servants came up trembling with excitement, saying, " Tembo karibu sana bwana "—an elephant is quite close.

Taking our guns we went to the fire round which the men had been sitting, but could see nothing in the

4

impenetrable darkness until, on putting some dry grass on the fire and creating a blaze, the brute trumpeted quite close, and we could just distinguish a great mass moving off.

The Zanzibari askari in charge of the gun detachment took up a safe position at once in the boat 20 yards from the shore, and loaded the Maxim gun, a most dangerous proceeding, for which he was duly punished, as next morning the gun was found aimed directly on the camp.

What with hippos in the water and elephants all round us, it was just like sleeping in the Zoological Gardens, except that there were no bars to keep the animals within proper bounds, and one went to bed expecting to see an elephant's foot appearing through the side of the tent.

However, when morning came there were no elephants to be seen, and we resumed our journey to Kibero. The many floating islands of *sudd* made it difficult to distinguish the mouth of the Victoria Nile, and there is always a mirage on the horizon.

The east shore continued very swampy until at Lukwai's we effected a landing. Here there is a long stretch of low-lying ground covered with bush, aloes, and euphorbia trees, which lies between the lake and the high hills about 3 miles away. It is uninhabited, and is consequently the home of many animals, such as water-buck, kobus kob, a few buffalo and elephant. One evening in July, when I was camped in the same spot, we distinctly heard the roar of a lion, which had evidently secured a very fine goat presented to us by Tukenda, a chief at Mahagi; tired of our company, it had rushed off into the bush the moment we landed.

The Wanyoro have many villages and much cultivation on the high ground. Several good-sized rivers make their way down the escarpment and across the low ground into the lake.

On a second journey on Lake Albert in July I visited the Sudanese post at Mswa, and the west coast up to Mahagi. At Mswa there is still a village of Lendus, who remained there when the Sudanese were taken away. These Lendus, of whom there are a good many employed in the Protectorate, are of the greatest value. They carry the same loads as the Zanzibari porters, and receive four rupees a month instead of ten. They are usually very willing and cheerful.

A river called Kakoi flows down from the hills into the lake close to Mswa, and there are banana groves and fields of sweet potatoes along it. The natives living there are very primitive, and do not require cloth; they are of a darker hue than any natives I have yet seen in Central Africa.

From here along the coast the mountains, streaked with silver by numerous rivulets, come sheer down to the water's edge, until at Mahagi the hills are not so steep, and some low-lying ground juts out into the lake. This ground, as well as the hills behind under the Nelia peak, is covered with villages and cultivation. The chief of the place, Tukenda, and his people are all very friendly, and seem to possess an unlimited supply of chickens, the average price of which is from one to two strings of beads. Our journey came to an end on the 25th, when we got back to Kibero, and we returned to Fort Hoima the next day.

The lake seems certainly unhealthy to people coming from the high ground, and on returning to Hoima the whole of the escort of ten men who had been left at

Kibero on the second journey (quite a short one) were very ill with fever, and one died. They had been indulging in sulphur baths and probably caught a chill. I was also ill with fever on returning. Baker describes how, on reaching Vacovia on the lake, not one of his party could rise from the ground, and says: "No one could live at Vacovia without repeated attacks of fever."

IV

FIRST EXPEDITION TO THE VICTORIA NILE

ON our return to Hoima we found that Kabarega's envoys had run away. This looked suspicious, and the reign of peace was not destined to last long in Unyoro, as on the 9th of February a letter arrived from Kampala to say that 1200 Wanyoro were reported to have raided the country near Toru, under our protection, and killed two friendly chiefs. Kabarega had taken advantage of the truce, and the fact of the patrols being relaxed, to send this force down to the south, across the road between the forts, in order to meet a large caravan of arms and ammunition which was being brought up by the Arabs from the East Coast.

Captain Dunning, D.S.O., and Captain Ashburnham, with a force of Sudanese from Uganda, were marching on Fort Kaduma, and a force of Waganda was at that time being mobilised to follow them.

From information received through natives it was found that a number of Wanyoro, under an important chief called Rabadongo, were at Misriandura, a place not far off on the old Arab trade route. Cunningham decided to attack them at once, and two companies with a Maxim-gun detachment paraded at 5 p.m. on the 10th to make a night march.

This was my first experience of the black soldiers

on the war-path, and they certainly presented an extraordinary appearance as they fell in on the parade-
ground outside the fort that afternoon. The men were
sized indiscriminately, some being very tall and others
very small. Their best uniform—consisting of a blue
jersey, a pair of white breeches, an occasional pair of
putties, and a much-worn fez, originally red—was never
very grand, but to describe their campaigning clothes
as ragged is to use a mild epithet. Their jerseys were
covered and held together by patches of the ordinary
white trade cloth, of every conceivable shape and size,
and in some instances they were replaced by a torn
and tattered shirt reaching down to the knees. Round
their waists were fastened native-made leather belts,
with an upper flap to protect the cartridges from the
rain; these were really very well made, and served
excellently for the purpose. Suspended from the belt
hung numerous charms and amulets, made up of
cowries, bits of bone, leather cases containing Arabic
writing, and other weird articles. Their breeches were
of much the same colour as the ground, and were
patched in the same manner as the jerseys. A fez, a
piece of cloth wound round the head as a turban, or a
straw hat, such as they make themselves, fastened
under the chin by a piece of leather, completed their
attire.

The black officers usually wore a khaki jacket with
brass buttons, breeches and putties, or a pair of trousers,
a red fez, or more often a straw hat. Like the men,
they were also armed with rifles, but on the march were
most often to be seen with an umbrella, followed by a
boy carrying their rifle.[1]

[1] Owing to difficulties of transport, barely enough cloth arrived all this
way to pay the men, so there was little left to serve out as clothing.

SUDANESE TROOPS, No 5 COMPANY: ESCORT TO A MAXIM GUN

Close at hand, and waiting for them to start, stood a number of their women, with loads on their heads containing their cooking utensils—all manner of kinds of pots and pans—together with perhaps a *tente d'abris* and a blanket and some food. It is a hard life for them, and they age prematurely, so that one seldom sees a good-looking woman. Forced to carry loads on their heads from childhood, they are well set up and have good figures, and march along with the heavy loads in a wonderful way. They are disfigured with lines and either tribal or slave marks on the face and the upper part of the body. Some of these marks are supposed to enhance their personal charms, and are made by cutting the flesh with a knife and by burning. They are a light-hearted and good-natured people, and always cheery under difficulties. Marching in single file is the only means of progression in this country, and we started off along the main road to Baranwa in this formation, with about forty irregulars—friendly Wanyoro and Waganda—under the chief Omara, and half No. 4 Company forming the advance-guard, and half No. 3 Company as rear-guard. It soon became dark, and when we turned off along the Arab trade route in a south-westerly direction we had to force our way through the dense grass overhanging the path, stumbling over roots of trees and obstructions on the ground, and in vain trying to avoid hitting our faces against branches and twigs which the moonlight, filtering through the thick foliage overhead, failed to light up.

The heavy rain during the night before and on the morning of the 10th had made the path muddy and slippery, and, to add to the discomfort, about midnight, when we halted for rest and to allow the rear of the column to close up, a cold drizzling rain commenced, and lasted until dawn, when our ardour was still further damped by having to wade through a slimy, cold, papyrus swamp.

As we approached the high conical hill called Msaga Nkasi we were astonished at seeing fires in all directions, and at once concluded that our column had been detected and that these were watch-fires to announce our approach. This illumination, which in flickering and fitful flames extended round the steep sides of the high hill in front of us, was caused, however, by the fires lit for the purpose of capturing the white ants at the period of their transformation into winged insects. These are eagerly sought after as food, and little straw conical sheds are raised over the small hillocks in which they swarm for the purpose of capturing them.

As we advanced the country became thickly populated, and was covered with fields of cultivation and groves of plantains. There were many villages about, and we were soon discovered; the alarm was given, and we were fired upon after crossing the swamp. We did not arrive at Rabadongo's village till 7.30 a.m., after fourteen hours' marching, so that the surprise was a failure, and the Wanyoro had had time to drive off their cattle and flocks, and the Arabs who were with them to escape with their goods. Patrols were sent out later on in the day in different directions, but, after the long march, everyone was glad of a rest and some food. It was pleasant also to lie and bask in the sun, and to get dry again. Amongst other curious articles found here was a hock bottle, the last thing one expected to find in Central Africa. We camped at Rabadongo's that night, and next morning marched back a short way to Msaga Nkasi. The natives collected on the top of the hill which commanded the road, and had to be dislodged by the Maxim, whilst a desultory attack was made on the rear-guard as it crossed the swamp.

From the top of this hill, Msaga Nkasi, 500 feet above the camp, which I ascended afterwards, there was a magnificent view of the country, and to the northward there extended a great marsh forming the source of the Kafu River.

We returned to Hoima by a different track, which, though much shorter, had the disadvantage of crossing many streams and swamps. At the fort we found a deserter from Emin Pasha's old army who had come in from Kabarega. He proved very useful in giving information as to the road to the Victoria Nile, and also regarding Kabarega's movements.

The start was fixed for the 20th, and on that day two columns marched for the Nile by different routes to meet north of Mruli. Our column from Hoima consisted of two and a half companies Sudanese, the irregulars, and one Maxim-gun detachment — about 400 men altogether; Dunning's force from Baranwa consisted of two companies Sudanese, one Maxim, and 2000 Waganda, and was to march along the Kafu River.

I was ill with fever for three days before the start, a result of the night march to Rabadongo's, and my condition was not improved by the constant fear that I should be unable to accompany the expedition and be left behind in the fort. However, I succeeded in coming to the fort on the 20th, and with the aid of a donkey got through the first march. Luckily, we left our ponies behind, as it would have been almost impossible to take them with us by the road the guide led us; he seemed to take especial care to cross all the deep swamps in the country. We reached a place called Kivari's on the 22nd, marching along the slope of some hills over a fine open grass country, where the irregulars looted, amongst other things, a French musical-box playing four tunes, which was, wonderful to relate, in excellent order. There was a well-posted ambush of twenty-five Wanyoro on the following day at the crossing of the Katagurakwa River, and as we came down to the bank in single file it was funny to see all the men in front suddenly bend down as the line of white smoke appeared from the papyrus rushes in front and the slugs and leaden missiles flew past overhead. Only one man was wounded by the fire, which was very erratic. One volley was enough for the Wanyoro, and away they all ran, followed by the Sudanese, who captured one of them. We camped early not far from the river, as the guide informed us that there was no water in front for some distance. From here we crossed the waterless plain, passing round Kaduku Hill to the Nile, which we reached near Kunguru Island. The country here is very flat and open, and dotted about with lovely Borassus palms. It was hard to believe that the Nile was really in front of us—it looked far more like a great papyrus swamp; and, indeed, it was not till reaching Magia Hill farther north that we were able to see the water and get a view of this magnificent river, over 1000 yards broad, and truly, to use Baker's expression, "a giant at its birth."

The other column had travelled by a good road along the Kafu River to Mruli, and joined us at Kunguru on the 25th.

Kabarega had moved to Kajumbura Island farther north, so on the 27th the whole force marched north-east along the Nile. Two canoes captured from the Wanyoro, and a berthon boat, were manned by some soldiers, and were ordered to move down the river, keeping parallel with the force marching along the bank. We reached Magia Hill about 11 a.m., and from here numbers of Wanyoro were seen on the opposite bank, and an attempt was made to capture some of their canoes, which were escaping down stream. The Maxim opened fire from the hill to support our men coming down the river, but the Wanyoro were too quick for them, and only one canoe was taken.

We marched on again, reaching Kajumbura Island at 4 p.m., and had to wade through the water for 100 yards to get to it. This island had evidently been occupied by Kabarega, and was covered with straw huts and enclosures.

The Nile banks were bordered by masses of *sudd*, the total breadth of the river being 1100 yards. From mounds or ant heaps near the side we could see plainly across to the right bank, where Kabarega with his followers had taken up his position, and the white-robed Warasura (soldiers) could be seen moving about among the trees. Continual drumming went on, and even our bugle-calls were imitated by men who must have been deserters from Emin Pasha's army. The river bank was thoroughly reconnoitred, and it was found that stockades and entrenchments had been made along the opposite bank for some miles to defend openings in the *sudd*, and that one crossing was as bad as another. The attack was therefore ordered to take place opposite Kajumbura Island at dawn on 2nd March. A raised platform was constructed at the edge of the water, on which the Maxim guns were placed, to cover the force crossing the river.

The Waganda were employed on the 1st enlarging the narrow channel through the *sudd* to the open water in the middle of the river.   It was rather a cold misty morning when the little fleet of five canoes, and a berthon boat with Cunningham, Dunning, and Ashburnham, and the Sudanese chosen to man them, pushed out from the bank to wait at the edge of the *sudd* till there was sufficient daylight to cross.

I was left on the left bank in charge of the Maxims to cover the attack.   It seemed that the mist hanging over the floating vegetation would never lift, and one strained one's eyes in vain trying to get a glimpse of the opposite shore, until at last the air became clearer and the canoes paddled across the open stream.   The Wanyoro were well on their guard, and soon opened a heavy fire on the advancing canoes, and, to make matters worse, two of these upset.   The Maxim was able to come into action on the Wanyoro to the right, but not on those in the immediate front.   The affair had a disastrous ending, as Cunningham and Dunning were both severely wounded; some men were killed and wounded, and Ashburnham had a narrow escape, receiving a bullet through his helmet.

It was now we felt the want of a doctor.   There had been no doctor in Unyoro for certainly four months, and even at this time the only one in Uganda, Dr. Ansorge, had left to take Colonel Colvile to the coast.

Ashburnham and I, who were now the only white officers not *hors de combat*, had to attend to the wounded, besides performing our other duties, and it was anxious work looking after our own brother-officers.

However, Dr. Mackinnon was known to have left the coast in November, and was to be sent on to Unyoro as soon as he arrived in Uganda. No further attack was feasible at present owing to the insufficiency of canoes, and it was decided to transport the wounded back to Fort Hoima, where it was hoped Dr. Mackinnon would meet them. Dunning had been shot in the chest and was in a critical state. The Maxim gun was regularly fired from the raised platform near the water's edge at any parties or groups of the enemy collected together along the opposite bank, and harassed them considerably.

On 4th March I left this feverish camp on the island, across which a canoe was dragged to help us in transporting the wounded across the creek. As, hampered with stretchers, we were only able to move slowly, Ashburnham, who was now in command, remained on the island with the rear-guard that day, and rejoined me at the village of Kalianongo on the 5th. We returned by a different route north of the one previously taken. It was a dismal march back, and I do not think Sir Samuel and Lady Baker, in their retirement from Masindi, could have execrated the fœtid swamps and dense overgrowth more than we did whilst striving to get the stretchers over and across these obstacles. On 9th March a black came up in haste to the front of the column to fetch me, and on going back a short way I found poor Dunning quite unconscious. His litter had been placed on the ground, and the bearers were standing round in a helpless manner. I made every effort to restore him, alas! in vain, and at length the sad conviction stole over me that he was dead. I had striven hard not to believe that this was the case, and must confess to giving way altogether, in grief at the loss of a brave and gallant comrade, and realising the utter sadness of such a death in this far-off savage country, where there was none of the pomp and panoply of war as a compensation.   It was a sad blow to Ashburnham and myself, as our comrade had seemed so much better in the morning, and had spoken to me quite cheerfully only a short time before.   Ashburnham, who was indefatigable in looking after him, had stayed in his tent the night before, and said he had had a much better night.   There were so few officers in the country at this time that one could ill be spared.

We were anxious about Cunningham, and he was not informed of Dunning's death till, on reaching Fort Hoima, the fact could no longer be concealed.   Here, to our dismay, there was still no doctor, and Dr. Mackinnon did not arrive till 30th March.   However, Cunningham, with rest and care, improved gradually, and was soon able to get about on crutches.

On the 14th instant Ashburnham went away to Uganda with the two companies of Sudanese which had been brought from there at the outset of the expedition.   The Waganda had already departed.

For the next four weeks I led a peaceful and uneventful existence at Hoima, where my time was principally occupied in drilling soldiers and farming. The rainy season was due, and the ground had to be got into order for sowing the crops—potatoes, Indian corn, and rice.   The garrison now consisted of 350 men, and they paraded from 6 to 8 a.m. every morning, when an endeavour was made to improve their shooting by unlimited firing exercise and aiming drill.   There was hardly any ammunition to spare for target practice.

Many men were daily reported sick and unable to attend parade. Having strong suspicions that some of these were malingerers, I was looking forward to the arrival of a medical officer, as, not being a doctor myself, it was difficult to make certain whether a man was ill or not. I had almost begun to fancy myself one, as I had been obliged to attend to all the sick for some time. The principal complaint from which the Sudanese suffered here was pneumonia, and they seem to be a very weak-chested people.

A great deal of lameness was caused by jiggers, little animals about the size of a flea, which burrow into the feet, usually under the toe-nails, and then lay their eggs there. If extracted at once there is little harm done, but if allowed to remain in for any time great irritation ensues, and a sore is caused which extends until toes and even feet are entirely eaten away. One of the Wanyoro here was in a terrible condition, and used to crawl across the parade-ground on hands and knees to have his wounds dressed. These jiggers are a frightful plague, and have come across Africa from the West Coast. They had only got as far as Kavirondo on the east of Lake Victoria at this time, but there is little doubt that they will eventually reach the East Coast.

One great method of keeping them out of the houses is to have the floors well brushed out, and then sprinkled with water, as they cannot stand the damp.

There was a good deal of fever among the blacks at Hoima, and the mortality here was greater than at any other station in the Uganda Protectorate. After parade the soldiers were employed on fatigue work till 5 p.m., with a rest of two hours in the middle of the day.   There was plenty of work to be done in making roads, building houses, and cultivation.

Besides dispensing justice in military offences, I was often called upon to adjudicate in cases of private dispute amongst the Sudanese, even so far as to settle the damages in divorce cases.   I remember in one case the outraged husband was made happy by being awarded 9 yards of cloth, which the co-respondent in a mean manner attempted to avoid paying, and severe measures had to be finally taken to enforce payment.

We were rather confined to the precincts of the fort owing to the hostility of the natives, and it was dangerous to go far without an escort.   On 22nd March two women who had gone out to collect potatoes were murdered only a short distance away.

V

UNYORO EXPEDITION, APRIL–JUNE 1895

THE fiat had gone forth, " Kabarega delendus est."
With this object, in spite of the rainy season, a
large force was ordered to concentrate at Mruli on the
15th April.   Owing to the great numbers of Waganda
taking part in the expedition, the force from Uganda
was delayed and did not arrive till the 20th.

Cunningham, who was now nearly well again, and I,
both took our ponies, as we were to proceed by a higher
and much better route than that previously followed,
viâ Katonesi and Kisoga, avoiding the bad swamps,
and we ultimately reached our destination in six days.

Mruli used to be the capital in King Kamrasi's time
(1864), and has always had a certain importance from
its position on the main road to Uganda.   This was
the most southern post occupied by General Gordon,
and I saw the site of the old fort on the right bank of
the Kafu River, which flows into the Nile at this point.
It is low and unhealthy, and there is a great deal of
sudd along the banks of the Nile here, which is also
continually blocking up the mouth of the Kafu River,
only about 30 yards broad.   A few miles up this
river there is a fine grass plain on both sides, where
are to be found elephant, kobus kob, Jackson's hartebeest, and also smaller antelope.   The river there is a

5

nice running stream between steep banks, and several villages and banana plantations are scattered about in the distance.   Whilst waiting for the Uganda column to arrive, I went out twice to shoot in this direction, with half a company as escort, and killed four kobus kob, two of which had good heads.   It is rather a disadvantage in stalking game to be followed by half a company of soldiers, but one had to make the best of it, and the Sudanese took a keen interest in the sport, and were very useful in carrying back the meat.

The Nile at Mruli is 900 yards broad, and had distinctly risen since I was there in February, and it was possible to see the water over the papyrus.   We heard afterwards that Lake Victoria had risen considerably, which would account for it; in fact, the pier built by Colonel Colvile at Port Alice was completely covered with water.   The Wanyoro were in large numbers along the opposite bank, and great preparations were being made to oppose the crossing.   The Nile makes a great bend here, forming a right angle and sweeping round a wooded cliff which rises to a height of 30 feet above the water.   At first sight the high ground contained in the right angle appears to be an island, and has been marked so in many of the old maps.

Along the cliff, lines of entrenchments had been dug by the Wanyoro, and we could hear continual hammering as stockades were erected.   A Maxim gun was placed on a raised platform at the edge of the *sudd*, and fired when working parties could be seen; this caused the work to cease by day, but it was resumed again at nightfall.

About 60 yards of *sudd* which encircled the promontory had been cut down to the water's edge to give the defenders a clear field of fire, and formed a nasty

WANYORO CHIEF AND FOLLOWERS

obstacle. Ashburnham reconnoitred down the river for some distance and found all the crossings guarded and Kabarega in his old position opposite Kajumbura Island.

On 20th April, Captain Ternan, D.S.O., and Lieut. Madocks arrived on the east bank of the Kafu with the Uganda column, consisting of one company Sudanese and about 15,000 Waganda.

The latter had brought with them overland a great number of canoes in pieces, which had now to be sewn together by the native canoemen. With this force also came two Hotchkiss guns, which had recently been sent up from the coast. They were wonderfully accurate and proved of great value, though the labour of dragging them through the swamps was enormous. A hundred Waganda were told off each day for the purpose.

Mr. Grant was expected daily with a fleet of canoes which he was bringing down the Nile from Namiongwa through Lake Kioja, and, at about noon on the 22nd, sharp firing commencing from the opposite bank denoted his approach. He took shelter under the left bank till 1.30 p.m., when, supported by the Katikiro (General of the Waganda forces) with ten big canoes which had been sewn together and launched, he advanced to the attack, covered by a heavy fire from the Hotchkiss guns and the Maxims. It was an extremely pretty sight to see the canoes suddenly advance across the river in line, and the cliff opposite was wreathed in smoke where the Wanyoro were firing from their entrenchments. It was a strong position, and in places there were two or even three tiers of fire.

As the canoes reached the barrier of the *sudd*, and could get no farther, the occupants had to get out and wade through the floating vegetation to the shore, and it is marvellous that not more men were hit.

It was an exciting scene, as the white-robed Waganda, and the Sudanese soldiers in Grant's canoes rushed forward to the attack, and stormed the central stockade. As soon as this was won, the enemy quickly retired from the other defences, and could be seen flying over the hill pursued by the Waganda. Three men were killed and twelve wounded on our side, and the Katikiro received a spear wound in the arm. The defenders had remained at their posts till the last, and forty-one killed were counted lying in the trenches.

As soon as the position fell, Ashburnham was ordered off to prevent Kabarega recrossing the Victoria Nile into Unyoro, and marched that evening for Kajumbura Island with two companies and a Hotchkiss gun. The crossing to the right bank commenced at once, and continued for three days, being much delayed by the *sudd* which was always blocking up the mouth of the Kafu, where the embarkation in canoes took place.

The noise and confusion were tremendous, and the Waganda boatmen were constantly running into each other, so that numbers of canoes were smashed. It was useless to expostulate, and they could not be prevailed upon to pass each other on any particular side, *i.e.* to the right or left. All day the canoes went to and fro, many of them leaking, and almost filling with water before they landed their freights on the opposite bank.

A stockaded post was built near the site of our old camp at Mruli, and in the middle of it there was a big tree, from the top of which a sentry could have a good view of the river and the surrounding country. A small garrison was left here under the command of a native officer. Cunningham and I left our ponies at Mruli until our return.

The total strength of the expedition was as follows:—

Major G. Cunningham—Derbyshire Regiment (in command).

Captain T. B. Ternan, D.S.O.—Manchester Regiment.

Captain Ashburnham—60th Rifles.

Lieutenant R. J. Madocks—Royal Welsh Fusiliers.

Lieutenant S. Vandeleur—Scots Guards.

Mr. Grant.

Dr. Mackinnon.

6 companies Sudanese (500 men).

20,000 Waganda irregulars.

2 Hotchkiss guns.

3 Maxim guns.

Lying as it did close to the scene of the action, the camp was in a most unsanitary condition, and we were all longing to be off, but a start could not be made until the canoes had been repaired, and the river column under Mr. Grant was ready to go. We were to march along the right bank, whilst Grant moved down the Nile with the naval forces. One of his canoes called the flagship was hewn out of a single tree, and held easily fifty men, with a Maxim gun in the bows.

Everything was ready by the 27th of April, and on that day we marched off at 6.30 a.m., along a good road made by the Wanyoro near the river bank. The country was thickly wooded with very fine trees, and ten miles to the east lay some high hills between Kalengari Hill and the high Mahorsi ridge. I noticed several traps for hippo formed by upright poles supporting a weighted spear point which was arranged so as to drop on the animal when he passed underneath. The spear point was of course poisoned.

There was a lovely bit of country at Kitao, opposite Kajumbura Island, covered with tall Borassus palms, feathery date palms, and shady trees, with a green lawn stretching down to the water's edge.

Kabarega had very wisely retired on hearing of the crossing having been successfully effected at Mruli, as the ground on the same bank was open and quite indefensible, but the remains of his residence, the site of which had been well chosen, were still to be seen, and on the rising ground among the trees about a mile off were some Wakedi villages. Ashburnham's column was encamped opposite on the left bank of the Nile, and he came across in the afternoon to see us, just recovering from a severe attack of fever. We halted a day at Kitao, and I went down the river with Grant and the canoes on a reconnaissance. The river was very winding, and there was a strong stream. A party of Waganda went out on the same day across towards Lake Kioja, and captured 220 cows and 300 sheep and goats, after a fight with some Wanyoro.

We continued our march on 1st May, and our troubles were now to begin ; between here and Foweira we had to cross deep swamps and rivers running into the Nile. I was in charge of the Hotchkiss gun this day. Two hours after the start we came to a broad and deep swamp reported to run for 6 miles inland. It took an hour to convey the gun across, and the barrel had to be lifted off the carriage and carried across by men resting poles on their shoulders.

The carriage was dragged through the swamp under water most of the time. One or more crocodiles were lying in the passage through the papyrus, and two men were bitten about 100 yards behind me. When the whole force had got across, it was discovered that, altogether, six men had been seized, and three of these were frightfully lacerated above the knee, and ultimately succumbed to their wounds from blood poisoning.

Luckily most people remained in ignorance of their danger until they were across the swamp, for the passage being narrow, everyone crowded into it from the bank, so that there was no means of retreat.

A crocodile scare occurred very easily after this, and it was alarming to see the great mass of people swaying from side to side in the deep water in their endeavours to get out of the way of the supposed crocodile. On one of these occasions a certain white officer, who was being carried through the swamp on the shoulders of a stalwart Mganda, found himself left close to the dreaded spot, and expected momentarily to be deposited by his bearer into the jaws of a crocodile, the man not being able to dash away with the others, owing to the weight on his shoulders.

Our next camp, Kosoka, was situated between the river and a curious hill called Kibuzi, on the top of which are strewn large blocks of granite.

It was reported here that a river in front was impassable, and that the enemy were holding the far side of it. I was sent in the afternoon with a company to find out the truth of this, and after going 2½ miles came to a broad sheet of water covered with papyrus rushes.

The only means of finding out whether it was fordable was to wade into it, and my feelings were far from pleasant, as I remembered the crocodiles in the morning. At every movement of the reeds one could fancy that one of these brutes was advancing to the attack. The water got deeper and deeper, until it reached the armpits; but the worst portion was over, and after going about 250 yards, we reached an island, on the farther side of which the channel was narrower, and not so deep. The enemy on the opposite bank proved to be some Wakedi with some spears and bows and arrows, with whom we did not interfere.

Having taken good care to carry my coat containing my chronometer, watch, and pocket-compass on my head, I was very angry to find that my Somali interpreter had walked through the river with my precious prismatic compass and aneroid slung round him, well underneath the water.

There was little difficulty in forcing the passage the next day. The Wakedi were soon dispersed by the Maxim, and the Waganda crossed and extended very rapidly on the other side, and their white dresses could be seen far off to the right and left. They are particularly good at executing this movement, and it is a pretty sight to see.

I was with the rear-guard this day, 2nd May, and it was hard work forcing one's way through the dense masses of Waganda, who blocked up the road. Many of the chiefs had their wives with them, and it was amusing to see these fine ladies in white dresses picking their way through the mud. After crossing the Kola River, we passed through a large Wakedi village, and then over some swampy ground, which delayed the gun very much, camping eventually at a village called Niambari.

The Waganda went on scouting far to the front, and messengers returned in the afternoon, who reported having fallen in with a force of Wanyoro 8 miles off. A prisoner whom they brought back stated that Kabarega was with them himself, and that he was retreating into the Wakedi country with a quantity of cattle.

Cunningham ordered Madocks to start with a flying column in pursuit at once. At 6 p.m., Madocks and I left with two companies Sudanese, one Maxim gun detachment, and 7000 Waganda. We marched in a north-easterly direction till about 11 p.m., mostly through swampy ground, where we were assailed by swarms of mosquitoes. We then halted near a deserted village for the remainder of the night, and started again at dawn the next morning. The tracks of cattle became very distinct as we went on, along a most abominable road, skirting a large river, and passing in and out of swamps. The pace became faster and faster, and the Waganda in front were just like hounds in full cry. It was impossible to keep up, and at twelve o'clock we halted for an hour, to give the men carrying loads a necessary rest. The Zanzibaris carrying the Maxim gun and the ammunition were quite exhausted with struggling through the swamps at this pace. There were several Wakedi natives hovering about the column, and we had to keep a good look-out not to be rushed by them.

On marching again, the cattle tracks were seen to be quite fresh, and there were marks showing where beasts unable to go any farther had been hastily killed and cut up.

At length, about 3 p.m., we came up with an immense quantity of cattle, which were captured very easily, and the Wanyoro offered little resistance, only ten men being killed and wounded on our side. Kabarega was unfortunately not with them, and, according to a deserter, had left the road with some of his followers, and gone in a south-easterly direction. It was a great disappointment, as we had hoped to come up with him. Everyone was far too tired to move any further for the day, and it was a relief to lie down. Strict orders had been issued for the villages of the Wakedi people, with whom we had no quarrel, to be left alone; but owing to their determined hostility, and the fact of several men having being speared by them from the high grass at the side of the road, it became impossible to restrain the Waganda any longer.

The people, as can be gleaned from their name, Wa Kedi, which means naked people, wear absolutely no clothes. They are a small race; the men have the centre teeth of the lower jaw taken out, and some have beads sewn on to a tuft of hair at the back of the head. They are a formidable race, armed with spears and poisoned arrows, and are fond of attacking at night. The Waganda have a great dread of them, and have invariably suffered reverses in their attempts to enter the country further to the south.

In 1877 a force of 200 Sudanese soldiers from the Egyptian post at Mruli was surprised and cut to pieces by them, and on another occasion a force from the same post was massacred by them in a night attack. They were just like snakes in the grass, and used to creep up close to the camp and spear men out fetching water or cutting grass. It was necessary to build a strong zariba every night.

The river whose course we had been following is called the Lenga and, according to a Mkedi prisoner, extends for a long way inland. Some days to the north-east, beyond the source of the Lenga, is a country said to be full of camels and donkeys and inhabited by natives who wear gold ornaments in their ears.

On our way along the Lenga we passed through several large villages, which consisted of a quantity of big cone-shaped huts, with a curious entrance, forming a porch about 3 feet in diameter. The interior of the huts was in some cases painted white and ornamented with rough patterns. They had no protection in the form of a fence round them, and apparently the people live in peace with each other, although they do not owe allegiance to any one man, and each village is quite independent of the other. This fact would make it rather difficult for any expedition entering the country, as although some villages might be friendly, the others could not be depended upon.

It seemed to be a land of plenty, and there were large quantities of mtama, dhurra, sweet potatoes, semsem, tobacco, beans, etc. We also found honey, which was a great luxury.

There were rumours that the Wakedi intended to attack us in force on our march back to the Nile with the cattle, about 1000 in number, so strict precautions were taken, and the cattle were divided up into lots of about 100 each and placed under the guard of a mixed escort of Sudanese and Waganda.

We marched by a shorter and straighter route than before, leaving the river to our right. The Katikiro with some Waganda led the way, and a force of Waganda brought up the rear of the column, which was a very long one. The Wakedi made no attack in force, but harassed the line of march, killing and wounding several men and also an unfortunate Wanyoro woman. It was impossible to see them in the grass, and difficult to retaliate.

There were some very fine beasts among the cattle, and the length of their horns was quite extraordinary, some being fully 3 feet 6 inches long, but they were sadly jaded after the way in which they had been driven and hurried along; and several had to be killed on the road back to Niambari, which we reached in two days. We enjoyed a well-earned rest here on the 6th, and continued the march along the Nile on the 7th. There was heavy rain and thunder, usually in the afternoon and at night, but, considering that it was supposed to be the middle of the rainy season, we suffered very little discomfort.

At Niambari two of the Zanzibari servants woke up one morning to find a great puff-adder curled up and asleep in their tent—not a pleasant bed-fellow. One day I also had an unpleasant adventure with a snake. On coming into camp after a march, I lay down on my bed to read. My servant entered the tent later, and to my astonishment retreated into a corner looking very frightened, and pointed to the bag at the foot of my camp bed. Here to my horror, close to my feet, was a great snake with part of his body and its head raised, just apparently about to dart on to the bed, where I was lying. It did not take me long to slip cautiously over the back of the bed on to the ground, and we killed the snake on the bag before it had time to move.

Although I have mentioned these incidents it was curious how seldom snakes were seen, as they must have thrived in this damp heat and tropical vegetation.

We continued our march along the Nile on the 7th, and on that day spent almost more time in the water than we did on dry land. The native officer who had been sent to reconnoitre the road for six hours the day before, reported that it was a very good one. So it was for four miles, and he had taken good care not to go further. Beyond that, the Lenga joined the Nile and formed a little delta, choked by masses of floating vegetation. But for this and the papyrus, which so soon forms a causeway, I imagine the river would have been unfordable.

Our march along the right bank came to an end on the 8th, when we camped opposite Foweira and again met Grant with the canoes. Ternan had gone away with Ashburnham and a small force to patrol the line of river down to the Murchison Falls.

The latter had made the fortunate capture, on the east bank, of the Namasole or Queen Mother, widow of Kamrasi the former king of Unyoro, and mother of Kabarega, an extraordinary-looking old woman who was reported to have great influence over the people. She was enormously fat and unwieldy, and was always carried about on an angareb (bedstead). She had escaped being thrown with the remainder of Kamrasi's wives into his grave, as described by Baker. With her were several members of the royal family, including sons of Kabarega. My Somali interpreter used to amuse me by calling them the royalties.

No further news could be obtained of Kabarega, and Cunningham decided to cross over to the west bank, and proceed to Masindi, where it was intended to build a fort with a view to keeping Kabarega out of Northern Unyoro. The river Dukhi flows into the Nile from the north-east just north of Foweira, and is swift and unfordable, so that a farther advance by land would have necessitated much delay in crossing this obstacle in canoes. The chief Kakunguru and a party

of irregulars were sent, however, across it after a number
of Wanyoro, who had retreated in this direction, and
succeeded in capturing 500 cattle.   A canoe upset
whilst crossing the river Dukhi, and a chief and four
men were unfortunately swept away by the strong
current, and drowned.   The inhabitants north of this
river are called Shulis, and live in walled villages,
apparently having no dealings with their neighbours,
the Wakedi to the south.   They did not show any
hostility but simply retired into their villages, and
waved flags, as the Waganda passed by in pursuit of
the Wanyoro.

Owing to the masses of Waganda, quite a town of
grass huts had grown up here, and it presented a curious
sight as we walked through it, though the smoke from the
green-wood fires was almost unbearable.   I noticed
several men studying their Luganda prayer-books, and
the missionaries have certainly done wonders in teaching the people to read and write.

We recrossed the Victoria Nile at Foweira, about
the spot where Sir Samuel Baker crossed in 1872,
and although the river is about 500 yards broad in
the open, and there is a strong stream, nearly all the
cattle captured from Kabarega, amounting now to
2000, swam safely over.   It was a strange sight to see
the long line of cattle struggling across the river with
their heads bobbing about in the water.   Many of them
were carried far down the stream and had to work
their way up under the lee of the shore to the only
place where the high bank was cut away sufficiently
to enable them to land.   A very few were seized by
crocodiles.   Navigation ends soon after Foweira has
been passed, when the banks of the river contract, and
the broad mass of water, suddenly confined to a narrow

space, assumes an alarming velocity. The floating islands are whirled rapidly down to certain destruction in the rocks and rapids below. The Nile making a great bend to the west soon dashes down over the Karuma Falls and onwards in a succession of cataracts to Lake Albert.

By observations, I made the height of Foweira 3470 feet, and Lake Albert 2113 feet above the sea, so that in the distance of 53 miles along its course between Foweira and the smooth water below the Murchison Falls, the river drops 1360 feet.

The crossing of the whole force to the left bank occupied nearly a week, and the *sudd* had to be cut away at first to make room for the canoes.

Every day one or two men were speared by Wakedi, and Mackinnon had a hard time in attending to the wounded. On the 11th a large party of Waganda, who had gone out without orders, fell into an ambush whilst crossing a swamp, and lost 150 of their number killed. They were returning back to camp in their usual careless manner, when the Wakedi suddenly charged down on them with spears. A *sauve qui peut* ensued, and but few returned to tell the tale.

As the numbers of Waganda on the right bank decreased, and all the soldiers except No. 4 Company were withdrawn, a perfect panic seized those left behind, owing to a rumour that the Wakedi were coming down on them. They rushed madly into the water regardless of the danger of being seized by crocodiles or of drowning, and fought with each other to get into the canoes. The Katikiro could do nothing with them, and another company had to be sent back to restore confidence.

We had a delightful camp on the left bank at

Foweira, 30 feet above the river, and our ponies joined us here from Mruli, whither an escort had been sent to fetch them. They were looking rather thin, owing to the bad grass. On 18th May, Cunningham left with a small force on a tour through northern Unyoro, and the remainder of the column started on the march to Masindi. Grant returned with his column to Usoga on the same day by river, with orders to leave ten canoes at Mruli, in case they were wanted. There was very satisfactory news from this place; it was reported that the natives were coming in to settle round the post we had built there, and to cultivate the plantations.

In the angle formed by the Nile at Foweira there is a dense impenetrable mass of vegetation and high grass which rises to a height of fourteen feet above the ground, and the whole country is thickly wooded. For the first three days we had to march through country like this. The great numbers of cattle trampled down the grass on each side of the track, so that there was soon a capital road, and the rear-guard and the Hotch-kiss gun came easily along. It was arduous work, however, colliding with and helping along sick persons, tired cows and refractory guns, and the rear-guard as a rule did not enter camp till late in the afternoon.

As we neared Masindi the country opened out, and there were many banana plantations and fields of green grass affording splendid grazing ground for cattle. On the 6th day we came to a halt in the Busindi district, and were joined by Ternan and Ash-burnham from the Murchison Falls. The former had been ill, and, hampered by a Hotchkiss gun, they had actually been eleven days on the march, although the distance is comparatively short. We spent two days here looking out for a site for the proposed fort, but were unable to find a suitable spot, and on the second day Madocks and I ascended to the top of Mount Fumbi, which lay about 3 miles north of our camp.

Although I have been unable to find this hill marked on any former map, it is quite the most notable landmark in Unyoro. About three-quarters of a mile long, and about 150 to 80 yards in breadth at the top, it has precipitous sides, covered with grass, low trees, and shrubs, and is 762 feet above Masindi Fort, the present headquarters, and 4640 feet above the sea. It can be seen distinctly from most parts of the country, even from close to the Murchison Falls. From the top of it one has a magnificent view over the country, which, however, looks decidedly disappointing. The dull green of the swamps preponderates; bits of yellow here and there mark the mtama cultivation, intermingled with banana groves, especially to the west and north-west, in which directions the country is very thickly populated. Close to the east side, between Mount Fumbi and the Kisoga line of hills, lies a small lake ringed with papyrus, from which rises the river Katagurakwa; this stream flows through the narrow gorge in the hills—where the Wanyoro laid an ambush for us in our first march—and then across a flat plain covered with low trees to the Kafu River. Far to the north-west several hills stand out, among which the Gisi peak is the most noticeable. The ground slopes gradually down towards the lake in gentle undulations. The valleys in the immediate vicinity of Mount Fumbi are very fertile, and covered with quantities of Indian corn, dhurra, mtama, tobacco, semsem, and banana plantations. The castor-oil tree is also often found. This hill is used as a refuge in time of war, and we

6

found some tusks of ivory hidden away on the top, one of them weighing no less than 164 lb. Kabarega is still supposed to have a quantity of ivory concealed in the swamps and rivers.

It was a hard climb up to the top, but I was well rewarded by being able to make some useful additions to my map and gain a splendid idea of the country. Some enterprising Wanyoro had the impertinence to fire on us when we got there.

Not being able to find a good place for the fort, we marched the next day, and I led the column in a south-westerly direction to a place I had noticed on returning from the previous expedition. Passing round the base of Mount Fumbi, we halted on a knoll 1½ miles west of it, which was an excellent situation on high ground, with a stream close by, and surrounded by many villages and much cultivation. Ternan finally decided to build the fort here.

It is exactly in the same latitude as Kibero, namely, 1° 41′ north, whilst Mruli is in 1° 39′ north.

This was then our most northern line of occupation; but since that time the whole of Unyoro has been definitely declared to be in the Protectorate, and advanced posts have been established near the Murchison Falls and at Foweira.

The Victoria Nile forms such a distinct geographical and strategical boundary that one wonders why this advance has been so long delayed.

The construction of the Masindi Fort was at once proceeded with, and, the operations being now concluded, the Waganda army left for Uganda under the Katikiro, travelling *viâ* the river Kafu and Bulamwezi, leaving, however, a small number behind to assist in building the fort. The contingent from Buddu was ordered to return there direct, with instructions to attack Rabadongo, Kabarega's Katikiro, at a place called Misriandura on the way. News was afterwards received that this attack had been entirely successful, and that Rabadongo had been driven out of the country and had thrown himself on the mercy of Kasagama, King of Toru.

During this campaign nearly 250 women and children who had been raided from Uganda in past years by the Wanyoro were rescued, and were able to return to their homes.

Although Kabarega had again eluded capture the expedition had been an entirely successful one, and he had sustained a severe loss in the 2000 cattle which had been captured from him. He had been driven out of his own country across the Nile, and the whole of Northern Unyoro had been traversed and patrolled for the first time since the establishment of a British Protectorate over Uganda. Numbers of the natives were coming in to make peace, and a market-place was soon formed near the site of the fort. This was to be a very strong one, and consisted of a parapet 4 feet 6 inches in height, with deep ditch outside, forming a large square of 80 yards inside, and defended at two opposite corners by strong flanks with a stockade 8 feet in height.

Ashburnham returned to Uganda on the 29th, and, leaving Ternan and Madocks at Masindi, Cunningham, Mackinnon, and I arrived at Hoima with Nos. 3 and 4 Companies on 5th June, after nearly two months' absence.

VI

CAPTURE OF ARAB SLAVE STATION IN SOUTHERN UNYORO

ON our return to Hoima we found that they had been having exciting times there as well, as the following grave but humorous entries in the diary kept day by day in the fort by Mr. Forster will show :—

"*April* 19*th.*—Lion visited camp during night and carried off woman (Bunyoro).

"*April* 20*th.*—Lion came again and took another woman.

"*April* 21*st.*—Lion carried off Bunyoro man. Seen by patrols and fired at. He visited cattle-house, and was wounded by guard.

"*April* 22*nd.*—Section went out to look for lion and found him near river. Badly wounded, but very fierce!! Was killed and brought into camp.

"*April* 24*th.*—Another lion (probably lioness) visited camp during night, and carried off Nubian child. Was seen by patrols and fired at.

"*April* 25*th.*—Lioness came again, and went to cattle-house, where guard fired at and wounded her. One of the shots struck house at considerable distance, and entered thigh of Nubian woman, where it still remains. Woman apparently little the worse.

" *May 3rd.*—Askari Kamsur Mohamed, No. 3 Company, broke out of camp at night in drunken state, and fired six shots at sentries. Attempts made to capture him, but without success." And yet some people think life in Africa must be so dull!!

Forster told me he found the tracks of the above lions passed one night 2 yards from the door of my house. As the door was only made of grass, and could easily have been pushed down, I congratulated myself on not having been at home. Lions had never been heard of here before, and it was an extraordinary circumstance that they should have come here through the dense grass and undergrowth. The inhabitants were naturally terrified. Precisely the same thing happened at Kitanwa in July, when a lion visited the place three nights running, taking a child the first night, a woman the next, and a child on the third night, when I happened to be camping there on my return from Lake Albert.

I went at once in the morning to the place where it occurred and found the poor mother in a state of frenzy, and her arms and breast were torn by the brute's claws as it had seized the child from her. The hole in the side of the native hut where it had forced its way in could be plainly seen. In this instance we were able to follow the tracks across some fields of cultivation, but they then disappeared into the long grass near a swamp and we could go no farther.

I was disappointed to find that my garden at Hoima, which we fondly imagined was going to supply us with so many luxuries, had turned out a failure, owing to the little rain there had been.

The queen-mother and suite were installed in a

house at Hoima, and many Wanyoro came in to see her and to make peace. She had been a great nuisance on the march, and at one time refused to be carried any farther. There were endless difficulties with her also about food. She insisted on having meat and milk; it was beneath the dignity of the royal family to eat potatoes and plantains. Women also in Unyoro will not eat chicken or fish, so the old lady was rather limited in her bill of fare. I used to pay her a visit occasionally, and once showed her the Christmas number of the *Graphic*, in which she was much interested, especially in the picture of a lion devouring a white man who had just taken a thorn out of its foot; she no doubt wished the white men in Unyoro could have been exterminated in the same manner. She was rather cheeky at times, and one day asked by what right we had come into Unyoro, and why we had not sent to ask Kabarega's permission. As long as she could get plenty of marissa, which is the intoxicating spirit made from bananas, she was quite happy. There were many reports of her cruelty in former days, and it was said that she used to think nothing of ordering fifty people to have their heads cut off in her own district, which used to extend south from Hoima to Bugoma.

I was destined to remain only ten days at Hoima, during which time my energies were devoted to laying out the new road to Masindi to connect the two posts. This was very much wanted, as the native path, by its eccentric bends and sinuosities, made the distance to be traversed nearly twice as long as it need have been. Starting up the centre of the densely overgrown valley to the north the road was to cross the high stony ridge on the east, and then, descending into another valley, to skirt the high ground which finally juts out into a point at Kibugumia.

At this time Southern Unyoro was still in a rather disturbed state, and the chiefs had not come in. Mr. Foaker had been sent from Uganda to establish the Nakabimba post on the Msisi River, with a view to intercepting the large Arab caravans which were known to be bringing arms and gunpowder into the country in exchange for slaves and ivory. On 15th June letters arrived—sent through with all speed from Uganda—to say that one of the patrols sent out along the Msisi River had been fired upon by Arabs coming into Unyoro, who had killed and wounded some of the Sudanese soldiers and effected a crossing. Another Arab caravan was also known to be on its way, and was expected daily. Cunningham had been ill for a week, suffering from a severe attack of hæmaturic fever, the most deadly of all African diseases, and it was fortunate he had Mackinnon to look after him. I was in consequence ordered off alone with Nos. 3 and 4 Companies Sudanese, one Maxim-gun detachment, and the irregulars; total strength about 250, and marched off on the morning of the 16th. It poured with rain the whole day, and the native track to Misriandura was in a frightful condition. We marched till dark, as it was important to get on as quickly as possible before notice could be given of our approach. No bugle-calls were sounded, and starting early the next day we made our way through the thick bush by little-used tracks, avoiding habitations, and passing to the left of some high hills which form the gate of Bugoma. We reached the Chief Chikakule's district at noon, effectually surprising the inhabitants, who were holding a market. The alarm soon spread, and

the natives collected to defend their villages, situated
on some rising ground in front, but were soon routed
by No. 3 Company and the irregulars, who extended
and advanced in good order up the slope. It was
getting late, so I halted here and sent out patrols
immediately to try and discover the whereabouts of
the Arab station, which was the *raison d'être* of the
expedition. The country to the south was entirely
unmapped, and it was very difficult to obtain any
information. However, by good luck it was ascer-
tained that the Arabs were at a place called Mwenda's,
farther to the south. To reach this we had to cross
two big swamps which form the head-waters of the
Kafu River. After crossing some fairly open rising
ground beyond them, it was curious to find, 5 miles
farther on, a river about 30 yards broad and, at the
time we crossed it, 4 feet deep, flowing in the opposite
direction towards the Albert Nyanza. This river, rising in the same swamp as the Kafu, is called the
Ravasanja, and would be impassable during the rains.
A very well-kept road led from this point to the Arab
station at Mwenda's, which I had the good fortune to
surprise and capture. The high grass round it enabled
us to approach unperceived, and the men then charged
into the enclosures, which covered a space about 400
yards square, with bugles blowing and an appalling noise going on. The loot proved too much for
the Sudanese soldiers, and, on the enemy being driven
out, my small army, mindful of old days, dispersed in
all directions, and it was a long time before I could
restore order. Some of them had to be severely dealt
with. I managed to collect scattered remnants of No.
4 Company to send in pursuit, and at the same time
opened fire with the Maxim on the Arabs, who were

retiring across the stream in the valley and up the far slope. Many could be seen carrying off tusks of ivory. Some of the huts were unfortunately set on fire, and a good deal of loot was, I fear, destroyed; but the capture proved a valuable one, including many bales of cloth, coloured silks, cowries, twenty-four tusks of ivory, guns, percussion caps, and thirty-three kegs of gunpowder.

The Arabs were completely surprised, and offered little resistance. Our total casualties were, two men killed, two wounded, and three severely injured by an explosion of gunpowder. One of the latter had all the flesh burnt off his face and hands, and presented a ghastly appearance, being quite unrecognisable. Most of the slaves ran into the bush on hearing the firing, so that only twenty were found. Eighteen prisoners were captured, but the Arab ringleaders unfortunately escaped. We also secured thirty-five cows, three very good donkeys, and some goats and sheep.

It is curious how this station had existed so long without having been discovered, and it shows the difficulty of ascertaining what goes on in this wilderness of high elephant grass and river swamps. Khalfan, the leading Arab, had been in Unyoro for two years, and employed a number of subordinates, who conducted caravans to and from the coast through the German territory south of Lake Victoria. It must have been a lucrative trade, as the price of slaves did not run high in Equatoria. One woman told me she had been sold for three goats, with one extra goat thrown in for her child. Another woman had been sold for a load of beads, and others for guns. Apparently there was a demand for extremely fat women, as there were four Waganda slaves who were of such mountainous proportions that they could hardly move about.

Slaves are most unsatisfactory individuals, and have a dread of the unknown. I left them at Mwenda's until my return from Southern Unyoro, and they all seemed quite happy, and glad to be free. However, on the first day's march back to Hoima, after my return, several of them disappeared into the bush, only to be appropriated by someone else. Needless to say, the fat Waganda did not run away.

In the enclosures there were a number of houses, built, like the Swahili houses on the East Coast, in an oblong shape with thatched roofs. Khalfan lived in a very nice one, and evidently led a life of ease and luxury, which was rudely broken by the arrival of the white man and the hated soldiery. Many documents in Arabic writing were found lying about, and everything was in confusion, showing the haste with which he had taken to flight.

I had received orders to establish communication with the post at Nakabimba, but it was very uncertain where this was situated, so we had to struggle blindly on in a southerly direction. A stockaded post was built at Mwenda's, in which all the cloth, ivory, etc. was collected and stored, and a small force of thirty men, under Mulazim Rehan Abdullah, was left behind to garrison it.

The country between Mwenda's and Kisimba is very fertile, and covered with banana plantations and cultivation. After crossing a deep swamp and river called Embaia, which was only just fordable, the country alters entirely, and one enters a line of rugged hills covered with blocks of granite in curious and fantastic shapes, two little peaks facing us as we entered the line of hills, bearing a strange resemblance to a native saddle. Streams rise in these hills, but rapidly become papyrus swamps. Passing through a gap in the hills we gradually ascended to a high mountainous plateau where there is a big village called Bianja, and here the inhabitants were friendly and brought us in provisions. I was delighted to hear that the fort was only about 9 miles off, and it was very satisfactory to find that we had come by such a direct route. Continuing our march the next day, 23rd June, through the same barren and mountainous country, we reached the Msisi River, flowing in a deep gorge below us, and winding in all directions as it forced its way through the high rocky hills towards Lake Albert.

We could see the Nakabimba fort, which had just been built by Mr. Foaker, on a high hill south of the Msisi, but it took us a long time to descend into the narrow gorge and cross the river. As we ascended the steep and stony path up the opposite hillside the discordant blasts of the Sudanese buglers re-echoed through the mountain and gave notice of our approach.

It was, indeed, a surprise for the garrison of the fort, but not equal to that which I experienced when, to my delight and astonishment, I saw my former adjutant and brother-officer, Captain Pulteney, coming down with Mr. Foaker to meet me in this wild and mountainous part of Central Africa, the last place in which I should have expected to see him. Leaving the coast on 20th March, he had, on arriving in Uganda, been sent straight on to take over the command at Nakabimba, where he had already been a week. Our mails and news from home had been very few and far between, so it will be imagined with what joy I met a brother-

officer who had only just come out.   It is said we
talked for two days consecutively, during which Foaker
learnt something about the brigade of Guards.   The
fort is in latitude 38' 24" north, and is 4582 feet above
the sea, so that the climate there was naturally much
colder and fresher than in other parts of Unyoro.   It
is a wild and rugged country, but there are a good
many Wanyoro living in the valleys among the hills.
Not far from here lie the far-famed Mountains of the
Moon, the snow-covered Ruwenzori range, which so
seldom deigns to reveal its splendour to the human
eye.   Foaker had only three times seen the snow from
the fort during a stay of six weeks.   After a day's rest
at Nakabimba I started with Pulteney, who intended
to come with me as far as Mwenda's, on my return
journey by a different route for the purpose of surveying.   Marching along the river for three hours we
reached the crossing known as Ruantomara, which is
made by heaping bundles of papyrus one over the
other so as to form a causeway.   It was in very bad
order, some of the papyrus having been washed away,
so that from only being in 2 feet of water one suddenly subsided into a hole almost up to one's neck.
Many loads were dropped into the water in consequence, including my tent and bed, and some of
Pulteney's tin boxes.   It took one and a half hours for
the small column to get across the river, which was
not more than 30 yards broad.

On the second day we left the granite hills at a
place called Bwiaga, and descended into the plain
again.   Now, it so happened that two Arabs named
Mse and Juma bin Fakir, with a large caravan, had
selected this very route to leave the country by,
thinking to avoid me by making a detour to the west,

as they considered that I was certain to return by my
old road. Scouts in front reported that a caravan of
some sort was coming along the road (a native track
one foot wide, buried in elephant grass 10 feet high),
so we halted to allow it to approach. Strolling leisurely
along at its head who should walk into our very arms
as we lay concealed in the grass but the two Arab
leaders. In a moment all was confusion,—Arabs,
Zanzibaris, Wanyamwezi porters with food and tusks
of ivory on their heads, and slaves, all dived into the
grass as our men rushed out with a wild hurroosh.
Some were pulled out by the legs, others by the arms,
but a great many escaped, as the attempt to find them
in the long grass was just like looking for a needle in a
bundle of hay. This mattered little, however, as we
had secured the leaders. I do not think I ever remember seeing men so utterly flabbergasted as Messrs.
Mse and Juma bin Fakir, as they stood trembling in
the hands of the delighted Sudanese soldiers, who, with
their customary lightning-like *leger-de-main*, were appro-
priating any little articles of value they could lay their
hands on, to keep as a souvenir of the occasion. The
rout was complete, and the road onwards for miles
was strewn with the débris of gourds, bits of cloth,
potatoes, Indian corn, and pots and pans dropped by
the flying remnants of the caravan, hotly pursued by
the irregulars.

We reached Mwenda's on the fourth day, and found
all well. Here Pulteney left me to return to Nakabimba, where he became a terror to Arab slavers
and a good friend to the Wanyoro; whilst I set
out the next day for Hoima, arriving there on July
the 1st burdened with the captured loot, prisoners,
and slaves.

My men were all made happy by receiving a present of two months' pay as prize-money, and there was rejoicing and a dance, or fantasia, in the fort that night. There was at last a mail from home, with letters dated up to the beginning of February. The Arabs were sent with an escort to Uganda for trial at headquarters.

The territory between Hoima and the Msisi River used to be under the chiefs Rabadongo, Chikakule, Abaswese, and Mwenda, who had been hostile so long; they had all come in to make peace now, and were making roads and cultivating their fields.

Abaswese came in to make peace on the 22nd, dressed in a gorgeous costume, and was quite the best-dressed man I have seen in Africa. He was tall, with very good features and a pleasing expression, and seemed superior to most Waganda chiefs I have seen. His dress consisted of a bright red " Johore," with gold embroidery such as the Arabs wear, underneath which he wore a shirt made of fine soft leather. A pair of tight-fitting dark blue trousers, beautifully made sandals trimmed with fur, and a smart turban completed the costume, which fairly eclipsed my own torn and tattered garments. He looked a chief all over, and had a very good manner. Events had proved, however, he was no warrior, and at the approach of an enemy he was always the first man to disappear into the bush and the last to emerge from it. As a result of making peace he was attacked by one of his former confrères, and sent piteous messages to us to come and help him, saying that he was living in the grass.

It appeared Kabarega had sent messengers from his exile in the Shuli country to tell the people not to make peace, and that he was going to drive the white men out by the aid of the dervishes, and burn any he could take prisoners. The natives had begun to mistrust him at last, and were tired of war, so that several hundreds had re-occupied their old villages and plantations near the main roads.

VII

JOURNEY TO THE MURCHISON FALLS, AND BACK TO UGANDA

NEWS came in August that Kabarega was trying to come back into the extreme northern portion of his country, and was occupying an island somewhere on the Nile below the Karuma Falls; so, on the 11th, I was sent with 150 men to reinforce Lieutenant Madocks with the same number of men at Masindi, and go on with him to the Nile. Cunningham at the same time left for Uganda, where his presence was required as commander of the Sudanese troops. I was very glad to have this opportunity of surveying some more of Northern Unyoro and seeing the Murchison Falls.

The new road to Masindi had made a great difference in the rate of travel, and we covered the distance in two days. I found quite a fortress had been made, with a ditch 10 feet deep all round. It seemed almost a pity that there was no daring enemy to come and attack it. Ternan had just returned from Lake Albert, and was soon afterwards going down the Nile.

On the 13th Madocks and I set out with a view to striking Kabarega's camp on the Nile. We travelled *via* Kerota and Paniatoli, both occupied by Sudanese posts in Emin Pasha's time, passing through dense jungle most of the way. For the first three days the people were friendly, but after that the sphere of influence decidedly changed, and occasional shots were fired at us, three men being wounded, one of whom died.

We were obliged to bear off to the east, and, on the 18th, reached the Nile at a place called Kidopo, where we found Kabarega's settlement, a collection of 500 huts, on our side of the river, which rushed past 80 feet below in a foaming torrent, whilst opposite there was a small island, also with straw huts on it. There was a ferry lower down, but it was a dangerous one for a native canoe.

The people had, of course, crossed into the Shuli country, and we only had the satisfaction of burning all the houses. Some shots were fired from the other bank of the river, where a good many natives were collected. We remained here one day, which I spent in making a sketch of the rapid and island opposite — a most picturesque spot. The Karuma Falls higher up are rather disappointing, and are in truth only a series of cataracts in which there is not a great fall.

From Kidopo we followed the course of the Nile to the west, and, on the 20th, reached the site of the old fort Mpino overlooking the Nile (here nearly 500 yards broad), which pours impetuously past numerous little islands, by which its course is impeded. Junker lived at this delightful place for some time, and between the bottom of the steep bank and the river there are traces of the old garden still left in the shape of lemon trees, plantains, and papaws. One of the native officers told me he had been here as a boy, and that the native canoemen used to ferry people across the river to the

right bank, where roads led to Wadelai and to
Fatiko.

The native tracks were always coming to an end,
so that we had great difficulty in finding our way in
this labyrinth of high grass and woods, in which we
rarely obtained a view of the surrounding country.

There were many elephant and hippo traps, great
holes in the ground covered over with a thin layer of
sticks and sand, into one of which I had the pleasure
of disappearing. It was a morning I was feeling
particularly unwell, and was riding a donkey, when,
leaving the path to avoid some thorns, I felt the earth
giving way under me, and in another moment fell back
into a hole full of cold, muddy water, with the donkey
on top of me; we were ignominiously extricated by
the Sudanese soldiers. This did not improve my state
of health, and I had fever for two days afterwards.

After a long march we eventually, on 24th August,
reached a place called Bajan, where one of the
irregulars was shot in the leg whilst going down to
get water. The next day Madocks and I went to
see the Murchison Falls, only 3 miles distant. They
are really magnificent, and quite the *pièce de résistance*
of Equatoria. There are two falls about 100 yards
apart, the main one of these occupying a narrow gorge
worn away in the rock hardly 20 feet broad at the
top, through which the Nile, wrathful at being pent
up in this confined space, bursts with uncontrolled fury
in a mass of spray and a million particles of foam,
to fall 100 feet into the seething whirlpool below.
Black rocks on either side, covered with dark green
bushes and stunted trees, accentuate the dazzling
whiteness of the foam, and the grandeur of the
spectacle is enhanced by the absolute peacefulness

MURCHISON FALLS

and calmness of the water a little way below the falls, its mirror-like surface being only broken now and again by an occasional ripple, as a monstrous crocodile propels itself along. An enormous volume of water was leaping over the second fall, which was much broader at the top, but this, I hear, at certain seasons of the year (December and January, as a rule) ceases to flow, and can be crossed on foot, proving the great rise and fall of the Victoria Nile, to which Egypt is in part indebted for her summer supply of water.

A sight which almost takes one's breath away, and is even more impressive than the falls themselves, is obtained by walking along the river for a mile or so above them. Here the Nile comes sweeping round a corner 250 yards in breadth, and, with waves tumbling over each other in their mad race to reach the falls, thunders past precipitous cliffs over 200 feet in height, through which it has worn its way in the course of countless ages; and on seeing this it is difficult to imagine how the Nile ever had another course, or could have flowed in the opposite direction, as a well-known geologist has suggested.

We clambered down the rocks to a little patch of sand below the falls, beloved of crocodiles, where stood two or three little grass huts containing fishing tackle. A rustling noise behind one of these made us turn round, and lo and behold! a great crocodile waddling off into the water. Madocks killed him before he had gone far, and we measured him, finding him 14 feet long. His inside was full of round stones and gravel picked up from the shore.

There was a ledge of rock running out into the river from here, which afforded a capital point from which to photograph the falls, and I scrambled out along it with my apparatus, and had just got it into position when a few of Kabarega's enterprising followers opened fire from the bushes on the other bank, about a hundred yards off. Our soldiers commenced firing also, which was attended with equal danger, so that it was photography under difficulties with a vengeance, and, in my first surprise, I nearly fell off the slippery rocks into the water. Madocks riddled the grass on the opposite bank with his .303 rifle, and we were not disturbed again.

About a mile below the falls the river becomes quite sluggish and the stream almost ceases to run, so that, but for the roar of falling water above, one would think it was but some far-reaching indenture of the lake. A station has now been built on a small hill near the river, about 1200 yards below the falls, and forms at present our farthest outpost in Equatoria.

On our march back to Masindi, all the streams flowed into Lake Albert, until we reached our old camp at Kimena. The inhabitants of one village amused themselves by putting short spikes, about 7 inches long, covered with poison, in the ground for us to tread upon. One man was very much hurt in this way on entering the village, so, having received this warning, everyone was told to look out for them. It is not a custom of the Wanyoro, and was said to have been done by people of the Lure tribe who were living there. On our way back several women slaves of the Wanyoro ran away to us, wishing to return to their homes. This, in a few instances, was quite impossible, as their homes were much too far away. Two women even belonged to the Madi tribe near Dufile, and said they had been sold for guns. Three came from the south-west of Lake Albert and two from Toru, and one was a Sudanese woman, who originally came with her husband, a deserter from Wadelai, whom the Wanyoro killed. We saw many tracks of elephant and two old heads of buffalo, which, however, are few and far between.

Before reaching Kimena we passed by, 6 miles on our right, a great peak called Gisi, which it is strange not to find on any previous map. We entered the friendly zone again, and the natives remained in their villages and brought us in plantains and potatoes. I asked a prisoner, captured near the Nile, why the people to the north continued to be hostile, and he answered, as was very true, that the last time they had made friends with and trusted to the white men and the soldiers who came from the north (namely, Gordon, Emin, etc.), they had gone away and left them to the tender mercies of Kabarega, whose capital was at that time at Ruampara, near Hoima, and who sent his Warasura to kill any of them they could lay their hands on.

An old chief, called Don Joke, came in to see us at Pakano, and said he remembered Sir Samuel and Lady Baker coming to Unyoro in 1874.

We reached Masindi on 30th August, and thence I went straight on to Hoima, arriving there on the 1st September. The old queen-mother had been misbehaving herself, and had sent word to Chikakule and Mwenda, who had not yet surrendered, to come and attack the fort, as there were very few soldiers holding it. Soon after this I received orders to proceed to Uganda with No. 4 Company of Sudanese, from the Unyoro garrison, to take part in the expedition against the Nandi tribe east of Lake Victoria, who had been cutting up caravans on the main road to Uganda, and had also treacherously murdered a trader named West. This meant a march of about 350 miles, and I said good-bye to Unyoro on the 10th September, leaving a native officer in charge of Hoima, which had now been discarded as the headquarters in favour of Masindi.

The climate of the uplands of Unyoro is a fairly good one, and is, I think, drier than that of Uganda. Nearly the whole of the country, except just in the north-western corner, is at a height of over 3500 feet above the sea.

The maximum temperature registered at Fort Hoima during the time I was there was 89° in the shade, and the minimum 49°; as a rule, the thermometer did not go below 60° at night. The rains are very variable. In September, October, and November there is usually most rain; and July is the coolest month.

The Wanyoro are not so fine a race as the Waganda, although a few of the men and women, in spite of their black colour, are strikingly handsome, and more resemble the Wahuma and the Somalis in North-east Africa. Missionary enterprise, although commencing in the south, has not yet reached these people, and they are all pagans, believing in a god called Rubanga and evil spirits, to whom they sacrifice goats, chickens, etc., in case of severe illness or at the time of war. They have the usual medicine-men, called "ubandwa," who perform magic by killing animals, or using the leaves of plants.

They used to try and bring disaster upon us by burying a sheep with its throat cut and head just out of the ground; also, by leaving a chicken in an earthen-ware pot on the pathway; the Sudanese were always chary of going near these.

Excellent pottery is made in the country, also

earthenware pipes, both men and women being inveterate smokers.

They make the same bark cloth as the Waganda, and dye it black by putting it into the mud of a swamp for one day, and then leaving it in the sun. This bark cloth, which is stripped off in large pieces from a species of fig-tree, is a curious characteristic of these lake districts. It is ingeniously made by soaking the bark well in water and afterwards beating it thoroughly with a wooden hammer indented with little lines, which form an impression on the cloth. The different pieces are then neatly sewn together. Their musical instruments consist of primitive stringed instruments, drums, horns, and whistles. In former days, when Kabarega held undisputed sway, executions were frequent, the mode of execution being to kill people by two or three blows on the head with clubs. For women, the only punishment was to be placed in a big hole in the ground and left to starve to death.

I travelled to Kampala by a new and most excellent road *viâ* Mruli and along the Victoria Nile to Lake Kioja. Although the company with me was not more than 106 strong, the women, children, and followers who were returning to Uganda with them amounted to quite 800, and were not very good at getting along, as they had to carry all their goods and chattels with them. After leaving Mruli, we marched across a plain covered with dried-up grass and a few cactus trees, which alone seemed to thrive in this parched-up wilderness. As the Nile opened out into Lake Kioja, a high bank, half a mile to the right, showed where the old water-line had been. The second day's march brought us to a long line of banana plantations and villages on some rising ground, overlooking Lake Kioja, over which there was a fine view towards the Wakedi country. It is difficult to estimate the size of it, owing to the papyrus and *sudd* floating about. There were many Wanyoro living here.

A little farther on, one reaches the Kisilizi post, where the small garrison have always the excitement of expecting the Wakedi natives to come over in their canoes and raid the surrounding country. The road leaves the Nile here, and goes in an almost straight line to Kampala, crossing an uninhabited desert, which formed the boundary between the Wanyoro and the Waganda.[1] One gets a very good impression of Uganda on entering it from this side, and we passed through lovely shady banana groves and well-kept villages, over an open and undulating country stretching away towards the blue hills in the distance. It is a little swampy in the hollows, but the road is carried across on causeways, and one can walk all the way without getting one's feet wet. The hills become steeper and more frequent as one approaches Kampala, the road, nevertheless, passing straight over the tops of the highest hills, according to the Uganda custom.

Many of the Waganda helped to carry loads for the Sudanese, on payment of a few shells or bits of cloth.

On arriving in Uganda I found that Mr. Berkeley, formerly with Sir Gerald Portal's mission, had become Commissioner, and was then at Port Alice. Kampala, under the charge of Mr. George Wilson, was in a very flourishing condition; the size of the town had increased, and was increasing daily, all the people seem-

---

[1] Uganda has been recently extended, so as to comprise all the country up to the Nile, as far as Mruli and the Kafu River.

ing very happy and contented. Owing to the orderly administration of the country, the cessation of war and internal strife, the population of Uganda is increasing largely. As the people become more civilised their wants will increase, and they will be forced to work to supply themselves with the necessaries of life.

It has been said that it will be impossible to get native labour, but at present in Uganda itself the people have been induced to carry loads in the Protectorate, and perform a certain amount of work; numbers of natives were bringing in timber at Mumia's; until the outbreak of the Masai, hundreds of Wa-Kikuyu were carrying loads to Eldoma; and at Machako's, on the Uganda road, the natives had been induced to work in the fields.

Mr. G. Wilson had a large garden at Kampala in which all kinds of trees, fruits, and vegetables were doing well. A great deal of rice has been grown of late by the people themselves, and the native coffee is very good. There should be a great future for coffee planters in these countries. A regular post had been established, which the chiefs avail themselves of to write to each other.

Pulteney arrived on the 27th with forty-two men from his post in Southern Unyoro, also to take part in the expedition against the Nandi, who had cut up yet another caravan on the road from the coast, and seized many loads belonging to the missionaries. A great event in Uganda was the arrival of the caravan with Bishop Tucker and fourteen Europeans, of whom five were ladies,—the first to accomplish this long and arduous march. They had experienced a frightful hailstorm on their way through Kabras, during which two or three porters actually died on the road from exposure to the cold. During a hailstorm which occurred at the same time at Kampala a Swahili servant filled his pockets with the hailstones, to keep them as a memento of the extraordinary occurrence.

As the white ladies approached Kampala there was great excitement among the natives, who went in crowds to meet them. Bishop Hanlon and the English Roman Catholic Mission had also arrived lately, after an adventurous march, and had established themselves on one of the high hills, of which Mengo is composed.

On Friday the 11th, a parade of the Sudanese was held, and the Commissioner presented the medals for the first Unyoro Expedition in 1893, after which the companies marched past.

VIII

First Nandi Expedition

WE started from Kampala with the troops for the Nandi Expedition on the 14th October, and marched round the lake, through Usoga and Kavirondo, crossing the Victoria Nile at Jinja, where we camped in a lovely spot, just above the Ripon Falls. The force consisted of Nos. 1, 4, 5, and 9 Companies Sudanese, with one Maxim gun, about 400 men altogether, including a Waganda contingent of thirty men and a sergeant, who had been drilled regularly at Kampala. The sergeant, called Chongo, appeared in a very nearly new Coldstream Guards tunic, which he had bought from a Swahili porter for seventeen rupees. He was a great man in consequence, and commenced the campaign by walking off with two of the king's sheep. The men were rather comical-looking soldiers, but behaved pluckily afterwards, as I shall relate. There were a good many water-buck (*Cobus defassa*) near Jinja, and I was fortunate enough to shoot one with a very good head; horns 30 inches in length, and very even. The road from Jinja avoids Lubwa's, passing through Kasija and Biendi to Wakoli's. Cunningham, who had gone to the former place by canoe, intending to meet us on the march, failed to do so, and had to lunch, dine, and breakfast off bananas, until he caught us up the day afterwards.

It became very hot as we entered Kavirondo and approached Mumia's. On the road we met Mr. Grant returning from an expedition with Captain Sitwell and Mr. Hobley against the Ketosh people, a tribe living near Mount Elgon, who had offered a strenuous resistance, and in the attack on one of their villages killed two native officers and several men. The length of our column of over 1000 men astonished the natives of Kavirondo a good deal, and it was the first time the Sudanese had been sent in any force to this country. We reached Mumia's on the 29th, and Mackinnon joined us there on the 1st November, having come all the way from Unyoro very rapidly, and crossed Lake Victoria in the steel boat. Two more caravans had been attacked lately on the road between this and Eldoma, so that the transport service to Uganda was endangered, and it was important to move into the country as soon as possible. The great obstacle to transport had always been the total absence of food between Kikuyu and Kabras, a distance of twenty-two days for a loaded caravan going up country, except at the Eldoma station, which had only been latterly established, and was unable to supply caravans with food. This difficulty was now further increased by the Wa-Nandi proving hostile, and waylaying caravans on the main route between the top of the Mau escarpment and Kabras, in consequence of which the Guaso Masa fort had been established, close to the junction of the Guaso Masa and Kepdong Rivers. We could get very little information about the Nandi country, and had to trust principally to two Wa-Kwavi (an inferior branch of the Masai), who had been in the

country years before; to a Zanzibari porter, the sole
survivor of West's party; and to a Nandi woman,
who had fallen in love with him, and helped him to
escape. He had been sent into the country by West
for the purpose of trading, and was away at the time
of the massacre; he was then taken before the "laibon,"
or head medicine-man, and kept a prisoner, until this
woman left her own husband, children, and country,
and assisted him to escape. These Zanzibaris have a
wonderful way of ingratiating themselves with the
ladies of whatever country they find themselves in,
and in this instance it had saved the man's life. He
had learnt to speak the language in a very short time.

Major Cunningham decided to enter the country
from two sides, and concentrate at an important hill
called Alagabiet. The main column was to move in
an easterly direction to this point, whilst Captain Sitwell, Mr. Foaker, and about 100 men marched south
from the Guaso Masa fort to Alagabiet. After a few
days' delay at Mumia's, to make the necessary preparations, we marched along the usual caravan road as far
as Kabras, before entering the Nandi country. There
was a small depôt here, garrisoned by Sudanese, for
the purpose of supplying the Guaso Masa fort with
food, the latter being in an utterly sterile rocky
country, where nothing could be grown. As usual in
Kavirondo, there was a heavy thunderstorm with rain
either in the afternoon or night; and at a camp on the
Lusumo River I woke up to find a small river running
through my tent, and just in time to save my boots
from being washed away from under the bed. The
Sudanese had been prevailed upon to leave a good
many of their women and belongings at Lubwa's, so
that we were now only burdened with about 350

followers. The road was a good one, along the high ground overlooking the valley of the Narogare River to the north-west. Foaker continued his march along the caravan road, to reinforce Sitwell at the Guaso Masa fort with No. 1 Company. From the point where we turned off the caravan road into the unknown country, a high black wall of mountains could be seen in front of us, running from north to south, in which latter direction it becomes less perceptible. The upper slopes were covered with dense forest, which in some cases extended a little way down the escarpment. We soon left the last Kabras villages, in one of which the Nandi had killed nine people two nights before, notwithstanding their high mud wall and deep ditch. Two of the Kabras natives came with us a short way to show us the path, but none of them would venture to accompany us far into the dreaded Nandi country. After passing through a small belt of forest, and then between some small hills covered with boulders of granite, we reached the place where West and his men were murdered—a gruesome spot, with several skulls lying about, also his table and chair. He had evidently been in no fear of a surprise, and had placed his camp near the edge of a thick wood, and close to a lovely stream of running water, which forms really the headwaters of the Narogare or Lusumo River. There was no zariba round it, and at the time of the attack the men's guns had been put away in West's tent, so that they were powerless to defend themselves. It is almost incredible how West could have trusted himself on the outskirts of the Nandi country, knowing, as he must have done, the people's reputation for brigandage and treachery. It would have been much safer to have entered some way into the country, and

placed himself under the protection of one of the chiefs;
but here he was in a no man's land, and a prey to any
of the enterprising young warriors.

Traders have certainly been unfortunate in East
Africa. Mr. Muxworthy died of hæmaturic fever in
Kabras at the end of 1895, and Dick, another trader,
was killed by the Masai.

We afterwards crossed the Anoldamwe and Katumbi
Rivers, and camped under a high rocky hill, known as
Kamobir, which is 2 miles distant from the escarpment. Our camp was 5260 feet above the sea, and
the country to the south-west was undulating and
covered with short grass. Here and there were large
clumps of forest, in which there are said to be a few
buffalo, and we saw tracks of these animals close to
one of the streams. We marched along the escarpment the next day, and discovered some small huts
and patches of mtama cultivation, the first signs of the
Wa-Nandi. We saw a few natives, and discovered in
one of the huts a cup and other articles, which had
belonged to West. After several ineffectual attempts
to ascend, we found a very steep path, which led to
an open grass-covered space close to the top, and we
camped here at a height of 6332 feet. A section of
No. 4 Company went out from here into the dense
forest behind, and captured sixteen cattle, including a
black bull, identified by the Zanzibaris as originally
belonging to West, and a few sheep. Our column consisted of about 250 soldiers, 300 followers, one Maxim-
gun detachment, and four Europeans—Cunningham,
Pulteney, Mackinnon, and myself; and we used to pack
into a thorn zariba, about 80 to 90 yards square, as
the Wa-Nandi were known to be fond of night attacks.
The officers' tents were together in the middle, and the

men used to build small grass huts all round. The smoke from the fires at night was unbearable, and it was difficult to pick one's way through the fires and the sleeping forms lying round them, as one went the rounds at night.

I happened to be visiting the sentries in this camp at midnight, when a fire suddenly broke out among the huts of No. 9 Company, and spread with the greatest rapidity, fanned by the strong wind that was blowing. Each man was carrying eighty rounds of ammunition in his belt, and many of these were left on the ground as the men, roused from sleep by the roar of the flames, rushed to get out of the way. The confusion was increased by the sound of the cartridges exploding, which gave many the impression at first that we were being attacked. The line of flames was advancing straight for the tents, so Pulteney's and Mackinnon's tents, which were nearest to the danger, were taken down, and their effects strewn about all over the zariba, being with difficulty collected again in the morning. By this time, however, a line of men had collected, and succeeded in stopping and beating the flames out just before they reached the tents, but not before much damage had been done, and two or three of the rifles and bayonets were destroyed.

The wind increased to a gale, and when morning broke it was intensely cold, and we sat shivering over a hurried breakfast. The Zanzibaris and Lendu porters were stiff with cold, and could with difficulty carry their loads. Fortunately they are the most light-hearted people, and soon became good-humoured, and began to chaff each other. It was found impossible to get through the thick forest in front of us, and we had with disgust to retrace our steps, and make our way right down to the bottom of the steep hills by the same rocky and stony path by which we had ascended. Two miles to the north we found another native track, which led up to the high ridge and then through the forest, passing over an altitude of 6850 feet, and we camped near some scattered houses at a place called Samwiti. The men of the Waganda contingent distinguished themselves by capturing forty-four cattle and some sheep and goats in the afternoon. As it was impossible to carry food owing to want of porters, and we were entirely dependent on the country for supplies, this was an important item. The following day we marched in a northerly direction through several belts of forest, with open patches of short grass between them, and over swampy streams to Kimong, and thence east along a grassy spur to Alagabiet Hill, which is one of the main features of the country. Small clusters of huts were hidden away in openings in the forest, and the last village occupied by the Wa-Nandi was near Kimong.

We had not seen many of the natives as yet, though poisoned arrows had been shot at us in the forest, two or three of the followers being picked off from behind the trees.

We reached Alagabiet Hill on the 11th November, and camped on its north side. It is 7126 feet above the sea, and from the top one has a very good view over the valley of the Guaso Masa River, and across a very open country to the eastward, which is uninhabited, and where hartebeest, water-buck, and oribi are to be found.

The second column did not arrive, and the next day a section (about twenty-five men) was sent to the Guaso Masa fort to see what had happened. Covering the distance of 32 miles in the day, they returned

8

at 11 p.m. and reported that the force had marched off three days before, led in a wrong direction by the Masai guides, and had passed through the forest which we had just traversed, and down the escarpment to the low ground towards Kabras. It was an unfortunate thing, as every man available was required for this expedition, in which so many had to be employed in guarding the followers and the baggage. A party of Sudanese sent out the same day surprised a village near Kimong, taking a Martini rifle, two sniders, and some crosses, etc., looted from the caravan of the Roman Catholic mission. They also brought in three prisoners, who stated that the Wa-Nandi had been down three times to attack the Guaso Masa fort at night, but had been afraid to do so on hearing the continual cries of the sentries, as in the customary dull and monotonous tones they called out in succession the number of their posts. This was invariably done to ensure the sentries keeping awake.

Food was running short, and all idea of meeting the second column, which might have necessitated wandering about for several days, had to be given up. The country immediately south of Alagabiet is very swampy, a characteristic caused by the streams running down this way from the forest, and we had to retrace our steps along our old road to Samwiti. It was more like being in Scotland than in Africa at this height, and the days were cold, with very often rain in the afternoon. From Samwiti we steered straight for a high bluff called Usun, to the right of which there appeared to be a gap in the long line of hills in the far distance. One of the principal objects to be attained by the expedition was to try and find a shorter route for the Mombasa-Uganda road, which at present made such a detour to the northward. After leaving Samwiti, villages became more numerous, and there were cattle tracks in all directions. There was still a good deal of forest, belts of which run out from the main forest to the south-west.

Many natives were hanging about the line of march, and attempted to interfere with the somewhat difficult passage of a swampy stream, but these were held in check by the Maxim, whilst the leading company crossed, and camp was formed on some rising ground on the farther side after only a short march. Patrols were sent out, and it soon became apparent that large bodies of the enemy were in the vicinity, and intended to try conclusions with us. A thorn zariba was made, in which the women followers and baggage were left, with a portion of the force to guard them, whilst the remainder of the Sudanese and the Waganda irregulars went out to cover the return of one of the patrols across the Kimonde River, which it was feared, from the heavy firing heard in this direction, had got into difficulties. The river, down to which the ground sloped steeply, was about 6 feet deep, and was crossed by a native bridge. To the east of it, open grassy undulations were here and there varied by patches of forest. Only a few natives could be seen on the ridge, and it was with astonishment we suddenly saw a crowd of about 500 coming over the top of the hill at great speed, apparently excellently organised, and formed in three sides of a square, above which a dense thicket of long-bladed spears flashed in the sunlight. Wheeling to the left as if by some common impulse, on they came in spite of a Maxim gun posted behind the river, and charged down with tremendous dash on to the force which was some way up the slope on the east bank, and which closed up as well as it could to face the impending attack.

It was a critical moment, but luckily the Sudanese stood firm, and as the great mass of natives approached closer the heavy fire began to tell. Nearer and nearer they came, and it almost seemed that they would overwhelm No. 4 Company, which had to bear the brunt of the attack; but at last, wavering before this leaden hail, which they had never before experienced, their ranks broke and they scattered in all directions, leaving many of their number on the ground. Half a company left at the bridge had, on the first alarm, advanced to the support of their comrades, and the flying natives had now to run the gauntlet of the fire from these men as they retired over the hill, leaving the ground strewn with their big shields and spears. It was a splendid charge, and if continued for 30 yards or so more would have been a successful one.

Fourteen of our men, including the sergeant of the Waganda contingent, were cut off and killed, and the red tunic, of which the unfortunate man had been so proud, was found rent with many spear holes. Truly this tunic, originally sold by some deserter, had had a curious history, and the possession of it, like the shirt of Nessus, may have been fatal to the owners, who would have been naturally singled out by the enemy. Saleh, one of my best porters, and Wonumbeni, one of the gun detachment, were also killed this day, and one Mganda had no less than four severe spear wounds. This charge was a revelation to us, after fighting the cautious Wanyoro and Arabs towards Lake Albert, and at once accounted for the warlike reputation and prestige amongst other East African tribes which the Wa-Nandi possessed. Such an onslaught would have

CHARGE OF THE WA-NANDI

annihilated any smaller force without firearms, or a weakly guarded caravan travelling in single file along the Uganda road, and it was providential that the natives should have selected this occasion to make their attack, instead of waiting until we were in column of route, hampered by carriers, followers, and women.

The Nandi are a fine-looking race, very black, strong, and muscular. They dress their hair like the Masai, whom they much resemble, and are fond of covering it with red grease, as also their bodies. The warriors wear big head-dresses made of monkey or goat skins, ornamented with cowries, and sometimes a sort of leather cape slung over the shoulder. Their only weapons are spears and bows and arrows. The spears are not so well finished and the shields are not so finely ornamented as those of the Masai; the latter are very strong, and painted a dull red colour, as also are, in some instances, the spears. They had captured a few rifles, guns, and ammunition in their recent attacks on caravans, but did not know how to use them; and the Zanzibari who escaped from their hands told an amusing story as to how the natives were all examining a rifle when it suddenly went off in their midst and shot one of them in the leg, since which they had been too frightened to touch firearms, convinced that they had got something to do with the evil spirit. He also said that, for some reason or other, a tin of corned beef was supposed to possess certain magical properties, and was preserved by the " laibon," or chief medicine-man, with great veneration. The women resemble the Masai very much, and distort the lobes of their ears, as a rule, with large pieces of wood. They wear a great many iron-wire rings round the arms and legs. On the 15th a reconnaissance was made to the south-east, to make sure that there were no large bodies of the enemy about, and camp was ultimately moved 6 miles in this direction. We halted here for a day and were attacked again by the Wa-Nandi in the early morning of the 17th. About three-quarters of an hour before dawn the camp was suddenly aroused by shots from the sentries round the inside of the zariba, and the sudden yelling and shouts of the natives outside as they found themselves discovered. It was still pitch dark, and there was an unpleasant cold rain falling. As I tumbled out of bed into my long boots my Swahili servant crawled through the door of my tent in a great state of excitement.

The soldiers had been all lying down with their rifles close to their appointed stations, and fell in very quickly. In a few seconds after the first alarm the blackness of the night was lit up by the red flashes from the rifles, as continuous firing commenced round the zariba. The Sudanese sentries, with their sharp ears, had been too watchful for the well-planned attack of the Wa-Nandi, so used to carrying out these night attacks. They were in large numbers and had crept up to within a hundred yards or less of the zariba before they were discovered. The strong thorn fence, 5 feet high, afforded ample protection to the men behind against any sudden rush, and the natives charging on towards this were soon thrown into confusion by the volleys of flame and smoke which issued forth from behind it. High above the ceaseless rattle of the rifle-fire sounded the savage yells and cries of the natives, and the stillness of the night was transformed into a perfect pandemonium. On finding themselves baulked in the object of their attack, and confronted as if by some supernatural agency, by here and there a sheet of flame, a panic seized them and they fled in all directions, some of them even throwing their shields and spears down in the first wild rush to get away, and many of these were picked up when, with the first light of dawn, we were able to issue forth from the zariba. It was still raining when morning broke, and the day was cold and dull. A company went out to reconnoitre in the direction the enemy had taken in their retreat, but returned, having only seen a few scattered natives, and we marched off at 8.15 towards a district called Kiture, which is a very populous one. Crossing the river Amai, we reached a fine open country with rolling hills covered with many huts, where there was fine pasturage for cattle, sheep, and goats, of which many tracks were to be seen along the paths leading down to the river. The Wa-Nandi dwellings—little circular huts lined with clay—were scattered about the country without any protection whatever, showing that the natives had never had anything to fear from their neighbours. They are great workers in iron, and near the Kimonde River we passed a large smelting furnace.

On the 18th we continued our march to the south-east, and crossed two channels of the river Kaimin by means of native bridges. The latter are made with big trees, and are quite the best I have seen constructed by natives. Our cattle and all the quadrupeds, including my faithful companion the pony, which was still with me, were able to cross by them. There was a piece of blood-stained cloth hanging on the bridge, which had been taken from one of the men who had been killed, and which was meant as a defiance, showing that the enemy were not as yet dismayed by the failure of their attacks on the 14th and the night of the 16th. Several bodies of armed natives showed in

front and on the flanks as we left the valley of the
Kaimin River and gradually ascended the opposite
slope.

The Maxim came into action at about 800 yards
range, and the column closed up and advanced very carefully, to prevent the large crowd of porters and Sudanese
followers, which are such an encumbrance, from being
charged.   These were all massed together like a flock
of sheep, and guarded on each side, whilst No. 9 Company skirmished in front and cleared a way for the
advance.   At several points along the ridge in front
spears waving on the sky-line, or a Nandi warrior
peering over the top in his uncouth head-dress, revealed
the fact that they were only waiting for a favourable
opportunity to charge down.   After their losses on the
14th they had, however, become cautious, and had
learnt to respect the Martini rifles.   At 10 a.m. we
crossed another small valley, and, marching for two
hours more, camped on a high hill called Teito, 7119
feet above the sea, from the top of which we had the
most lovely view.   We had been gradually ascending,
from 6627 feet at Samwiti, until we had now come to
the end of the high plateau, marked by a precipitous
drop of nearly 1000 feet into the valley beneath.
Away to the south-west stretched the great plain watered
by the Nyando River, which runs down to Ugowe Bay,
and far away in the distance could be seen the blue
waters of Lake Victoria.   To the south, again, on the
farther side of the plain, the country towards Sotik and
Lumbwa appeared hilly and mountainous.   We were
now in the heart of the Nandi country, and the sides
of the numerous hills around were dotted with clusters
of little huts and marked by patches of cultivation;
but a few miles beyond this to the north-east there

extended a bare open plain, uninhabited, and with hardly a tree on it. From our point of vantage it was easy to scan the various hillsides, and we could see a number of sheep and goats being driven off in haste. About 400 of these were ultimately captured by the Sudanese, two hours' march from camp.

From Teito I was glad to be able to fix our position on the map very accurately by bearings on Alagabiet Hill, which we had left on the 12th, and Eldalat a little to the north of it, both of which appeared clearly defined on the horizon.

A good path led down to the plain, into which we descended the next day, and it was quite like going from winter into summer. There was a great amount of cultivation, principally mtama, which was ripe, and also a few sweet potatoes, which we had not yet found in this country. At the bottom of the steep ridge we found ourselves in a little valley shut in by the hills, through a narrow opening in which flows a small stream which joins the Enolgotwe River. We gradually ascended again up the valley towards the gap in the range of hills, until the high bluff called Usun, which we had been steering for during the last few days, was close to us on our left. Here we camped at a place called Kabarer, or Kamwentowe. No. 4 Company climbed up the steep side of the Usun peak in the afternoon, and captured some cattle and sheep which we had seen moving along the top. There were a good many natives about, and at night they fired across into the camp, wounding one man and some of the cattle.

On leaving this camp we suddenly reached the edge of a deep ravine, on the far side of which there appeared to be a series of buttresses jutting out from

the Mau escarpment, and the country looked very
rugged and mountainous.   Below us lay the Sagane
River, which works its way almost from the very edge
of the mountains through a lovely valley, completely
enclosed by enormous hills, to the north called En-
gorobobi, and to the south, Tinderet.   A path led
down the steep declivity under a high peak to our
right, and joined the Sagane River at a point 5352 feet
above the sea, soon after which it flowed through a
gap in the hills to Ugowe Bay.   The caravan, launched
on its descent, was serpentining down the precipitous
side of the mountain, when suddenly from overhead
came a noise like thunder, as a huge boulder, crashing
downwards, broke into fragments on striking another
rock, and the pieces flew harmlessly over the heads of
the caravan.   Almost immediately another came hurtling down, and the cause of this miniature avalanche
became soon apparent, as the natives above looked over
the top of the cliff to see the result of their efforts.   A
porter had been injured by a splinter from the last
boulder, and his load went tumbling down the side of
the cliff, striking terror into the hearts of the other
porters, who, rushing either forwards or backwards,
endeavoured to retreat from the danger zone and seek
the protection of a friendly ledge of rock.   It was an
unpleasant predicament to be in, as yet another and
another boulder or piece of rock thundered down over
the path, wounding two more men, until at length the
range of the crest-line above was obtained, and a well-
directed fire grazing over the summit made it too hot for
the enemy, who desisted from their attempt, and the
remainder of the caravan was able to pass in safety.

The descent occupied an hour, and we then marched
in an easterly direction along the river to a place

called Mitete, in the valley, surrounded by houses and cultivation.

At the head of the valley we commenced the ascent of Mau by a native track through the forest, which commences almost immediately. After a climb of 2860 feet, very trying for loaded porters, we eventually camped in an open space almost at the top, surrounded by clumps of bamboo forest, and 8900 feet above the sea. It was bitterly cold, and we were glad of big fires outside our tents. Although at this height, we were not safe from the Wa-Nandi, who hung round the column, and killed one woman and wounded another who had gone out a short way to draw water.

The top of Mau consists of an undulating plateau, broken up in places by deep ravines covered with short grass, and in places by clumps of forest. There are no inhabitants, except some occasional Wanderobbo hunters, and the few tracks we saw were the paths used by Nandi raiding-parties.

The next day we ascended for a mile or so more through the forest, and then entered a series of small valleys covered with short grass, passing at times through clumps of forest and over swampy streams. It was a miserable day both for man and beast, and there was a cold sleet driving in our faces all the morning, which completely petrified the unfortunate porters and caused a few of them to collapse by the roadside.

Some " Jackson's hartebeest " were seen, and there were also a very few tracks of buffalo, rhinoceros, and elephant, which had been crossing the mountains. To the south there seemed to be some very thick forest.

Our next camp was 9122 feet above the sea, and from here the main body returned to warmer climes in

the Sagane Valley, whilst I was sent on with fifty men
to try and reach the Eldoma Ravine, which it was
known could not be far off.

Nearly a whole company of the Sudanese were
unprovided with greatcoats, and it was dangerous to
expose these and the scantily clad followers any longer
to the rigour of the climate at this height.

It was intensely cold, and the mountains were
enveloped in a dense mist, when my small party
marched off on the morning of the 23rd, led by one of
the Wa-Kwavi guides, who at best possessed only a
vague notion of the country. The track passed close
to a small lake, and, an hour after the start, became
almost imperceptible as we dived into the forest on
the eastern slope of the mountains. For the first 1000
feet of the descent masses of bamboos, replaced farther
on by dense tropical forest, clothed the slopes, and the
fallen trees and broken canes formed an intricate and
rotten entanglement under foot, through which it was
difficult to find a way. A perfect shower-bath descended at every wave of the delicate branches overhead, which were laden with moisture from the thick
white mist. As we descended the bamboos disappeared,
and huge trees festooned with creepers, and a perfect
network of branches covered with white moss, did their
best to keep out the meagre daylight above. Some of
these fallen giants, surrounded by a labyrinth of small
trees and sharp-pointed branches which had accompanied their fall, defied all attempts to force a passage.
A man had then to crawl to the farther side of the
obstacle, and, having been placed in the direction of
our march by a compass bearing, we cut a way round
to him. This was the only way to avoid being lost in
this primæval forest, as the guide was no longer sure of

the way, and every hundred yards or so of our course were checked by compass. We were much hampered by having to carry two sick men along with us, and also a certain number of loads. The whole day was passed in continuously cutting, and not an opening appeared to relieve the gloomy solitude of the forest. The men were getting very tired, and I was anxious at the prospect of spending the night in this unpleasant place, without any water except that which dripped from the trees. A horrible thought also struck me, that my compass might be wrong, or that a mistake had been made in plotting the route. Just at night-fall, however, when I had almost given up hope, we emerged from the gloomy blackness of the forest into an open glade, through which, to my delight, ran the regular well-beaten caravan road; and there was joy among the Zanzibaris when, a little way off, they recognised the familiar camp known to them as Campi ya Mwiba, and to the Masai as Ngare Lekonge, about 7 miles from the Eldoma Ravine station. We had thus found a route from Lake Victoria, saving a distance of about 80 to 100 miles.

It took under three hours the next morning, in pouring rain, to reach the Eldoma station, where I found Mr. Martin, who had built a very strong fort on a hill not far from the ravine, from which, on a fine day, Lake Baringo can be seen flashing in the sunlight, and there is a lovely view across to the Leikipia range. Martin entertained us with the best of everything, and it was pleasant to revel in the luxury of a station again. My men were also made happy by being able to fill themselves to repletion. By a great piece of luck the mail had arrived at the station from the coast the day before, so that I was able to take back letters and papers for our party in the Sagane Valley. The Eldoma Ravine station has become an important place now, the whole district being under Mr. Jackson, who was for so long Acting Commissioner after Colonel Colvile left. A great quantity of food-products has been planted, and Masai (Kamasia) have been induced to settle around. It is a healthy place, 7000 feet above the sea, and very suitable for colonists.

Time was precious, and I could not afford to tarry at Eldoma, so on the 25th we started to scale the mountains again, accompanied by two Masai. Our return journey was much easier, owing to the road being cut through the forest, and in two days I was able to rejoin the main column at Mitete, to the joy of my men, who were glad to leave the bleak and inhospitable Mau plateau and bask in the sunshine again. Just before the steep descent on the western side into Sagane Valley the sun came out, and a lovely panorama unfolded itself. Looking down over the dark green forest, which extends and becomes thicker to the south, the different valleys could be distinctly traced leading to the great plain. Beyond the Sagane Valley the rugged hills near Usun showed up plainly in the foreground, and over them one could see in the far distance the blue waters of the Victoria Nyanza.

I found the main body encamped about half-way down the valley, and it was a pleasant surprise to everyone when I produced the mail.

The next day we climbed up to the top of the range of hills known as Tinderet, and travelled across an open and very hilly country inhabited by the Wa-Nandi, who throughout tried to harass the column, and on the 27th killed two of the porters. A company of the Sudanese skirmished in front in extended order, and the Maxim had several times to be brought into action.   We were much delayed by small streams and rivers running down from the mountains, and we eventually camped on the third day close under the Endubo Mountain, on a range running down towards the valley of the Nyando River, called by the Masai Kedowa or Merto.

There were a few people living on the mountains in the vicinity, but this is about their limit, and there were no houses in the plain to the south or towards the lake.   It is 59 miles from here to Lake Nakuro, and the Masai with us said that there was a fairly good track over the mountains, and that it was open until the descent through forest on the farther side. This track would probably bring one out close to the Guaso Masa River, and if it could be used for road or railway would shorten the route from the East Coast to Lake Victoria very considerably, as there is no difficulty in going along the Nyando Valley to Ugowe Bay, where there is a harbour.

We marched in a westerly direction from here into the big plain, 4000 feet above the sea, which is covered with short grass and a few thorn bushes and small trees.   There are no inhabitants until one approaches the lake, where there are several villages belonging to a chief called Kitoto.   A few antelope, Senegal harte-beest, water-buck, and some small gazelles were seen, and Pulteney shot a large python coiled round the branches of a small tree.   Towering over the plain to the north-west rises the great Nandi escarpment, which runs right down to Ugowe Bay, and then round by the Wa-Tiriki and Maragolia Hills.   It was very hot and steamy in the plain, and there were thunderstorms in the evening and night.   After four weeks spent on the high ground and the mountains we felt the change in the climate very much, and were glad to leave the hot plain.

We crossed the river Enolgotwe, flowing between steep banks, and 4 miles farther on reached the base of the hills, where we found a very well-marked road, evidently used by the Wa-Nandi for driving their cattle and flocks down to graze. It was too late to commence the ascent, and we camped here almost at the foot of the escarpment. An old Kavirondo man, who eked out a miserable existence in the plain, came into camp here, and from him we heard our first news of Sitwell's column, which he said had come to Kitoto's, and had left four days before.

On the 2nd December we climbed to the top of the plateau again, over 2000 feet, along a small watercourse, and on arriving there found the hills covered with boulders of granite, and very bare. There was a dense mist most of the day, and it was very cold and damp. The country reminded me exactly of Mr. Rider Haggard's description of the unknown country in his book *The Children of the Mist*, excepting that we failed to find the beautiful Princess, and were received with poisoned arrows instead. The poison did not have much effect when the arrows were taken out at once, and under the skilful treatment of Dr. Mackinnon the patients nearly all recovered. We were now heading straight for Mumia's, and 9 miles from the edge of the plateau reached the forest. We travelled along its edge for some distance before entering it, which we did by a very bad path, frightfully muddy and steep in places. Every now and then an arrow whizzed across the track, and the men halting and turning outwards fired a volley into the bush, in order to put to flight our unseen enemies. This road brought us out at a place called Kavaren, 6000 feet above the sea, where we camped on an eminence near some small hills covered with blocks of granite. Although at the edge of the high plateau, we still found a good many Wa-Nandi here, and captured some more cattle. A belt of forest about 5 miles broad separates them from a large Kavirondo tribe called the Kabalusia, and it was curious to emerge from the forest into this populous and most fertile district, inhabited by an entirely different type of natives, with thick lips, curly hair, and very ugly. On all sides extended fields of mtama, telebone, potatoes, and banana plantations, so that it was difficult even to find a place to camp. The natives were very friendly, and crowded into the camp in great numbers. Some of them wore an apology for a costume in the shape of a small skin slung over the shoulder, which was principally used for sitting down upon. The remainder did not even have that. They became such a nuisance that a sentry had to be posted in front of our tents. It was amusing to watch the stalwart Sudanese, who had put on his medal for the occasion, strutting proudly up and down, driving them off like so many sheep. One old woman had a small round stone fixed into her chin by way of adornment. The people possessed a great many cattle and sheep, and must pay a large tribute to their formidable neighbours the Wa-Nandi.

Between these people and the Kakamega, another section of the Wa-Kavirondo, we crossed the river Rukus or Rukuse, a very fine stream 25 to 30 yards broad, which emerges through a gap in the Nandi escarpment, after it has received the Kimonde, Amai, and Kaimin Rivers, and flows into Lake Victoria.

9

Although it was fordable, there was a delay of nearly two hours in getting the whole column across. At a camp 4 miles beyond the river three porters were speared by the natives when out looting, a fate which they richly deserved, as strict orders had been given against it. They had, however, become so accustomed to foraging for themselves in a hostile country that they continued to do the same in a friendly one.

We did not arrive among the usual walled villages of Kavirondo until we reached the Asori people not far from Mumiās.

On the 9th December we came down to the Lusumo River, a swollen torrent about 20 yards broad, which we crossed by means of a capital native bridge made of creepers. The cattle and donkeys managed to swim across farther up, with the exception of one of the latter, which was swept past us down to the rapids below the bridge, where it was tossed about like a cork among the rocks, and we were astonished and pleased to find him alive at the lower end of them. The river swarms with crocodiles, and one of the people from the fort was carried off in the act of drawing water at the crossing, the last seen of him being his arm above water in a strong stream. About 5 miles beyond the river we reached Mumiās, and found quite a party assembled—Hobley, S. Bagge, F. J. Jackson (who was on his way from Uganda to take over the ravine station), and J. P. Wilson, leaving for the coast. We remained here till the 14th December, and after incessant marching for twenty-three days I was very glad of a rest.

Nothing had been heard of the second column since 24th November, when it was reported to be at Kitoto's, close to Lake Victoria. Two days afterwards, however, it arrived from the south. Having ascended the escarpment near Kitoto's, it had been attacked at night by the Nandi, some of whom succeeded in penetrating into the zariba, owing to two of the sentries being asleep. They were fortunately driven out with a loss on our side of three killed and five wounded. Sitwell was grazed by a spear, and had a narrow escape, shooting one of the enemy at his tent door. For the first few minutes the occupants of the zariba had a lively time, as in the darkness it was difficult to tell friends from foes.

IX

PACIFICATION OF NANDI—FINAL EXPERIENCES

IT was considered that the Wa-Nandi had not been sufficiently quelled, so that on the 14th December the combined forces—total strength, 410—marched into their country again. We had a long march through the forest on the 17th, eventually camping not far from our old camp at Samwiti. Travelling along our former road, we camped at Kiture on the 19th, and Cunningham parleyed with some natives on a hill, through one of our Masai guides, without much result. With the usual native diplomacy, they wanted us to go all the way to the Eldoma Ravine, when they said their leaders would then come in to make peace. Even whilst this conversation was going on, a Sudanese and a Wanyamwezi porter were speared close to the camp. Marching in a south-westerly direction, on the 22nd December, we camped at the head of the escarpment overlooking Lake Victoria, passing on the way a hill called Kisaiga, not far from the river Kaimin, from which we had a splendid view over all the country round. At the bridge over the river a live goat disembowelled, a dead chicken, and a hand cut out of leather, were placed in the pathway for magic. On the 22nd, after a running fight with the natives, during which only a few men were wounded by arrows, we captured a large number of cattle in an enormous ravine leading up from the plain, 1000 feet deep, and about a mile broad at the top.

Turning in a westerly direction, we now kept along the edge of the plateau, through what proved to be a densely populated country. We halted near Moraba Peak on Christmas day, 1895, which we celebrated as best we could. An extraordinary piece of magic, consisting of a live dog, and a snake with its head fixed in a pumpkin—the two tied together, was found outside the zariba in the morning; and the prisoners agreed that this portended some great disaster, and that we were to be attacked that night. Sure enough we were not allowed to rest in peace after our Christmas dinner, but were turned out about midnight by the sentries firing on natives round the zariba. No organised attack, however, took place, owing to the bright moonlight. We continued our march the next day, and the head of the column was attacked whilst entering a narrow gorge. A few friendly irregulars, who were in front, were seized with a panic, and throwing down their shields and spears, ran back on the soldiers, who, advancing into the rocks, commenced firing wildly in all directions, and it was some time before order could be restored. Curiously enough, the kettle carried by Cunningham's cook was pierced by an arrow and rendered useless. The enemy were soon dispersed, and we were eventually camped under Kevillat Peak, at the edge of the Nandi country. We returned to Mumia's through Tiriki and Maragolia, having traversed the Nandi country in every direction. On the 29th, we missed the proper track, and had to cross a regular papyrus river swamp, such as one sees, as a rule, only in Uganda and Unyoro. We returned on the 31st

December, just in time to spend New Year's day at
Mumiās.

The Nandi are ruled by a medicine-man or "laibon,"
who lives near Moran, close to the edge of the plateau,
where we had been on the last journey. Under him
there are several "seigunanis," or leaders of bands.
The people consult the "laibon" in everything, and he
advises them as regards their expeditions and war
parties. It was said that he told his people that they
had nothing to fear from us, as the powder would
soon get damp, and then our cartridges would not go
off. His reputation had rather suffered in consequence,
and we heard he had been obliged to leave the country
in haste. The Nandi war parties have been in the
habit of raiding the country far to the north, and, as
is the case with the Masai, their custom is to attack
at night. The people speak the same language as
the Sotik, Lumbwa, and Kamasia tribes, and intermarry
with them.

The Nandi country lies, as we have seen, at an
average height of over 6000 feet above the sea, and
is excellently adapted for colonists. There is perfect
grazing-ground, and the natives possessed large numbers of cattle, sheep, and goats. Horses should do
well there; and my pony, which was with me the
whole time, was never sick or sorry. The soil is very
fertile, except in the northern portion beyond Alagabiet, where it is stony and barren. The climate is a
very good one. It is cold at night on the high
ground; the thermometer rarely went above 80°.
There was a good deal of rain at night when we were
there. In a column of 270 soldiers and 330 followers, the average total of sick per day was only
thirty-three, and of these few were bad cases. This is

a very small number, when the extremes of climate experienced, from the hot plains at the level of Lake Victoria to the cold mountain-tops 9000 feet above the sea, are taken into consideration. The expedition was brought to a successful conclusion, by the Wa-Nandi making peace, and sending in presents of ivory soon after we returned to Mumiās. What surprised them more than anything was the fact of the Sudanese women accompanying their husbands on the war-path, opposed as it is to their own ideas of fighting; and it was evident they considered it futile to resist any longer a power whose women waged war as well as the men.

The results of the expedition have been most important. Not only have all attacks on caravans ceased, but the main road from the east coast has been carried straight through this hitherto unknown country, from the top of the Mau Mountains, after the ascent has been made by the usual route past the Eldoma station. At a point on the escarpment the ground slopes gradually down towards the Rukus Valley, forming an open, slightly undulating plain, until the Nandi villages are reached. A belt of thick forest, from 8 to 10 miles in width, forms rather an obstacle, but after this Kavirondo and a fine open country is attained. Instead of passing through an uninhabited desert as before, the road now very soon reaches an extremely fertile country, and there is a great saving in distance.

The opening up of the Nandi country has also made a great difference to the Eldoma Ravine station, as it is only a two days' march to the fertile Sagane Valley, where food can be obtained.

With a railway from the coast, and steamers on the Victoria Nyanza, timber and fuel will be in great demand, and this Nandi forest will be of inestimable value. Some of the trees are very fine, and the supply would last for a great number of years. As will be seen from the map, the forest stretches a long way from north to south, and the edge of it is not far from Ugowe Bay. In Kavirondo, with the exception of Kikelelwas Forest, hardly a tree is visible, and great difficulty is experienced in getting wood.

The great obstacle to the railway is the Mau escarpment, but it seems probable that a shorter way will be found to Lake Victoria over the mountains than the one at present suggested and surveyed. As communication with Uganda will in any case be continued by steamer, it seems immaterial where the railway reaches Lake Victoria if the length of the line is lessened, and there is thereby a proportionate saving of expense.

It has been found that a harbour could be formed at Ugowe Bay or near the mouth of the Rukus River. If a route could be discovered over the Mau escarpment to the west of Lakes Nakuro and Elmenteita, or up the valley of the Guaso Masai River, there is a fairly easy descent along the valley of the Nyando River to Ugowe Bay, and a great distance would be saved.

In the event of the railway being carried over Mau by the proposed route past the Eldoma Ravine, it will be feasible to continue the line through the Nandi country to Mumiās and Berkeley Bay, or along the Rukus River to Lake Victoria.

With the difficulties in front it seems improbable that the railway will reach the lake till the year 1903. It is strange to think what a difference this will make to Uganda, which will be thus suddenly brought into direct communication with the civilised world. Towns of brick houses will spring up, shops will be opened, steamers and launches will ply to and fro on the lake, and numbers of Europeans will come to the country from all parts. Horses and donkeys will be transported rapidly through the belt of country infested by the tsetse fly, lying between the Tsavo and Kibwezi, and ought to reach Uganda in good condition. Animals do well there if properly looked after, though dangers exist in the form of snakes and bad grass met with in places.

At a future date there will no doubt be a light line of railway through Unyoro, connecting the two important lakes—the Victoria and Albert Nyanzas. There is a good route, only 73 miles in length, from a port on Lake Victoria near the capital, through the dry, level country of Bulamwezi to Mruli, a mile or two above which the Kafu is easily bridged. The route hence to the Murchison Falls is the only one by which the great drop to Lake Albert can be overcome, unless the railway stops at the edge of the high plateau, and all freight is carried by hand up and down the enormously steep cliff. From Mruli to Kimena — 27 miles — there is a fall of 40 feet only, but between this and the Murchison Falls, a distance of 25 miles in a direct line, the descent of 1360 feet to the level of Lake Albert is negotiated. This, however, is only a gradual descent, and the gradient is not more than one ninety-sixth. The total distance from Lake Victoria in a direct line, *via* Mruli, would be 125 miles, so, allowing for obstacles, a light railway of say 150 miles ought to connect the two lakes. Once this is done, the whole of Lake Albert, on the west of which there is a vast amount of ivory, and all the Upper Sudan down to Dufile, will be in steam communication with the east coast. and a journey from Mombasa to Dufile ought not to take more than nine days. It is to be hoped that a steam launch will be placed on this portion of the Nile before long.

We only remained at Mumiās a short time. It took two days for the force to cross the Nzoia River by means of a ford where the water was only 4 feet deep, and on 5th January we started on our return march to Uganda. The direct route to Port Victoria lay along the Nzoia River, and this had hitherto been closed by the hostility of the Wanipa tribe, who had been foolish enough to murder any messengers sent through their country, and to threaten any small caravans passing near it.

The country along the river is very bare and open, and there is no firewood at all until the Wanipa country is reached. The people live, like other Kavirondo tribes, in walled villages, and a great many of them had collected with their cattle in a large village surrounded with a very thick wall made of red clay and a big ditch. The only entrances to it were small gateways through the wall, now blocked with beams of timber and thorn trees. A few shells into the gateway soon convinced the people of the futility of resistance, and they were allowed to escape, whilst the chief and his relations were fortunately captured without bloodshed. If truth be told, we were rather sorry for these people, though their folly had to be punished in some way or other. A native officer reported that a sergeant had been killed whilst looting one of the houses, but next morning the said sergeant arrived in camp, having apparently risen from the dead. He had received two or three spear wounds and been rendered unconscious, but was able to walk into camp in the morning.

The ground became rocky and hilly, as we neared Port Victoria; this is an extremely pretty place, and there are several islands dotted about in the lake. We spent an afternoon shooting duck on the Nzoia River in native canoes. The river is about 70 yards broad here, and along the banks, covered with dense entanglements of high grass, are numerous little tunnels about 4 feet in height, through which the hippopotami climb up when they go for their evening walk.

It was in one of these that Mr. M'Allister met a crocodile, disturbed by human footsteps and rushing down to the water. It was a nasty predicament, and without a rifle he would have been in a bad way, but he luckily killed the brute when it had almost reached him.

On our march round the lake into Usoga, we met the three Frenchmen, M. Versepuy, Baron de Romans, and M. Spörch their secretary, who were journeying from the East Coast of Africa to Uganda with the intention of reaching the West Coast, and had heard all about the disaster with the Masai in the Kedong Valley.

A large caravan of Wa-Kikuyu with about 140 Swahilis were carrying bags of food to the Eldoma station. There were many Masai kraals in the Kedong Valley, where the Masai were pasturing their cattle, and the caravan on passing through the kraals proceeded to annoy the Masai by interfering with their women and cattle, and brought on themselves a fearful retribution. The blood of the younger warriors was up in an instant, and they seized their spears and rushed on the unfortunate caravan.

Those of the Zanzibaris who had guns may have offered a short resistance, but the Masai do not stand in much awe of fire-arms as used by Zanzibaris, and the few bullets that whistled over their heads would not delay their rush.   In a few moments the massacre began, and did not cease till no less than 456 Wa-Kikuyu and 99 Zanzibaris had been killed.   The course of the flight could be plainly traced, as I passed through the Kedong Valley in March, by the bones, skulls, and blood-stained bits of cloth lying along the path for several miles.   The Wa-Kikuyu bore no arms of any description, and were absolutely defenceless.

The Frenchmen were encamped with a trader named Dick, a day's march from the Kikuyu station.   On hearing of the disaster, the latter insisted on going to punish the Masai, and, the Frenchmen finding that he was bent on going, decided to support him.

The former was a private trader and of course utterly in the wrong, but was to pay the penalty by his death.   They captured a certain amount of cattle, but on their return the Masai collected from the hills around and a running fight with them had to be maintained, during the course of which Dick's revolver jammed and two Masai running in speared him in the chest, killing him instantly.

We arrived at Jinja, the crossing of the Victoria Nile above the Ripon Falls, on the 17th January.   There were many tracks of elephant about, and we heard that they had been seen by natives close to a place called Ukasa on the caravan road, about four days previously.   I went on ahead with a company of Sudanese the next day, arrived in Kampala on the 21st January, and on the 23rd went on to Ntebi.   This march I had to do as usual in pouring rain; the streams rushing down from the hills play havoc with the road, and the path becomes very slippery. Animals find it difficult to keep on their legs, and one is compelled to walk. Mr. Berkeley, the Commissioner, kindly asked me to stay. I remained at Ntebi till the 13th February, and my time was fully occupied in completing the surveys of the Nandi country, and leaving copies of the maps before my departure. During a heavy thunderstorm at Kampala, Mr. Mallek's house in the fort was struck by lightning and burnt to the ground. Two little columns of smoke were seen to rise up from the grass roof, the house being in flames a few moments later. It was struck in two places, but fortunately the room in which Mr. Mallek was at the time was not struck. The danger was added to by the nearness of the powder magazine to the house, and it was only by strenuous efforts that the flames were prevented from setting fire to this as well.

I was very glad to meet Ashburnham the day before I left for the coast. He came in from Toru that morning, having been very unwell since December. Amongst many other adventures, he had been obliged to dive into a river to escape an infuriated elephant which he had wounded. He had also been a long way up Ruwenzori by the Mupuka Valley, but had turned back on account of his food supply running out.

Kasagama, the King of Toru, was now at Kampala, and also Chikakule and Mwenda, the Wanyoro chiefs, who had held out for so long, and whom I have mentioned before. Chikakule was an old man and was evidently much impressed with what he saw at Kampala, and must have wished he had made friends with the white man before.

The Frenchmen were still here, and were in a great

state of mind about their porters who refused to go through the Congo Free State, even on double pay, such being the effect of Stokes' execution on the minds of the natives. Many black traders were leaving the country, and passing by the Salt Lake at Katwe into Uganda. However, an arrangement was eventually come to, and they reached the West Coast about July. I am sorry to say that Mr. Versepuy died shortly after his return to France from typhoid fever.

The poor Kātikiro lost all his goods and chattels in a big fire, which destroyed his houses and enclosures. When once a fire gets hold of these Waganda houses, they are so combustible that it is difficult to check it. A supply of gunpowder, the explosion of which could be heard during the fire, added to the confusion.

Cunningham was to cross the Lake in the steel boat, and meet me at Mumiās, and I started on my return home, with the porters and loads, on the 15th February. There was great competition for the privilege of coming with me, among the Zanzibaris at Kampala, all of whom are very glad to get back to the beloved coast, or " pwane," as they call it.

At Mondo's a leopard skin was brought me for sale, in which there were almost more holes than skin, and the man explained that it had killed nine men, so everyone put his spear into it. There were some very pernicious small flies here, which had only arrived lately, and would seem to have been brought out by the very hot weather. The men covered their legs with grass and banana leaves to avoid being bitten by them. I crossed in canoes this time to Lubwa's, where I found Mr. Grant. This fair and peaceful looking spot, already desecrated by the murder of Bishop Hannington, has been recently further sullied by the massacre of

Major Thruston, with Messrs. Scott and Wilson, owing to the regrettable mutiny of a section of the Sudanese troops, aided by some Waganda Mohammedans.

It was sad to see the swarms of locusts eating everything up in Usoga. The people had given up driving them off in despair, and where before there were nice shady groves of banana trees, there remained only the bare stalks and stems, looking very wretched and miserable.

At the Sio River, some natives said an antelope lived in the marshy ground near its mouth, and I went with them to look for it. It seemed a strange place to find one, and after a man had waded in and walked through the high grass I had almost given up waiting, when a fine animal with horns suddenly bounded out, and I secured him, to the delight of my caravan, who had a good feed that evening.

The weather was very hot indeed at this time of year, and the country was completely burnt up. The two dogs, although native ones, felt the heat very much, and it was curious to see them rushing on ahead to get every bit of shade they could see. After resting here they used to catch me up and run on again if they saw another small bush. Nur Fahil declares that black dogs feel the heat more than others, but I do not know what he bases this theory on.

The Kavirondo natives strike one as more extra-ordinary than ever, every time one sees them, and people at home can little picture to themselves what they are; the "mashers" were now wearing a sort of mask, made of beads or shells, and were bedaubed with red paint.

I arrived at Mumiās on the 26th, and found Hobley, who had just returned from an interesting

trip to Mt. Elgon, having visited the caves in which
people live. The country in this direction is very
fertile and full of banana plantations. Cunningham
came in the next morning, having travelled along the
Nzoia with only a few porters, and found the Wanipa
people quite friendly.

On the 28th, everything had to be got ready for
our journey to the coast, and the food had to be
weighed and served out. Every man received three
days' "posho" in beads, and eight in flour, which he
had to carry himself, and which was to last him as far
as the Eldoma station, whilst in addition, loads of flour
were carried for the journey on to Kikuyu. Some of
the men proved unfit to travel, and others had to be
found to fill their places.

On the 29th February we left for the coast, and
we were indeed glad to think that our faces were at
last turned towards home. On 3rd March we reached
the Guaso Masa station, and I have seldom seen the
Union Jack floating over a more barren, inhospitable-
looking place. Round the stockade there was a high
thorn zariba, and inside grew one solitary tree, perched
up in which was the Sudanese sentry. The soil was
so rocky that cultivation was impossible.

Mr. Foaker said that two headmen and about
thirteen Wa-Nandi had brought in a large tusk of ivory,
weighing 90 lb., as a peace-offering three days before.
We saw antelope and zebra on the march the next
day, and I killed a hartebeest and a bush-buck. The
latter is one of several small antelope, which make a
curious whistling noise when startled. The height of
our camp this day was 6700 feet, and we were
gradually ascending. We now travelled over the
big open plain, following the course of the Nollose-

geli River. Herds of hartebeest and zebra were seen, and Cunningham shot two of the former.

On the 6th inst. we left the plain, and ascended through woods and across rushing streams until we reached an open space, where we sat down for our usual halt after going for three or four hours. Every day we had been expecting the mail, which was now two months late, and now a few men could be seen coming over the brow of the hill in front of us, which we at once conjectured must be the precious mail.

However, more and more forms could be seen coming over the hill, then spears glinted in the sunlight, and we knew this was either a Nandi or a Masai war-party. Were they friends or enemies? It was an anxious time for our small party, and resistance for any length of time would have been out of the question. We took our rifles and waited for them to come up. They came straight on, and as the leaders approached they came and shook hands with us, proving to be at the head of a Masai war-party, composed of the same El Moran, or warriors, who had massacred the caravan in the Kedong Valley. It was a curious sight to see, and the column passed rapidly on in single file, threading its way through the mountains. They were divided up into detachments, wearing different kinds of head-gear; some had great head-dresses made of monkey skins, others of goat skins, whilst some had capes of ostrich feathers over their shoulders. They carried lovely spears and shields, most of the former wrapped in rags or painted red to avoid detection. Their leaders were friendly enough, and wanted us to go with them to raid the Kimariongo tribe, who live near Ingoboto, east of

10

Elgon, but two or three of the El Moran were insulting, and brandished their spears as they went by. I counted 484 in all; and following the column, which had several long gaps in it, were some cattle and sheep, to provide food on their journey. On arriving at their destination, they collect together at nightfall for the attack, and in the early morn fall on their enemies, killing man, woman, and child; stabbing right and left with their long sharp spears.

The Masai are certainly a disturbing element in this part of Africa, and will have to be dealt with some day. As civilisation advances, and they are gradually enclosed by the advancing Protectorates, their happy hunting-grounds become smaller; and it is almost too much to expect the Masai El Moran to settle down as peaceful British subjects without a good deal of compulsion. They have been accustomed to roam over an enormous extent of country, and it is not so many years since their raids extended nearly to the East Coast. Latterly, they have been obliged to confine themselves more to the north and northwest.

The Nandi tribe, who resemble the Masai so much, have been always more than a match for them, and the Masai have never dared to raid into their country, preferring probably a less warlike and more defenceless enemy.

At Naivasha we met Captain Sclater and Lieutenant Smith of the Royal Engineers, with a party, making the waggon-road from Kikuyu to the lake. Their carts had reached this point from the coast. The road down the Kedong escarpment was nearly completed, having been cut with great labour out of the rock. There were many Masai kraals between the Gilgil River and Naivasha, where we met the great chief Terari with his old father, who weighed twenty stone.

The country was so completely dried up that there was little game to be seen. On the Athi plains I killed a rhinoceros, and ought to have shot a lioness, who walked past me among some rocks only forty yards away, but I was chagrined to find that my gun-bearer had taken out the cartridges from my rifle, and at the click of the hammers the lioness bounded off into the rocks with a growl, and was not seen again.

Three days from Mombasa we met a detachment of the 24th Beluchistan Regiment, under Captain Mellis, employed in hunting the rebel chief, Mbaruk, who shortly afterwards gave himself up to the Germans in their territory.

On arriving at the coast, it was astonishing to see the change which had taken place in Mombasa owing to the railway, work on which had just been begun. The place had increased very much in size, and now possessed a club, hotel, and various shops. The East African Company had been bought out, and a Protectorate established over the whole territory, from the coast to the Kedong Valley, north of Kikuyu, where it marches with the Uganda Protectorate. Limited to a diminutive area at first, the latter has now rapidly been extended to include the whole country bounded by the Victoria Nile, the Albert and Albert-Edward Nyanzas to the west and north-west, and a large extent of country southwards to the Kedong Valley, twenty miles south of Lake Naivasha.

Embarking on the mail steamer at Mombasa, I arrived in England at the end of May 1896, after nearly two years' absence.

As a result of the recent expeditions in Unyoro,

commencing with Colonel Sir H. E. Colvile's in 1894, the whole country has been pacified, and at the present time a white man could walk across in comparative safety, with two attendants, from Mruli to the Murchison Falls. Kabarega and his myrmidons have been driven into exile across the Nile, which now forms a perfect frontier.

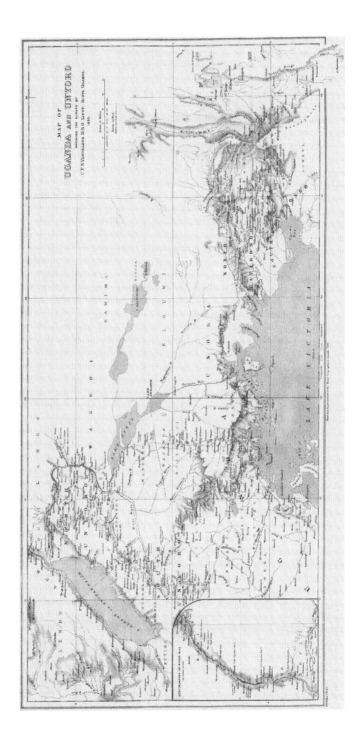

MAP OF
UGANDA and UNYORD
SHEWING the ROUTE of
Cᵀ F. D. LUGARD D.S.O. Late in Service Uganda.
1893.

X

European Enterprise on the Niger

I MUST now transport my readers across to the western side of the African Continent, where another great river, the Niger, little inferior in importance to the Nile, flows into the Gulf of Guinea, and with its fine waterway affords splendid facilities for trade and communication with the interior.

In 1796, after months of horrible privation and bad treatment by the natives, Mungo Park reached the upper portion of the Niger at Sego, and was the first European to look on the waters of this river, whose source and mouth were for so long such a mystery to geographers. That a great river existed in the Western Sudan was known even in the days of Herodotus, who tells of the journey undertaken by the Nasamones from their native country to the west of Egypt, and how the five young men, after crossing the Great Desert (Sahara), found themselves in a fertile country, and discovered a large river flowing from west to east.

Mungo Park, utterly destitute, was forced to make his way back to the coast, but returned a few years afterwards with a Government expedition, and, on reaching the Niger, constructed a craft with which he could sail down the river, which he called the Joliba, by lashing two large canoes together. After floating down for over a thousand miles, through a country inhabited by equally hostile and fanatical Moors and Tuaregs, the craft was dashed to pieces in the rapids below Yauri, near Bussa, and Park, with the few remaining survivors of his unfortunate expedition, threw themselves into the water, in preference to attempting to land and being seized by the hostile natives lining the banks.

Many English explorers, amongst others Oudney, Denham, and Clapperton, made strenuous efforts, after Park's death, to solve the riddle of the Niger, until, in 1830, Richard Lander, who had originally travelled as servant to Captain Clapperton, reached Bussa by land from the coast, and thence descended successfully in two canoes to the Atlantic, proving the accuracy of a book written by James M'Queen in 1821—"Containing a Particular Account of the Course and Termination of the Great River Niger in the Atlantic Ocean."

With wonderful insight M'Queen lays down the course of the river, which he came to the conclusion could only find its outlet in the Bights of Benin and Biafra. He points out the importance of the "Niger" to the commerce of England, and maintains that Bussa is the inner key of the situation. "Granted," he says, "that the navigation of the Niger was interrupted at Bussa by reason of rapids or rocks rising amidst the stream, still we know that the river can be navigated in safety from Bussa upwards and from Bussa downwards. [This is rather inaccurate.] Therefore on this commanding spot let the British standard be firmly planted, and no power on Africa could tear it up. A trifling land carriage would then give this nation nearly all the advantages of an open navigation, and by such a natural barrier place the Niger completely under her control. Firmly planted in Central Africa, the British flag would become the rallying-point for all that is honourable, useful, beneficial, just, and good."

These are curious and noteworthy words, written over seventy years ago about an unknown spot in the middle of Africa, which has been thrown into prominence lately. It is wonderful with what accuracy he foretold the dangers of a French advance from the Senegal to the Niger, and its far-reaching consequences, if carried out, to our commercial and political position in West Central Africa, in the following words:—" France is already established on the Senegal, and commands that river; and if the supineness and carelessness of Great Britain allow that powerful, enterprising, and ambitious rival to step before us and fix herself securely on the Lower Niger, then it is evident that, with such a settlement in addition to her command of the Senegal, France will command all Northern Africa. The consequences cannot fail to be fatal to the best interests of this country. . . ." He concludes as follows:—" By means of the Niger and his tributary streams, it is quite evident that the whole trade of Central Africa may be rendered exclusively and permanently our own. . . . To support and carry into execution the measures necessary to accomplish this undertaking, is worthy of the Ministry of Great Britain, and worthy of the first country of the world. It will confer immortal honour on our native land—lasting glory on the name and reign of George the Fourth—bring immense and permanent advantages to Britain, and bestow incalculable blessings and benefits on Africa. . . . Let but the noble Union Ensign wave over and be planted by the stream of the mighty Niger, and the deepest wounds of Africa are healed.

Round it and to it the nations, from Balia to Darfur, from Asben to Benin, would gather for safety and protection; the slave would burst his fetters, and the slave trade be heard of no more."

This view of the situation on the Niger, taken at the beginning of the century, seems so important, that I trust I shall be pardoned for dwelling on it.

No consideration of natural difficulties seems to limit the French in their advance. In 1880 the Tricolor was planted on the Upper Niger, and at the same time a railway was commenced to connect the highest navigable point on the Senegal with Bamako on the Niger, and a gunboat was carried over in sections and launched on the river, exactly as is being done now between the Congo and the Nile.

The Niger is a curious river, rising as it does not more than 150 miles east of Sierra Leone, and then making a great bend to the northward to Timbuktu, almost at its most northern point, before starting on its southward course to the Atlantic.

The first European to enter Timbuktu—setting aside accounts of doubtful authenticity—was Major Laing, who reached that place from Tripoli on 18th August 1826, and was murdered only a month afterwards, two days after his departure from the city. He was followed shortly afterwards by the French traveller René Caillié, who made a wonderful journey from Senegal to Timbuktu, where he stayed two weeks, and then on across the Sahara to Morocco, disguised as an Arab. The most interesting epoch in the history of the Western Sudan has been the invasion of the Fulahs at the commencement of the present century. Resembling the Wahuma in Uganda and the lake regions, they are lighter in colour, taller and finer-

FULAHS ON THE MARCH

looking people, than the indigenous population. Mungo Park says of them: "Far different, too, were the Fulah inhabitants. A tawny complexion, small, well-shaped features and soft silky hair distinguished them at a glance from the Negro races round them." Everywhere he found them remarkable for their industry, and no less successful in agriculture than in pastoral pursuits, which seem to have been their original speciality. Their history is unknown, but they would seem to be an offshoot of the great race of Gallas in the lands to the south of Abyssinia. They had for years been gradually working westwards with their flocks and herds, until the Niger seemed to have imposed a limit to their advance. Gradually increasing in numbers in what are now known as the Hausa States, they combined together under a religious leader called Othman dan Fodio. The Mohammedan religion, which had found its way across the Desert into the Sudan in the ninth and tenth centuries, had spread among the Fulahs with great rapidity, and under the influence of this sheikh they were now roused to a great state of religious fervour and enthusiasm.

Their peaceful vocations had hitherto unfitted them for the use of arms, and they suffered many defeats at first, but, on gaining experience in war, they were gradually transformed into a disciplined army of warriors, and their victorious cavalry swept across the Western Sudan, conquering the natives until the whole of this vast empire acknowledged the political supremacy of the Fulah.

On the death of Othman in 1817, the huge empire he had raised was divided between his sons, Bello and Abd Allahi.

To the former was given Sokoto and all the east

and south, while to the latter fell the western provinces along the Niger, with Gando as capital. The countries to the west of the Niger, including Massina, became independent under Ahmed Lebbo, one of Othman's lieutenants, who conquered that region immediately before the death of Othman (see *Mungo Park and the Niger*, by Joseph Thomson).

Although the tendency of the Fulahs of late years has been to push southwards towards the sea—and the country of Ilorin is ruled over by a Fulah, and is a great Mohammedan centre—yet the people of Borgu and Bussa have always successfully resisted the invasion of the Fulahs, and have remained pagans.

The mortality amongst white men belonging to Government expeditions, etc., which at first endeavoured to open up the Niger, from fever caused by the germs contracted in the pestilential mangrove swamps, or in the damp clammy mist overhanging the river at night, is terrible to contemplate. In fact, no European seemed able to live there for any period, however short. In 1832, Macgregor Laird placed two steamers on the Niger, which ascended the river as far as Rabba, and the Benuë for 100 miles from its confluence with the Niger. Out of 49 Europeans who went out, only 9 survived, the remainder falling victims to the dreaded climate. A Government expedition to Lokoja in 1841 was equally unfortunate.

It is extraordinary what an advance has been made of late, owing to medical science, and the improvement and greater portability of food, in the methods of resisting the insidious malaria and excessive heat and moisture of a tropical climate, and how much improvement has taken place in the general health of the Europeans on the Niger.

In 1852 another attempt was made by Macgregor
Laird to establish trade on the Niger; but his stations
were sacked by the natives, and, on his death, commerce on the Niger came to a standstill. New firms
were gradually started, until they were amalgamated
into what was known as the United African Company
in 1879, from which period dates Sir George Goldie's
connection with the Niger, and a new era. On applying to the Government in 1881 for a charter, the first
difficulty raised was that the capital of the Company
was too small. To meet this, the capital was increased
from £125,000 to £1,000,000 sterling, the Company
was thrown open to the public, and the name changed
to the National African Company.

The French companies on the Niger were at last
bought out, the final deeds of transfer being signed only
a few days before the meeting of the Berlin Conference
(see *Partition of Africa*, by Dr. J. Scott Keltie). In
1885, Mr. Joseph Thomson was sent up the Niger to
secure treaties with the Sultans of Sokoto and Gando,
who practically placed the dual Fulah empire under a
British Protectorate, and gave all commercial privileges
to the National African Company. In the next year
the Company received a Royal Charter from the
Government, and at last the whole of the navigable
portions of the Niger and the Benuë were secured for
England, and the National African Company became
the Royal Niger Company, with Lord Aberdare as
Governor, and Sir George Goldie (the real creator of
the Company) as Vice-Governor.

The Company, whilst endeavouring to secure the
territories over which it sought for a charter, had been
continually hampered by the efforts of both the
Germans and the French, to cut away the ground

from under its feet. From 1883 to 1886, Herr Flegel, aided by the German Colonial Society, struggled vigorously to extend German influence; but the British Company made no less than 400 treaties with the tribes amongst whom the country is divided. Shortly after the Charter was granted, Herr Hönigsberg entered the Niger, and visited the Emir of Nupe, with whom he made a treaty, in defiance of existing treaties, securing this country actually on the left bank of the navigable Niger, and which the Germans contended was not dependent on the Sultan of Gando.

In 1890, Lieutenant Mizon ascended the Niger with a view to securing the *Hinterland* for France, and, after failing to do this, he again set out in 1892 for Adamawa up the Benue.

At the Berlin Conference it was agreed that there should be freedom of transit for merchant ships on the Niger, but this does not apply to the war ships of foreign nations. The Company have a right to make their own customs regulations as to landing on their own territories.

There are several ways of reaching the main river by the numerous branches into which it expands as it nears the Atlantic, and winds through the swampy Delta.

British traders have been settled on the Oil Rivers, so called from the oil palms growing in the Delta, for a century, at first for the purpose of carrying on the slave trade. Since that ceased, an equally lucrative trade has been carried on in the oil derived from the palms, and, until a government was established, the traders lived for the most part in hulks anchored off the villages. In 1884, Consul Hewitt secured treaties with the native chiefs along part of the

coast between the Rio de Rey and Lagos, and in 1891
this portion, the valuable Oil Rivers, became practically
a British colony, and is now administered by the
Foreign Office. First known as the Oil Rivers Protectorate, the name has now been changed to the
Niger Coast Protectorate, with Old Calabar as the
seat of government. British missionaries had been
at work in this region for over fifty years. It seems
a pity that this district should be under à different
régime from the Niger itself, but it was felt that it
would have been unjust to compel the traders to
amalgamate with the Company, as they preferred to
remain separate.

It must be understood that the territories over
which the Royal Niger Company holds its charter,
extend behind the Niger Coast Protectorate, but the
former possesses two ports at the mouth of the Niger,
called Akassa and Burutu.

The Niger, from Sego to the sea, may be divided
into three fairly equal portions. The term "Upper
Niger" is generally applied to the long stretch of
navigable river flowing downward from Bamako past
Timbuktu to the first rapids. Great Britain has
always admitted the political claims of France to the
regions on both banks of this section, owing to the
proximity to the French colony of Senegambia, from
which that part of the river can be best approached for
the practical purposes of commerce.

The name "Lower Niger" is given to the section
navigable for purposes of commerce from the sea to
the lowest rapids. The political rights of Great
Britain over the regions on both banks of this section
are not disputed by any person of authority in France.

The Middle Niger is the section, from 600 to 1000

miles in length, which, though navigable in parts, is not practicable for the transit of commerce by water from the Lower Niger to the Upper Niger, or *vice versâ*. It has been asserted that the Middle Niger is navigable for commercial purposes, and that the rapids are not impracticable, but this question has been finally settled by the recent journey from Bamako to the mouth of the river by Lieutenant Hourst and his companions. The difficulties encountered by Lieutenant Hourst, owing to the natural obstacles of the Middle Niger, rendered his journey one of the most remarkable among recent travels in Africa.

XI

En Route for Nigeria

AFTER a dinner, at which I met Mr. H. M. Stanley, who had no great opinion of the salubrity of the Niger regions, and gave me some very sound advice as to precautions to be taken in those parts, I left London the same evening by the midnight train to Liverpool, and embarked on the *S.S. Coomassie* the next morning, 28th November.

Major Cunningham, Lieutenants Pereira and Dr. Castelotte were also on board, and we were the last detachment to leave England for the Niger expedition, most of the officers having gone on before us. We entered Las Palmas, the harbour of Grand Canary Island, on December 7th, and were glad to get on shore after a very rough and stormy voyage from Liverpool. It had been almost impossible to stand up on deck until two days before reaching the Canaries. A ride here made up for a great deal of previous discomfort; one day we rode through the town past the Cathedral to Monte, and on into the mountains, a picturesque road, past banana groves which lay in the valleys; another day up to the lighthouse station at the end of the island, where we had a splendid view. In the evening of this day, as we were getting under weigh, a blue mass of hills suddenly appeared in the distance, and as the sun sank the blue outline appeared so clearly defined against the red sky, that the great Peak of Teneriffe almost seemed part of the island before us, though in reality sixty miles away.   Now began a long, monotonous voyage round the coast of Africa.   The sea was almost invariably calm, and the temperature gradually increased as we made our way to the south.   At Dakar we stopped to land the Consul, and were interested to see the place, which is the French port for their enormous possessions in the Western Sudan.   A railway runs from here to St. Louis, the seat of government, situated on the Senegal River.   The main street, bordered by a nice avenue of trees, is called the *Boulevard National*, and, thronged by natives wearing variegated coloured cloths, is a pretty sight.   On one side were the barracks containing the " Spahis," or black cavalry, and outside stood a sentry, such as Detaille would have loved to paint, dressed in a red serge tunic, white baggy pantaloons, and long black boots, armed with a long sword and rifle.   Through the verandahs on each side could be seen their small white Arab steeds, and as the guard turned out at four o'clock we could see that some of them, as well as the sentry, wore medals won in Dahome and the numerous African campaigns which the French have had in the Sudan.

We arrived at Sierra Leone on December 15th, and stayed three days there.   It is a pretty place as seen on entering the harbour, and the dark green hills rise up to a great height behind it.   The railway now being made had reached for six miles inland, and will be of immense value in opening up communication with the *Hinterland*.   There are no animals excepting small cattle, and the usual mode of progression is in a hammock with four bearers, which we were glad to avail ourselves of in climbing the steep hill, on which are situated the barracks, occupied by the West India Regiment. Two curious secret societies existing among the natives have been recently brought to light—one known as the Leopard Society, the members of which go out at night in leopard skins with gloves provided with steel claws, and get rid of anyone objectionable to them by strangling him and tearing his throat; the other is the Ju-Ju, or Crocodile Society, which exists some distance inland, for the purpose of still continuing the practice of cannibalism. It was very hot and sultry lying in the harbour, and a great relief to everyone when we had finished discharging the cargo and weighed anchor on the evening of the 17th. We reached Monrovia, the capital of the Liberian Republic, on the morning of the 19th, and remained there long enough to go ashore and walk through the place, which is a small, untidy town of scattered houses, lying on some rising ground along a small promontory jutting out into the sea. The State was founded in 1822 by 20,000 freed slaves, sent over from America by President Monroe. The Government is quite a farce; all the members are styled right honourable, but notwithstanding this they have proved quite unable to govern themselves. They have a diminutive fleet, consisting of two small gunboats, which occasionally demonstrate their power by firing across the bows of the mail steamers, for some unknown reason. The Liberians have a very great opinion of themselves and the influence of their State on the affairs of the world, though their knowledge of history is rather vague, as will be gathered from the following story:—A senator met a Frenchman one day in the street, who knocked up against him, when the former, in an indignant manner, turned round and said, "You d—— Frenchman, what for you shove me? what for we give you at Waterloo?"

We made our way slowly along the West Coast, stopping at all the different places—Cape Coast Castle, Accra, etc.   At the latter (which is now the seat of government for the Gold Coast) I met Sir W. Maxwell, the governor, and Sir Francis Scott, commandant of the Gold Coast Constabulary.

Kotonu, where we touched on the 24th, is the French port for Porto Novo and Dahome, and is a ghastly-looking place.   Along a strip of yellow sand there are a series of corrugated iron-roof warehouses, and houses occupied by the French officials.   Behind the sand is the native village, and then the lagoon, in which were lying two stern-wheelers, which run twice a week to Porto Novo.   A well-constructed iron pier 270 yards long runs out into the sea, having a large pier-head with five cranes on it.   This must have been a busy place during the campaign in Dahome, conducted by General Dodds.   At the present time the flags were all flying half-mast high, owing to the death of the wife of one of the officials in Porto Novo, and the place presented a mournful appearance.

Christmas Day was spent lying off the bar outside Lagos, which is unfavourable for large steamers, and only allows the smaller branch boats to pass at nearly high tide.   There was a certain amount of swell rolling in towards the bar from the open sea, and I can imagine few more unpleasant places to spend Christmas at, though this was the fourth winter I had spent on or near the Equator.   We were thoroughly tired with the inaction of the long sea voyage, and were longing to arrive in the mysterious reaches of the Niger

LANDING IN THE SURF

and learn for certain the object of the expedition, the secret of which had been so carefully guarded.

Countless had been the various objectives put forward by the press, not the least amusing of which was that given by the *Figaro*, to the effect that Sir George Goldie, having subdued the various States in the Western Sudan up to Kano, was then going to march across to Khartum. It was a fairly general opinion that the Mohammedan State of Ilorin would come into the sphere of operations, and this was strengthened on hearing that 100 men had been despatched from Lagos to strengthen the garrison on the Ilorin frontier, but there was great difference of opinion as to whether we were first going up the Niger or the Benuë, which joins the former at Lokoja.

The mouth of the Forcados River is no easy place to find in a coast like this, where one strip of land is exactly like another, and we went past it during the night, but turned round and found it at 9 a.m., eventually crossing the bar and anchoring within it at 10.30. Here we found the Niger Company's launch *Nupe* waiting for us, on board of which was Mr. Flint, the genial agent-general for the Lower Niger. Stores, saddlery, ammunition, and loads of all sorts had to be transferred from the ship to the launch, and it was a sad moment for us when we were informed that our own stores could not be found, and were probably under the remainder of the cargo, which would take several days to get out. This luckily proved untrue, and everything was eventually discovered in some hidden corner. Soon after daylight on the 27th we transferred ourselves to the *Nupe* and steamed rapidly off into this weird-looking region of creeks and mangrove swamps, looking back to see the outline of the mail steamer, our home for the last four weeks, soon vanish in the white mist of the early morn, and felt that we had broken the last link connecting us with the civilised world.

In place of the long interminable stretch of sand, topped by the dark green line of trees and bushes, which forms the West Coast of Africa, the eye now rested on a multitude of creeks, or rivers, intersecting interminable mangrove swamps, and merging themselves in the thin mist overhanging the horizon; and one could not wonder that the mouth and outlet of the great river Niger was unknown for so many centuries, and that almost as much mystery was attached to it as to the source of the Nile.

Times have altered since then. Now large steamers and speedy launches ply to and fro for hundreds of miles up the river, though in the dry season—lasting eight months—vessels exceeding 4 feet draught can navigate only a short distance. It was difficult at first to see how we could keep in the right channel, as in the launch we passed countless islands of mangroves, and every turn appeared just the same as another. To a newcomer the latter would seem to be nice green woods, but on closer inspection they prove to be nothing but thousands of white roots growing out of the slimy, yellow sand, in which they find a treacherous foothold, and above them, interlaced together, stretch the branches and green foliage which have given rise to the deception.

In an hour or two we come to the first station of the Royal Niger Company, called Burutu, where a small piece of *terra firma* has been utilised in this submerged region; and there are several warehouses, also a house in course of construction for the official in charge. As we proceed, the banks become more defined and harder, and on rounding a corner we come to the first signs of the natives. A few small square houses or huts, made of wattle and mud, with roofs of dried palm leaves and reeds, lie clustered together, the inhabitants of which maintain themselves by the fish they catch. Farther on, the scenery alters entirely. The mangrove swamps have given place to high banks, covered with long green grass and fine trees. Large villages are thronged with natives of rather an ugly and repulsive type, most of them wearing coloured cloths round their loins. Formerly they were undoubted cannibals, and accustomed to kill and eat their captives taken in war; and it is rumoured that even now a morsel of human flesh is not despised when obtainable, and I am told the human foot is a great delicacy. Behind and on each side of the village are banana groves, with their long, broad, shady leaves, and over all rise the lofty, thin palm trees, the feathery leaves of which taper gradually to the end, and droop gracefully over. Sometimes pretty acacia trees, and cotton trees with coloured blossoms, meet the eye.

Some of the women are painted with cross lines of blue or red, and in a few instances they have brass-wire bangles, or are covered with a slate-coloured chalk—a strange mode of adornment. Fishing-nets and baskets lie scattered about on the bank, and a number of dug-out canoes are fastened to the side. Here is one in course of construction. A man is shaping it out with an adze, after which the inside will be further burnt away by means of fire. Some of these canoes are really almost miniature ones, and so small are they that their sides appear nearly level with the water's edge. About 12 inches in width, they must be hard to balance, yet natives can be seen glid-

ing along in them under the banks at a great
pace.

To anyone of an adventurous turn of mind there is
something very taking in thus rapidly steaming up a
great waterway into the heart of Central Africa. At
every turn, new sights and strange beings meet the
eye, and one wonders what there can be behind the
apparently trackless bush and jungle which line the
banks, except where the human hand has made a
clearing for habitation. On the sandbanks, which are
now exposed in this the dry season, lie enormous
crocodiles, which waddle off into the water with a
splash at our approach; and on the second day, hippopotami can be seen poking their big goggle-eyed
heads out of the water at a safe distance from us.
This day we reached in the early morning a station
called Asaye. It was near here that Lieutenant
Mizon, after making his way up the river in a steam-
launch, unknown to the Company's officials, was surprised by the natives at night, and severely wounded,
some of his men being killed. The nights are dark,
and we have to anchor until morning; even now the
Maxim gun is loaded, and a watch is kept to guard
against surprise. Though there has been such success
in doing away with strife and bringing peace to these
regions, it is still just as well to be ready for emergencies. In old days villages used to raid one another,
and native traders plied up and down the river in their
canoes at the risk of their lives.

The farther one ascends up the river the more it
improves. Stations are passed where palm oil and the
valuable rubber are collected in readiness for transport
to England. Not until the third day do we arrive at
Asaba, the administrative headquarters—a pretty place,

situated about 40 feet above the river, which is here just over a mile broad. The grounds are well laid out, and mango trees, baobab trees, and feather palms line the walks.

Farther on, the country becomes drier and burnt-up-looking. Great sandy islands obstruct the channel of the river, and the course is more difficult to find. Twice we ran aground, and were delayed for three hours, having to pull ourselves off by means of a wire cable. The scenery on approaching Lokoja is very fine; high hills, some cone-shaped, rising up on each side. And here, on the fifth day, we reached our destination, the base of the forthcoming expedition.

Lokoja presented a very busy appearance, and the bank of the river was crowded with fatigue-parties of soldiers and natives, engaged loading the stern-wheelers and launches for the forthcoming expedition. After the naked savages we had seen along the banks of the Lower Niger, it was a change indeed to see the natives here all covered with cloth, tobes, and enormous turbans. Two or three horses were waiting for us, and we rode up to the barracks, which lie a little above the town, where we found all the officers collected. A line of tents extended along one side of the parade ground, an open sandy space in front of the mess-house, from which at times clouds of dust would sweep across and cover everything in one's tent with dust.

In the afternoon of our arrival I took over my Maxim - gun detachment, consisting of four Hausa soldiers, and paraded with the other Maxim guns for practice on the range at 500 to 300 yards.

The old chief at Lokoja, called Abbega, got up an entertainment for our benefit, which consisted of dances

by people of the different races in the town.   He is a
remarkable man, having accompanied Barth in his travels
through the Sudan, and having also been to London.
Squatting round in a circle outside the chief's house
were a large collection of natives, swathed, as is their
custom, in an enormous quantity of cloth, large folds
of which were also wound round their heads.   The
native cloth made at Kano is valued very highly, and
is mostly dyed blue, some of it being dyed red with
white stripes.   The dances were, as a rule, slow and
monotonous, but not the least curious was one called
the devil dance.

Some rather fat and unwieldy-looking women, who
were supposed to be possessed of the devil, danced
about, and finally jumped up in the air, coming down
with a bang in a sitting posture.

This was supposed to squash the devil, but must have
occasioned them a good deal of pain.   Another curious
entertainment was given us by some men, who heated
an iron red-hot and then rubbed their feet along it,
until the hissing of the burning flesh could be heard,
and the air was filled with the smell of burning; one
man even licked the red-hot iron with his tongue.

XII

PREPARATIONS AT LOKOJA

SIR George Goldie arrived on New Year's Day, and preparations were at once made for the departure of the column. Major Arnold, who was to command the troops, had arrived out a fortnight before; he had been in command of the Niger Constabulary for the last two years.

It was now known that the object of the expedition was to overthrow the Fulah power in Nupe, the most important State of the Sokoto Empire (ruled over by the Emir of Bida), which had made overtures to the Emir of Ilorin and the King of the Bussa country to combine together to overthrow the power of the white man on the Niger, though the King of Bussa not only remained faithful to his treaty, but informed the Company of the conspiracy.

In the last eighteen years British power has been gradually built up and established in the valley of the Niger, and an enormous and important territory secured to Great Britain by the Royal Niger Company. That a conflict was bound to occur sooner or later with the Mohammedan slave-raiding rulers of the interior, as has happened all over Africa, was recognised years ago, and a trained force of Hausas, well

armed, had been in process of organisation under
English officers for ten or twelve years. These soldiers
are the real Hausas from Hausaland itself, and form
the best fighting material in Africa: they are short,
sturdy-looking men, and excellent marchers; some of
them had served for a considerable time. The first
period of service is for five years only, but many
engage for a longer time, some even returning to their
homes and then enlisting again. A large number
come from the direction of Kano, about 700 miles in
the interior. Although little had been heard of them at
home, they had distinguished themselves in many small
expeditions and combats against slave-dealers, recalci-
trant chiefs, etc. This was the first time, however,
they were to be called upon to face the wild horsemen
and Mohammedans of the Western Sudan, and many
doubts were expressed as to their standing up before
them.

The Emir, confident of not being attacked, had
divided his army, and the moment had now arrived
for striking the blow. For 200 miles above Lokoja
the Niger makes a great bend to the west, and on the
farther side of the river lies the northern portion of the
Nupe country, the capital, Bida, being about 25 miles
from the river, almost on the sixth degree of longitude
east of Greenwich.

The Governor and the Earl of Scarborough had
visited the capital about four years before and inter-
viewed the Emir, who was informed that a repetition
of the raiding for slaves on the southern bank, into
the country under the protection of the Niger Company, would not be countenanced, and would lead to
measures being taken to stop it. The high ground
in the interior had been devastated for years by the

Fulahs, who had been accustomed to cross the Niger and settle down in some fertile spot which formed a good centre for their depredations. These used to extend even as far as Asaba in the south.

Few people at home can realise the enormous population existing in Hausaland, which forms the larger portion of Sokoto and Gando. It is estimated by Mr. Robinson at 15 millions, or one per cent. of the world's population, and of these a large proportion are slaves. The latter form a species of coinage in the country; and if a man goes on a journey he takes so many slaves with him, according to the length of the journey. With these he buys food and pays his way, with the result that a slave may be owned by several masters in a short space of time, besides changing his abode many hundreds of miles. The farther he advances into the Sudan from the West Coast the more valuable he becomes. Slavery may be said to flourish in Hausaland unchecked, and the slave trade on the East Coast of Africa cannot be compared with it.

The Emir of Bida, after three years of comparative tranquillity, had sent one of his leading generals, the Markum Muhammed, across the Niger with a large following, estimated at about 6000 to 7000, to a place called Kabba, where he had established a large war-camp not far from the native town, and was encamped there at the present time.

It was a magnificent opportunity to attack him, and a most essential point was that the Emir of Bida should remain ignorant of the mobilisation and concentration of the expedition till the very last minute, so that he should not have time to withdraw the southern army and concentrate his whole force in

one spot.   The mystery in which the aim and object
of the expedition was enveloped was therefore one
of the most important factors of its ultimate success.
News travels with great rapidity in Hausaland, where
traders are continually travelling from one place to
another, and there was little time to be lost now.

Lokoja is the headquarters of the Royal Niger
Company's Constabulary, and a position of great
importance, both from a commercial and a strategical
point of view.   It is situated at the confluence of the
two great rivers the Niger and Benuë, and consequently is the centre of all trade in these regions.   To
the eastward there is a waterway up the Benuë as
far as Yola, about 450 miles.   Large quantities of
ivory come down from this district, and it is only
250 miles from Yola to the south end of Lake
Chad, which is connected by trade routes with, one
may say, the whole of Central Africa.   Passing to
the eastward through the provinces of Wadai, Darfur,
and Kordofan, the Nile is reached at Khartum, and
this, until the dervish rule commenced, was formerly
a well-used road.

To the north lies the great Sahara, across the
waterless tracts of which large caravans find it worth
their while to bring European goods for sale in the
Hausa States, all the way from Tripoli, Benghazi, and
the Mediterranean coast.   A dangerous road this, and
one in which the terrors of thirst and attacks by
Tuaregs, the savage brigands of the desert, have to
be faced.

Launches can ascend the river Niger for another
200 miles from Lokoja as far as Rabba, in a north-
westerly direction, and beyond this in the rainy
season there is more or less broken water-communica-

MARKET ON THE WEST COAST

tion as far as the great capital and State of Sokoto. A glance at the map will show what a magnificent waterway this is, and what opportunities it offers for the development of these territories.

The force at the disposal of the Royal Niger Company consisted of about 1000 Hausa troops, but of these nearly half were required to garrison other portions of the territories, and also our long line of communications with the sea. It was only the year before that the Company's station at Akassa was attacked by the natives of Brass, and there is always a likelihood of trouble with the savage tribes inhabiting the Lower Niger and the Delta. Any disaster or reverse in our rear would have been very serious. The defence of Lokoja itself was most important, as all supplies and ammunition were stored here.

Two hundred men were to be left behind for this purpose, under the command of Captain Sangster of the Leicester Regiment. Lokoja lies on rising ground, which slopes gradually up to the edge of a high table mountain, called Mount Pati, 1200 feet above the sea, which I ascended one day. It is a steep climb up, but the view well repays the trouble. Immediately below one, and at the head of a valley, seem to lie the barracks, with the native town between them and the river, whilst in the distance the great sheet of water denotes the confluence of the Niger and Benuë, the latter of which can be seen stretching away in great bends to the eastward. A large extent of sandbanks is exposed to view at this season, and on one of these lay the wreck of one of the Company's large steamers, now half buried in the sand.

The country is covered with short trees and scrub,

and presented at the time a brown and parched-up appearance.

To guard the exposed flank towards the valley on the south-west was a small fort called Church Hill Fort, which was armed with a 9- and a 7-pounder gun, whilst to the north, to prevent an advance between the hills and the river, lay the magazine fort on Stirling Hill, which held two 7-pounder guns.

The Agent - General's house was also put into a state of defence, and armed with a Maxim gun. In addition to this the S.S. *Ribago*, one of the Company's largest steamers, was anchored in the river with a 12-pounder on board, enfilading any advance from the south. An electric search-light was also put up to aid the garrison in the defence.

Parades were held morning and afternoon, and the force was divided up into six companies, with each of which there were two English officers; attached to each company also there was an officer with a Maxim gun and the detachment belonging to it. The artillery consisted of five 7-pounder guns with short barrels, which were carried by porters, the barrels being slung on to a pole and carried by two men, one in front and one behind. All the officers were mounted on ponies— small, wiry little animals, very much like barbs, such as we were to see in such numbers later on. These were all under the charge of Lieutenant Chaworth Musters, 3rd Hussars. We were allowed to select our own, and I secured a very good pony, which afterwards won me a race at the race-meeting held outside the walls of Bida.

During the few days before we started, my time was fully occupied in taking and working out observations to rate the chronometer watches, of which I had three. The instruments supplied me by the Company,

consisted, besides the above, of a large and very good
sextant and artificial horizon, also a telescope for fixing
longitudes by occultations and eclipses of Jupiter's
satellites.   Owing to the rapidity with which the
column moved, and the few halts there were, it
proved impossible to use the latter.

XIII

Start from Lokoja

ON the 5th January the force paraded in marching order at 8.30, and the final preparations were made for the start on the following day. Maxim-gun belts were filled, and with each gun were carried four boxes with belts containing 250 cartridges, so that every gun had 1000 rounds for immediate use. Officers were allowed two loads of 60 lb., one containing a wooden bed and bedding in a kit-bag, the other a bath, in which one carried a change of clothes, boots, etc., and any luxuries one could stow away. It is a difficult matter to decide on what to take and what to leave behind, and the actual starting on an expedition is always a most troublesome matter. There are a hundred and one things which one would wish to take, and which one is obliged at the last minute to throw away.

We were now going to march into the country to the west of the Niger, with the probability of not reaching the river again for about three weeks, and the organisation of the transport even for a force of 500 men, where all food and supplies have to be carried, is no easy task. There were 900 carriers, 600 of whom were Hausas and Yorubas drawn from the country itself, while the remaining 300 came from the West Coast, among them being Fantis and Ashantis and natives from Accra and Lagos. Our own servants also came from the West Coast, and a very large and thick-set individual, like a prize-fighter, named Don Pedro, was told off to me, and was soon afterwards known throughout the camp as Samson. He did not, however, bear out the reputation of his name, and it was with difficulty he could be got to carry a small basket on the march, when he usually came into camp with the tail of the column. He said he had been with an officer in the Ashanti Expedition.

Executive-Officer Watts and Lieutenant Thompson were in charge of the transport, and had their work cut out for them. An African porter is an annoying person to deal with at any time, but when there are 900 of them the work becomes very trying, and the difficulties are increased enormously.

The carriers were divided up into eight companies, and on the morning of January 6th all the loads were laid out on the parade-ground, and the various companies told off to them, when the usual fighting and uproar commenced, each man trying to seize a load which he thought was lighter than another one. The organisation of the expedition had been carried out in a most perfect manner, and we were carrying rockets, blue surprise-lights, and strands of wire to place round the camp at night, also some specially made incendiary rockets for setting fire to thatched roofs.

Sir George Goldie marched out of Lokoja on the 6th, with a force composed as follows—

Officers and other Europeans, .	.	30
Rank and file in seven companies,	.	513
		543

There were unavoidable delays at starting, and it was eleven o'clock before we finally filed out through the narrow streets of the town, which were thronged by a wondering crowd of natives, and after being saluted by the guns from the forts, we made our way past the magazine fort and along the base of the high hills, with the Niger on our right. There were the usual breakdowns at starting, owing to the heat and the heavy loads. After going for two miles, we turned north-west, and followed one of the valleys running down from the high ground of the interior, camping at a place called Felela Busa. Looking back over the undulating sea of brown grass, the long line of carriers and soldiers, with here and there a European on horseback, could be traced winding along the native track like a great serpent, and it was curious to me to find myself on the tramp again, this time on another side of Africa, and I could not help wondering what the end and result of this expedition would be. As I looked round me, I could almost fancy myself on the East Coast again, and but that the porters seemed much better clothed and quieter on the march, they bore a striking resemblance to the Swahilis and Zanzibaris.

On the same day that the land column started to march, the flotilla of armed stern-wheelers and launches, which was lying off Lokoja in readiness, steamed off for the upper bend of the Niger under Mr. Wallace, the Agent-General for the Niger Sudan regions. No man possesses such a knowledge and experience of this country and its inhabitants as he does, and he is one of the few white men on whom the dangerous West African climate seems to have no effect. With an experience of twenty years up the Niger, he was invaluable on this expedition, and to him was entrusted the blockade of the River Niger between Egga, situated at the bend of the river, and Jebba. This was all part of a preconceived plan to prevent the southern and northern Nupe armies from effecting a junction. To carry this out the river between these two places was divided into six sections, and a system of patrolling instituted, which had the effect of stopping all communication from one bank to the other.

The flotilla consisted of the following vessels— *Empire, Liberty, Muri, Sudan, Florence, Borgu, Zaria, Bornu, Argus,* and *Ribago,* with two despatch launches, *Frances* and *Busybody.* The two stern-wheelers *Empire* and *Liberty,* which were to play such an important part in the campaign, had only recently been sent out from England. They were provided with an upper deck, with four cabins, cook-house, etc., on the sides, with a light sun-deck above, and though drawing only two feet six inches, were able to carry from 300 to 400 men, horses, guns, etc., besides a quantity of stores, and steamed from seven to eight knots an hour. They were fitted with some steel plates, and with two Nordenfeldt shell guns on wheeled carriages.

Three of the fastest launches were ordered to patrol the whole length of river to be blockaded, and so keep up a communication between the various sections.

The town of Kabba lies almost due west of Lokoja, and there is a path connecting the two places, on which the enemy's scouts had been seen not far from the river. It was determined, however, to move in a north-westerly direction, and thus interpose our force between Kabba and their line of retreat to Bida, so that they would be forced to make a detour to the west.

Owing to the thick bush and scrub with which this part of the country is covered, the column was necessarily obliged to move in single file, and the great danger to be apprehended was an attack by cavalry on the long line of carriers at any open spot on the march.

The order of march was as follows: The advance guard consisted of two companies and a Maxim-gun detachment, and was commanded by Major Cunningham. This body moved off early, and proceeded independently to the next camping-place, where always a lot of work had to be done in clearing the ground and preparing a site for the camp. The main body was headed by a company with Maxim gun, which was followed by four companies of carriers; then came the centre-guard consisting of two companies with Maxim gun, four more companies of carriers, and a rear-guard of one company and Maxim gun.

One company was always told off as baggage guard, and provided detachments for the protection of each company of carriers on the line of march. The marches were long and tedious, owing to the long line occupied by the column in single file, and the frequent halts necessary to close up the gaps, the rear-guard seldom reaching the camping ground till late in the afternoon. Fortunately the Harmattan wind was blowing, which brings minute particles of sand with it from the Sahara, and keeps off to a certain extent the hot rays of the sun, the atmosphere being at times so clouded that it was difficult to see hills a mile off.

The 7-pounders were carried by porters with the main body. The native guides who were with us, mounted on their thin wiry little ponies covered with gaily-coloured trappings, presented an extraordinary appearance, and gave us an inkling of what our adversaries would look like. Their heads were enveloped in voluminous folds of cloth, which was also wrapped round their necks, and the whole was crowned by an enormous plum-pudding-shaped straw hat with broad brim. Their flowing garments bulged out over their high-peaked saddles, which were usually covered with a gaudy saddle-cloth, made to cover the peaks in front and behind. Two "mallams," or native priests, who also accompanied us, were similarly dressed to the guides; they are regularly enrolled in the force, and amenable to discipline, and were liable to be brought up in the orderly-room if they were late for reading prayers. Three times a day they used to read out the prayers in the camp, which were responded to by the soldiers. Great attention was paid that no offence should be given to their religion, as it was assumed that the Fulahs would endeavour to entice our soldiers to their side by making a Jehad or religious war of it, and preaching destruction to all the Christians. This was the first time that the Hausas had been asked to fight against their co-religionists.

One of the mallams used always smile to benignantly on me, and usually attached himself to me on the march. As my knowledge of his language was rather scanty, we did not improve our acquaintance, but I am convinced that he looked upon me as a white mallam, and thought that my observations of the sun and stars with a sextant had something to do with the supernatural. When engaged in this, I used always to see a wondering and astonished little crowd of soldiers and carriers, who had collected to gaze at the proceed-

ings. They would always keep a respectful distance
off, principally I think with the idea that there was
something uncanny about them, and that it might be
dangerous to go any nearer.

The country through which we passed had been
devastated by slave-raiders, and was entirely uninhabited until we crossed the small river Gadwanga on
the third day, and reached the nearly deserted village
of Emu. A few poverty-stricken inhabitants came
out, who said that the Nupes had been at the village
the day before, that the representatives of the Emir of
Bida had only just left, and that they had taken away
a lot of food with them. Owing to the Harmattan
wind little could be seen beyond a mile, and the hills
loomed up in the mist as in a London fog. It became
an arduous task to keep the direction of the march, as
no point could be selected in front, a circumstance which
entailed continual stopping and looking at the compass.

On the 9th we climbed a rather rocky hill, on the
top of which a nice village called Jakuro was buried
among some lovely trees, and surrounded by small
fields of dhurra. The houses were oblong, and very
similar to the Swahili houses on the East Coast, made
of mud and wattle with thatched roofs. An annoying
delay took place, owing to the head of the column
taking a wrong track, which is an easy mistake to
make in this country. After descending the hill on
the other side, we had to retrace our steps again and
proceed by another path, and it took some time before
the column could be got into proper order again.

The sun was extremely hot, and after we left Jakuro
the country became very uninteresting and dried up.
The grass was about three feet high, and what trees there
were gave absolutely no shade. The Fanti carriers

ON THE MARCH TO KABBA

from the Gold Coast travelled very badly, and although we covered only 10½ miles, the main body did not reach camp till after four in the afternoon.

These long days in the sun, with frequent halts, are invariably far more trying than a march of double or even treble the distance which is covered in a shorter space of time.

The camp was laid out under the high peak of Akpara. The site was always marked out with flags by Lieut. Burdon, the camp quartermaster, who accompanied the advance-guard, and, if the ground admitted, it took the form of a square of 110 yards side.

Each company and Maxim-gun detachment had its own flags, and was therefore able to march straight off to its place in the camp on arriving in at the end of the march. Behind the troops on the front and rear face, there was a line of tents, one to every two officers, and behind these were picketed the horses, about forty in number.

I was fortunate in having a tent to myself, to enable me to carry out my surveying work without hindrance.

The centre of the camp was occupied by the carriers and loads, and was often the scene of turmoil and disturbance, caused by the porters quarrelling over the division of food or some triviality.

The quiet of the night was often broken by the horses stampeding and fighting with one another. Many of them were vicious brutes, and it was risky to pass too near to their heads or their heels, as one of our doctors soon discovered. He was going through the lines, when one of them suddenly seized him by the hand, and did not let go until it had bitten him to the bone, severely lacerating his hand.

At night two strands of wire were fastened up round the camp at a distance of about forty yards, to prevent a sudden rush.

Surprise-lights were also fastened to trees or stakes fifty yards off, and were connected by cords with the sides of the square, usually at the places where the Maxim guns were stationed. In the event of an attack, these could be fired in a few seconds, and burned for seven minutes with a bright blue light, throwing everything into relief round them. Maxim guns were always loaded and placed ready for action during the night. The smoke from the fires was very trying to the eyes, and one was nearly blinded if one had to find one's way from one side of the camp to another.

Every five or six officers used to mess together, and a cook was told off to each mess.

The English, as spoken by one's personal attendants, was somewhat bewildering, and was almost as difficult to understand as the Hausa language itself. If I called my servant, Samson, I usually received the answer, " I live for chop," which meant that he was eating his food, and could not by any possibility be disturbed. Another quaint expression was, " I find him I no look him." This was the invariable answer if one asked one's servant to get anything, and meant that he was unable to find it.

Goats and sheep were difficult to obtain, and we had at first principally to live on tinned provisions. There was little chance of killing any antelope, though two hartebeest did dash past the camp early one morning.

When the carriers began to settle down to their loads, we travelled much better, and usually covered over ten miles a day. The next biggest place we came to after Jakuro was Akpara, which we passed

through early on the 11th.   This village was also
situated on a hill, where there were rice, groves of
plantains, also yams and oranges.   We had ascended
a good deal since leaving the Niger, and were in quite
a lofty region for West Africa.   The nights became
much cooler, and the thermometer used to go down to
about 59° or 60° Fahrenheit, but it was very hot in the
middle of the day.   On the 11th January we reached
our first important point, called Sura, and camped
about two miles from the high hill which bears the
same name, and under which lies a fairly large native
village.   This lies on the regular raiding road used
between the capital Bida and the war-camp near
Kabba.

XIV

FLYING COLUMN TO KABBA

ORDERS were now given for the greater portion of the fighting force, total 403, with 300 porters carrying light loads, to leave the next day and make a forced march on the Markum's camp. Tents to be left behind, and each officer allowed one 40-lb. load.

The majority of the carriers and loads were thus left at Sura, where a strong zariba was to be built, and a company was left behind under Lieutenants Pereira and Neale to hold the post. Captain Hatton was at the same time sent with 150 carriers and a small escort north to Egga, to fetch some supplies. The sun was well up before a start could be made on the 12th inst. with the flying column to Kabba. Loads had to be divided up and readjusted, and porters told off to them, and no end of those little details seen to, which, apparently so unimportant, yet conduce so much to the ultimate success. We travelled the whole day, with a halt of two hours, over a dry and burnt-up country covered with low trees, first passing through the village and then southwards along the base of the Sura Hill. The river Mimi, near which we halted, is a lovely stream, and is bordered by beautiful trees, which afforded a grateful shade in the midst of this

HORSE PICKET AND CARRIERS IN CAMP AT SURA ON THE KABBA MARCH

sweltering heat. The river is said to run into the Niger about two miles below Lokoja. The monotony of the journey was broken only by the capture of a " dankari," or Nupe soldier, in the grass at the side of the road, who was probably a spy watching our movements. He was seen by one of the keen-eyed Hausa soldiers, who immediately gave chase, backed up by other soldiers and carriers near him on the march, who threw down their loads on the pathway, and all rushed off eager for some fun. Two or three of the fleetest of them came up with him, and brought him back in triumph, having torn most of his scanty clothing off him in the struggle, during which he bit a carrier very badly in the mouth.

Late in the afternoon we entered a dense bit of forest, ensconced in which was the village of Epi, hidden away from the outer world. Open glades round the habitations were filled with plantains, yams, and cotton, and the natives stood gaping at the doorways as we passed through. On emerging from the forest, it was a relief to see the head of the column halted on a little rising ground not far from a stream, which soon presented a busy scene, as everyone began to settle down to bivouac here for the night. The grass had to be cut down round the camp, and precautions taken to guard against a surprise. The position of Kabba was uncertain, and we were trusting entirely to the native guides with us. There was therefore no knowing how near the enemy might be. I sat up rather late to find the latitude, which was N. $7° 56' 15''$, and to plot the course of our march on the map, and had not turned in long when I was suddenly awaked by the noise and rushing of feet; my first impression that we were attacked was strengthened by seeing forms rushing past my bed in the dusk, and I bent down to get hold of my revolver.

It turned out, however, that the prisoner was the cause of all the disturbance, having effected his escape from the guard, which was posted just in front of my corner. Notwithstanding that he was fastened with cords to a soldier of the guard, he managed to wriggle himself out of them during the night, and was clever enough to dash through the back of the camp where he could not be fired at. In doing so he stampeded the carriers, who went with an alarming rush from one side of the camp to the other; and in the meantime he was making good his escape, though he must have hurt himself severely against the strands of wire, which were found bent and twisted up.

On resuming our march, the white mist and the wet grass—which was here very luxuriant, and soon wetted one through and through—reminded me of Uganda; but after going eight miles in a south-westerly direction the country improved, and we marched along a lovely grass valley covered with scattered palm trees. In this valley there were many traces of huts and enclosures, and it was no doubt the abandoned site of a Fulah war camp in previous years. A curious little rocky hill was pointed out to me in the distance as our destination, and about 12.30 p.m. we reached the outer wall of Kabba, which lies under the hill.

Great disappointment was caused by the news that our march had been in vain, and that the Nupe army had preferred to defer the engagement, and was now retreating in a north-westerly direction to the river Niger. As it turned out, everything was for the best, and during these three weeks of hard marching in the bend of the Niger the soldiers got to know their officers;

their discipline and mobility was proportionately increased, and all ranks received good training for the arduous work which was before them. A halt was called outside the town, and the few palm trees dotted about were soon surrounded by little groups of officers and men, seeking shelter from the tropical sun and a shady place to have the mid-day meal. Between us and the town lay another wall, made of red mud, now broken down in places and overgrown with green bushes. Passing over the ditch in front of it by a small causeway, the force defiled through the town after the mid-day halt, headed by Sir George Goldie, who received quite an ovation. He was met by about 2000 people, and the chief and leading people threw themselves on their knees before him, and thanked him for having rid them of their oppressors. The women and children emitted shrill shrieks of joy as each white man passed, and seemed very glad to see us; but this demonstration must be taken for what it is worth, as far as concerns the old chief, who would have welcomed either side impartially. He is known to have received a subsidy for collecting so many slaves and tribute from his own people.

Kabba is a picturesque place among pine woods, and evidently a shadow of what it has been once upon a time. The mud wall plainly shows the former extent of the town, over a mile from one side to the other, but it has been so reduced by raids and slavery for the past century, that now there cannot be more than 5000 inhabitants. It had been a sore tax on the inhabitants, having this war camp of the Fulahs at their very doors.

The Rev. C. E. Wating, who was travelling in this district with Bishop Tugwell and Bishop Phillips in December 1894, writes as follows:—

"At Ayeri, a town close to Kabba, the king came to call on us about seven o'clock, and told us the English king was the ruler of the world, and he besought us white men to come and help him. He said that four years ago, on his coming to the throne, the Nupes came and took away 300 of his people. He told us that oppression has been the rule here for forty years; that at first the Nupes only demanded couriers, then farm produce, and that now they will have slaves as well. As all their own slaves are gone as tribute, they have to give their own children, and many, after giving their wives and children for tribute, have left the town and not come back—among others his own brother and cousin; that there are hardly any young people in the country, and that their nation is becoming extinct. We had to assure them that we could not help them, but sympathised most fully with them."

Cotton, tobacco, and various kinds of grain were growing in the fields, and there were many plantain trees. After passing through another thick belt of wood and vegetation, we reached the wall on the south side of the town, and another fine open country lay spread out before us.

It was too late to reach the Fulah camp this day, but early next morning, soon after starting, we could see an enormous collection of thatched huts and enclosures, covering over a square mile of country. Rocky hills with precipitous sides rose up on each side about two miles distant, and the top of one of these overhung the base to such an extent that one wondered how it did not overbalance and tumble over. These hills formed a sort of line of outposts to the camp, and between them and where we were a sea of yellow grass was only broken by the few palm trees scattered about in solitary grandeur, which for the most part preferred the green banks along the stream watering the valley.

Although the camp was deserted and some of it had already been burned, half a score of horsemen and some people on foot could be seen hurriedly making off in the distance. Little remained to be done, except to complete the work of destruction, and two companies in extended order first marched through and returned, setting fire to all undestroyed huts, in which an occasional old gun, or sword, or basket of grain was found. Some of the enclosures were very neatly arranged, and I noticed very good wells of water.

We returned to Kabba, and camped in the place at which we made the mid-day halt the day before, and in the afternoon an imposing ceremony took place in the market-place of the town, where Sir George Goldie met the chiefs of Kabba and the neighbouring towns, and formally proclaimed the freedom of Southern Nupe from the Fulah power, and the cessation of slavery.

The whole force paraded and formed up in two columns facing the town, and the seven-pounder guns were mounted on their carriages and drawn by ropes.

It was a picturesque scene, and Kabba Hill was covered with groups of natives perched together on the rocks, who looked down with wondering eyes on the display in front of them, a sight such as they had never seen before—the regular lines of the Hausa soldiers, in khaki and red tarbooshes, the barrels of the Maxim guns and the bayonets flashing in the sunlight, and in front of these the short wicked-looking 7-pounders.

The old chief, dressed in a red and gold gown, very

much faded, and wearing a red tarboosh with blue tassel, sat in front of the assemblage, surrounded by other chiefs in variegated coloured costumes; and when Sir George Goldie arrived, and had been received with a salute, these came forward and threw themselves down before him.

He then addressed them in the most inimitable pigeon English, which was translated by his own interpreter Esa into Nupe, and by one of the sergeant-majors into Yoruba, and informed them that they would be henceforth taken under the protection of the Niger Company, whose aim and object was to promote peace and trade in these countries; that any disputes between them and other towns must be referred to the white man, and that slavery would be at an end from this time, and all the Fulahs driven across the river. The above was received with great applause by the people, and the chief made a suitable reply.

He was then asked if he had any horses to sell, some more of which were badly wanted for the expedition, but here there was great difficulty in getting anything out of him, owing to his fear of future punishment by the Nupes if the white men were beaten. He at first denied having any at all, and then said that those he possessed were lame or unfit for use. At length, after a great deal of talking, he produced two very weedy-looking animals, which were said to belong to some of his subjects.

He was a most unsatisfactory old individual, and, like all Africans, was very glad to get rid of his enemies by the means of someone else, but was very chary of putting himself to any inconvenience in lending assistance to do so.

After he had been presented with the British flag

the force returned to the camp, and the march to Sura was continued the next day.

The heat and continued marching had begun to tell, and Lieutenant Rigby, an under-officer, and several men had to be carried.

About a mile before we reached our old camp of the 12th there were marks of a good many horsemen crossing the road. We arrived back at Sura at two o'clock on the 16th and found all well, though Lieutenant Neale and Sergeant Murfit had been ill with fever. A high zariba had been made, which was now pulled down, and we reoccupied the old camping-ground.

Sunday the 17th was a rest-day, and the first day we had halted since leaving Lokoja. In consequence of information obtained, however, Lieutenant Festing, with Lieutenants Pereira and Neale and a company, started off at midday to Lukki, a village where Nupes were reported to be. This detachment ultimately rejoined us on the second days' march from Sura, having driven a small party of Nupes out of Lukki and captured a small store of gunpowder.

On the morning we left Sura the soldier in charge of my horse was nowhere to be found, and I discovered, after some difficulty, he had been ordered to remain behind, on account of a sore foot, with twenty-five other sick men, under a sergeant at Sura. These horse-boys were selected from the most inefficient and idiotic of the soldiers, and mine was without doubt the worst of them all, so that I was not sorry to get rid of him.

We were obliged to march to the village to get on the right track, and then turned due north, and descended gradually to the river Feraji, which flows to the eastward north of Akpara. The soil was very rocky and gravelly until we came to thick woods surrounding the village of Feraji, where there were lovely wells of clear water. A great deal of cotton was grown in the fields around, and I noticed women in a house at work on the looms, which are most ingenious. We camped about two miles farther on, and much delay was caused by having to clear the thick bush away.

On the 19th we reached a watercourse and re-entrant into the hills, up which we advanced, and camped beyond the village of Shale. This was an interesting point for us, as we noticed the water was now flowing the other way, in a northerly direction, into the Niger. The country became very barren and arid as we approached the Jakpana Hills, which we ascended by a steep path over stony and volcanic ground, some of the lava rocks over which we marched being extremely hot and trying to the naked feet of the porters; and it was a difficult march for them. We were, however, agreeably surprised, as we had been led to believe that it was a very bad march indeed, and that there was no water for a very long way. I started with the advance party at 6 a.m., and we reached the camping ground at 10.45.

There are three distinct peaks, the centre being a triangular rock without a particle of vegetation on it, which is visible for many miles. Before leaving the ridge we had a fine view over the valley to the west, and, on looking back, two twin peaks of an inconsiderable size, which we had hitherto missed seeing owing to the thick bush, now came into view, forming a gateway at the end of the valley. From this elevation, 1180 feet above the sea, the track led between two of the small peaks, and descended into the plain which

borders the Niger; and as we left the rugged sides of
the hills, fields of cultivation appeared, and the country
became much more prosperous-looking. Here we first
came upon a Nupe village—Kosobeji by name—
utterly different from any village we had yet seen, and
remarkable for the neatness of its walls and the struc-
ture of its houses; these were nearly all circular, and
made of red mud walls, with very neatly-thatched roofs.
Intermingled with little structures of the same sort for
grain, raised from the ground, they were crowded
together into the smallest space imaginable, so that
one wondered how the natives could move about
among them. Nearly every house had a miniature
courtyard, separated from the next house by a small
wall, and usually occupied by a goat or two and a few
chickens.

An enormous quantity of corn was found here, and
it proved to be a food depôt of the Southern Nupe
army, which had been dispersed at Kabba.

From Kosobeji a very gradual descent across a
great plain, covered with dry grass 4 feet high, led to
the Kampi River, at this time only a few yards broad,
but which is evidently a very fine river in the rains,
about 150 yards broad, flowing between sandy banks,
and emptying itself into the Niger near Egga. This
country presents an utterly different appearance in
the rains; little ravines and sandy river-beds, which we
crossed dryshod, become seething torrents, and render
travelling very difficult, if not impossible, for caravans
loaded as we were.

It was fresh and delightful marching in the early
morning; and soon after the sun rose, as we approached
the Kampi River, a peak towards Egbon loomed up out
of the mist in the distance, the very image of one of

the pyramids in Egypt, the side turned to us being lit
up by the sun's rays with a beautiful, soft, yellow colouring, strengthened by the blue shadows on the edges,
whilst away over the brown dried-up grass a belt of
dark green palm trees indicated the course of the river,
making a brilliant contrast with the surrounding
country. An hour farther on we reached Padda, a
large Nupe town of 4000 to 5000 inhabitants, which
contained many fine circular houses and markets, and
from which the people came out bringing plantains,
chickens, and eggs for sale to the camp, which was
posted on an undulation to the west of the town.
Detachments of the Fulahs were reported to be in the
towns not far off to the westward, and at a place
which lay close to the Pyramid Peak. They, however,
never harassed the line of march, and the advanced
guard became tired of looking out for an enemy which
up to now had pursued such Fabius-like tactics.

It was a short march from Padda to the Niger,
which we reached the next day, 22nd January, passing
to the right of three of those curious flat-topped hills
peculiar to West Africa, which rose up almost perpen-
dicularly from the ground, echeloned from right to left.
These are called the Egbon Hills, and are visible from
a ridge near Bida; the Pyramid Peak lies to the south
of them. Between Padda and the river several small
farms, with fields of cultivation around, lay scattered
about, the property of the Nupe princes, and worked
by their slaves sent across the river for the purpose.

It was pleasant to see the great river again, and we
camped at the small village called Egbon, where there
was an open space in the woods which border the river,
and where the bank shelved steeply down to the
water's edge. Close to the side lay some of the

stern-wheelers and launches which had been patrolling
the river, and were now waiting to convey the force
across to the northern bank.

So effective had been Mr. Wallace's blockade of the
Niger that not even a messenger could pass, and to
this co-operation must be attributed the retreat of the
Fulahs from Kabba without fighting, their one object
being to get back to the river and effect a crossing
before it was too late; and in this they were defeated
by the excellence of the arrangements for carrying out
the blockade. Mr. Wallace also succeeded in rousing
to revolt the people living on the banks of the river
known as Ganagas, who had formerly rebelled against
the Fulah power in 1882. Hereby a number of
native levies were secured, and, landing with these
and the small force available from the steamers, he
was able to seize several Fulah towns within striking
distance of the river.

The result of our march in the bend of the Niger
had been that the Southern Fulah army was now completely dispersed, and had scattered to the north-west
through the Yagba country, with the hope of reaching
the left bank of the Niger by one of the upper
crossings. We were running rather short of supplies,
and were very glad to see the steamers again, where
we knew we should be able to refill our provision-boxes,
and also obtain, what was a great luxury after the bad
water on the march — a few bottles of soda-water.
Each officer was also allowed to have a reserve box,
which was carried on one of the steamers.

XV

Expedition to Bida

NOT an hour was lost in preparing for the march to Bida, and on January 23rd, the day after we arrived at Egbon, two companies under Major Cunningham, D.S.O., crossed the river with the Governor at daylight to reconnoitre, and report upon the crossing of the creek, which was known to exist about two and a half miles from the left bank of the Niger. I had just settled down to complete some of my mapping work, and work out observations, when the order came for the company to which I was attached with my Maxim gun, to cross also. The men were soon ready, and it is wonderful how little kit these Hausas require on the march; the men were not allowed to carry anything but a blanket and their ammunition, and a few odds and ends which they managed to stow away in their haversacks. Most of them were plentifully adorned with charms and amulets, to keep off bullets and avert disaster. These consisted of little leather cases containing a piece of paper with a verse from the Koran, also pieces of wood, or shells fastened together by a bit of boot-lace, and were hung either round the neck or on the sword-belt, and sometimes fastened round their arm with the wrist-knife which is so common in this country. If worn under the clothing, they were

PART OF THE COMPANY'S FLOTILLA AT EGBON

always drawn out and ostentatiously displayed on coming into action. Their arms consisted of the Snider rifle and three-cornered bayonet, and the latter seemed to me very inferior to the sword-bayonet I had seen used in previous expeditions for cutting down trees, bush, and grass, and even for making a trench, where other implements were not forthcoming. It entailed having porters to carry choppers, axes, etc., for cutting wood, and even with these it would have been almost impossible to make a zariba without a considerable loss of time.

We filed down the steep bank on to the *Liberty*, but it required time and a good deal of persuasion to make the officers' horses cross the little bridge of planks which connected the ship with the shore. The river is 850 yards broad at Egbon, and the left bank was also steep, and necessitated a ramp being cut to enable the guns to be drawn up from the steamers. A road had to be cut from here to the creek, through the high grass and thick bush which lines the river-bank. The creek itself was a formidable obstacle, and, though only 40 yards broad, was deep and unfordable.

Fortunately, two rather rickety canoes were found not far off, and with these, and a large steel canoe, which was transported here from the river, the whole force was able to cross on the following day. On arriving I found a camp pitched on the other side of the creek, and heard that a mounted patrol of the enemy's had been seen in the morning.

The Governor was also encamped here, and, inured as he is to the climates of the Eastern and Western Sudan, had not escaped a touch of the fever which is so apt to assail one on coming down to the valley of the Niger from the high ground. Limiting himself throughout, he carried as little luggage as any of us. He kept in his own hands the Intelligence Department, and was constantly engaged cross-examining spies, guides, and messengers—an arduous task where African natives are concerned. With a wonderful prescience as to how events would turn out, he had planned everything long before in England, and the organisation of the expedition was complete down to the smallest detail.

This camp would have been a nasty place in which to be attacked at night, but the ground was not suited to the tactics of our enemy, a fact of which we were unaware at that time. Thick grass surrounded it on all sides, except where the creek lay, and in this grass a clearing had been made for the encampment. Not a hundred yards could be seen on either side, and it was just such a country as the tribes of the Lower Niger and Delta would have chosen for making their attack. Our adversaries, however, preferred the open ground round Bida, where they could attack with their cavalry, which they believed to be invincible.

In a reconnaissance from here it was found that a large swamp 250 yards broad existed about two miles farther in, over which no easier or more practicable way could be found than by the direct route. This was bad enough, in all conscience, for a large force with porters carrying loads, and it was difficult at first sight to believe that the two heavy guns could be dragged through. Consisting of a mass of fœtid mud and rank grass, it differed only from the river swamps in the Equatorial Lakes Region in the absence of the ever-multiplying papyrus, which forms such a feature there. Beyond this swamp one or two small villages were met with, where a few natives were captured, who were brought back into camp to be interrogated as to the enemy's movements.

The force was organised now as follows, in seven companies and gunners :—

Staff—
Commander—Major A. J. Arnold, 3rd Hussars.
Adjutant—Lieut. Festing, Royal Irish Rifles.
Galloper—Lieut. Carroll, Norfolk Regiment.
Transport—Lieut. Thomas, Leicester Regiment.
  „ Under-Officer Sergt. C. Bagford.

*Medical—*Drs. Cargill and Castellote.
*Executive—*Senior Executive Officer, W. Watts, H. J. Drew.
*Station Agent—*R. Marmon.
*Political—*W. Wallace, C.M.G., Special Commissioner for Niger Sudan Regions.

	Rank and File.
No. 1. Lieut. M'Clintock, Seaforth Highlanders .	60
Lieut. Day, South Wales Borderers	
Lieut. Bird, Royal West Surrey Regiment .	(Maxim gun).
No. 2. Major Cunningham, D.S.O., Derbyshire Regiment.	64
Lieut. Musters, 3rd Hussars.	
Lieut. Thorpe, Bedfordshire Regiment .	(Maxim gun).
No. 3. Lieut. Burdon, 2nd Lancashire Regiment .	68
Lieut. Tighe, West Riding Regiment.	
Lieut. Vandeleur, D.S.O., Scots Guards .	(Maxim gun).
No. 4. Lieut. Gillespie, South Wales Borderers .	63
Capt. Anderson, 3rd Middlesex Regiment.	
Lieut. Margesson, South Wales Borderers .	(Maxim gun).
No. 5. Capt. Sangster, Leicester Regiment . .	65
Lieut. Pereira, Coldstream Guards . .	(Maxim gun).
No. 6. Lieut. Neale, Royal West Surrey Regiment	64
Lieut. Parker, South Wales Borderers .	(Maxim gun).
No. 7. Capt. Hatton, 4th Lancashire Regiment .	64

Gunners—
Sub-Commandant Robinson.
Under-Officer Corporal A. E. Bosher.
Under-Officer Bombadier J. Halfpenny.
     Total 59

Total Strength.

Europeans 32
Constabulary (rank and file) . . 507 ⎫ Natives . 1072
Carriers . . . . . 565 ⎭

                              Total . . . 1104

Armament.

One 12-pounder Whitworth B.L. gun.
One 9-pounder Whitworth B.L. gun.
Five 7-pounders R.M.L. machine guns.
Six Maxim guns, 45.

Stores and Supplies—Artillery.

12-pounder . . . . . 50 rounds common shell.
9-pounder . . . . . 50 rounds common shell.
7-pounder . . . . ⎰95 rounds double shell.
                  ⎱35 rounds shrapnel shell.
                   16 rounds common shell.

Small Arms.

Maxim . . . . 18,000 rounds.
Snider . . . . 50 rounds per man, by troops.
       30,000 rounds reserve, by transport.

Rations—Ten days : three days by troops, seven days by transport.

The force marched off at 6.15 a.m. on the 25th inst. in the following order :—

Advance-guard . . . . . . 2 companies.
Baggage-guard . . . . . . 1 company.
Centre- guard . . . . . 1 „
Rear- guard . . . . . 1 „
       Guns in rear escorted by two companies.

After successfully crossing the swamp, we passed several villages and plantain groves, the country being very flat and wooded, and, on nearing the village of Lokitsha, a few shots were fired at the head of the column. A good deal of drumming and blowing of horns could be heard in the vicinity, and, as soon as the main body came up, camp was formed here, and the two companies of the advance-guard pushed on. A body of the enemy, including some horsemen, were met with and soon routed, one gunner on our side being slightly wounded.

It was now certain the Nupes meant to fight for their capital, and the next day, the 26th of January, when the force marched off at 6 o'clock, one could soon tell by the silence kept that something exciting was expected, yet no one could have foreseen the hard fighting that was to last through the day. I was lucky this day to be attached to the advance-guard, which was under command of Major Cunningham, and consisted of Nos. 3 and 5 companies, and was also accompanied by Sir George Goldie and Mr. Wallace. The main body followed up half a mile in rear with the carriers and the guns. As the march progressed in a northerly direction, the country became more open, and we passed through large fields of cultivation surrounding numerous villages. The half company in front, under Lieutenant Tighe, now extended, and advanced in skirmishing order, carefully examining the different villages *en route*, from which a surprise might be effected. At 7.30 a party of the enemy's cavalry could be discovered on the far side of a small swamp, concealed to a great extent by a fringe of palm trees and a fold in the ground, where they were evidently waiting to swoop down on the head of the column unperceived, and take it at a disadvantage as it emerged from the swamp. A few rounds from the Maxim in close proximity to their heads soon scattered them, and a cloud of dust was raised by their flying horses. Continual skirmishing took place from this point for another four miles, during which the enclosed country gave way to enormous open undulating plains, with here and there a village or farmstead nestling among a small clump of trees.

It was an ideal battlefield; and as we came down to the ravine, or nullah, through which flows the Rafi Shaun stream, the Nupe army could be seen extending in their thousands along the top of a low undulation in front, looking at a distance in their white dresses like flocks of sheep grazing on the green grass, whilst away to the flanks bodies of horsemen could be seen trotting about, conspicuous in their flowing garments.

A halt was now called, to give time for the main body to come up, and the two Maxim guns came into action so as to clear the ground on the farther side of the ravine. As the carriers arrived, camp was formed, and the loads were stacked in the centre, the men lying down round them, and the two companies of the advance-guard were then pushed forward across the ravine.

These were again reinforced by Nos. 4 and 7 Companies, which were thrown back in echelon on each flank, and the whole then advanced under command of Major Arnold, with the object of reconnoitring the ground on the reverse side of the slope, and to drive the enemy back, and, if possible, prevent them harassing the guns and the carriers still in the rear on the line of march.

It was a pretty sight to see the men of the first two companies doubling down the path to the ravine, on which some of the enemy's marksmen were now making rather good practice, little spurts of sand testifying to the accuracy of their range; and as they ascended to the top of the opposite slope, headed by their commander, Major Cunningham, they rapidly extended on either side of the path, and lay down to await the two companies which were to reinforce them. When these had crossed, the order was given to advance, and the line moved forward, halting every now and then to open fire. Volley-firing was carried out with precision, and the Maxims fired with telling effect on the enemy's line at ranges of 300 to 400 yards. Two of the latter were posted between the two centre companies, and one accompanied each company in echelon on the flanks. Every inch of the ground was disputed ; and whilst the two centre companies steadily advanced, those on the flanks were busily engaged driving off the bodies of cavalry, who took advantage of small woods and villages to approach close and threaten the safety of the small force. The country, entirely different from any we had yet seen, was admirably adapted to cavalry.

The long, low undulations led up to a ridge, on the top of which a magnificent sight met our eyes. Outside the great wall of the capital, made of red mud, crenulated, and about 10 feet high, stood masses of people, who extended a long way to the south, and were now being joined by those we had just driven back. These were retiring rapidly across a stream of water flowing in the valley which runs through the eastern portion of the town.

The great capital, holding from 60,000 to 100,000 inhabitants, according to the estimate of the few English and German travellers who had been there, seemed a mass of lofty thatched houses and high clay walls, forming enclosures, which intermingle with pine trees extending to the north as far as the eye can reach.

Emirs and chiefs in their brilliant robes trotted

about at the head of their troops of horsemen, and bands of footmen armed with guns and spears, and the air resounded with the drumming and blowing of horns and roar of the dense multitude ready to give us battle.

The walls of Bida were now 2000 yards off, and a halt was made to give the 7-pounders, which had been sent for, a chance to get up if possible. It was a welcome rest; and, after cleaning out my Maxim gun, I sat down to gaze at the crowds on the opposite slope. There was a large concourse under the branches of an enormous tree about 200 yards from the main wall, and many more were in and about some small villages lying outside the town. It was a sweltering hot day, and the midday sun beat down from a perfectly cloudless blue sky, making everything in the distance appear shimmering and indistinct, whilst the dust and powder all combined to make one very thirsty, and I luckily bethought me of a very green orange which I had stowed away in my holster two or three days before.

Like the knights of old days, every horseman seemed to be followed by two or three squires carrying his gun and some spears, and, where the horsemen were banded together, they were usually followed by similar parties of footmen.

Occasional shots were fired from the Maxim, but, to judge from the increasing noise from the enemy's masses and the activity of their horsemen, our halt was evidently considered a confession of weakness. I had not long gone out in front of the line with Lieutenant Thomson to take the range of the big tree, when the order was given to retire, and we returned to our places—this being the last I ever saw of Thomson. He apparently rode out to the rear to see if the guns were coming, and must have been almost immediately cut off by the enemy's horsemen, as his body was found soon after we started, and was carried with us in the square.

The moment the retirement commenced, a great shout went up from the multitude, who proceeded to cross the watercourse and rush up the ridge after us. It was a most difficult operation in the face of a bold and determined enemy, and admirably conducted by Major Arnold. The slightest mistake or panic and the little column was lost, as every white man knew; and the greatest praise must be given to the black soldiers, who behaved splendidly, kept quite cool, and obeyed their officers' commands. It must be remembered that they had never had to face cavalry before, the moral effect of which, even on white troops, is very great, as recognised by all European armies. The Maxims had in most cases expended a great deal of their ammunition, and were ordered only to fire in emergencies, owing to the delay unavoidable in mounting and dismounting, so that everything depended on the fire - discipline of the black troops, whose aim was far more effective than might have been expected from soldiers surrounded on all sides, and exposed to a constant, though ill - directed, fire from the enemy's riflemen. These fortunately aimed too high, or they would have inflicted far more damage than they did, the bullets usually whizzing harmlessly over the square. There were only five casualties besides poor Thomson at present, and the danger was slight, provided that the horsemen could be prevented from breaking the square, which they could have done so easily if they

had only possessed the courage to face the last
hundred yards which separated them from our ranks.
As the companies closed in to form square, No. 5
Company under Captain Sangster, formed the rear
face, and had its work cut out in stopping the ugly
rushes of the now elated and triumphant enemy,
who closed in upon us from all sides. The men
were also controlled by Major Cunningham and
Lieutenant Festing, it being now almost an impossi-
bility to make oneself heard above the din of the fight.
Though many of them were Yorubas, who were supposed
to be the least warlike of our soldiers, and were looked
down upon by the Hausas, they behaved very well.

Lieutenant Pereira had a narrow escape of being
cut off with his Maxim, the men being very slow
in dismounting the gun. It was now nearly two
o'clock, and the men were very tired, which is not
to be wondered at, as we had started from Lokitsha
soon after dawn, and had been fighting throughout
the day in the trying damp heat which exists in the
valley of the Niger. The men who carried the guns
were ordinary African porters, selected principally
for their strength and physique, and it is astonishing
how well they behaved. My own porters used to
watch the result of each shot with the keenest interest,
and were sometimes seen dancing about behind the
gun in their excitement. The actual detachment
consisted of four soldiers, who were responsible for
mounting and dismounting the gun, and acted besides
as a guard to the porters on the march.

Slowly but surely we made our way back to the
camp, No. 3 Company, under Lieutenant Burdon,
clearing a way for the advance, Lieutenant Tighe
of this company having already had to ride for his

life whilst carrying a message. On his way back to the camp he saw horsemen on the flanks, evidently closing in with the object of cutting him off, and setting spurs to his horse just got through in time, emptying his revolver at the leading horsemen as he dashed down towards the ravine covered by the fire from the camp. Our movements were necessarily slow, and halts had to be continually made to open fire and drive off the more daring of the enemy encircling the square, before a fresh advance could be made.

It was a strange sight to see these Fulah horsemen firmly fixed in their high peaked saddles, with enormous brass and iron stirrups, as they galloped along on their long-tailed ponies, covered with gay trappings, waving their swords or spears in the air, with their white robes flying in the wind, accompanied at the same time by the clamour of their small drums and the deep-bassed horns which were encouraging them to the attack. Very often an enormous straw hat surmounted the turban, which was wound round their heads, or was allowed to fall back and hang over the shoulder, whilst many of their leaders were very well dressed, and wore flat-heeled riding-boots of red leather, which are excellently made in this country.

Some of them showed reckless audacity in galloping up, brandishing their swords, to within 100 yards of the square, and at times they were even nearer to the rear face than this, rushing up over every fold of the ground; and their faces could be plainly distinguished, some of the officers even using their revolvers. As we descended along the open slope towards the camp, it was an exciting scene for the few white men in it, and they all agreed that the square was kept in the most perfect formation, surrounded by masses of people, who gradually cleared off to a respectful distance, as the square was supported by the fire from the camp, which covered the crossing of the ravine.

Everyone in the square was immensely relieved, when they saw that the camp, with all the reserve ammunition, was safe, and there is no doubt that the Nupe army lost a grand opportunity. If, instead of devoting most of their attention to the square, they had crept up the ravine, or had established themselves in force in the village near, they would have had the camp at their mercy. Fortunately, it was well posted, and the small force in it was able to ward off the attacks by smaller bodies of the enemy, whilst the four companies were engaged in front.

Whilst marching in square we had missed the track, and had now to bear off to our right to find the path leading down to the ravine. Luckily we were encumbered with no baggage or carriers, and could move easily across the rough ground, and the fields of cultivation. The enemy were still pretty close, and Nos. 3 and 5 Maxims were sent across the ravine to take up a position on the rocks in front of the camp, and cover the crossing of the remainder of the force. It was now about 2.30 p.m., and the position was as follows:—The camp was well situated, and commanded the water 150 yards off. On the farther side of the ravine the enemy was divided up into large bodies and small groups about 1200 yards off standing near villages or under trees, and behind them again on the ridge were masses of people and the less bold of the warriors awaiting events.

The only weak point of the camp was the rear

side, where the ground did not admit of a good view, and where some riflemen had posted themselves in the bushes, and fired into the camp, wounding two or three of the carriers. These, and also the servants, lay huddled up in the centre, many of them burying their heads in the ground in fear of being shot. After some difficulty, I found my own servant trying to conceal his elephantine proportions like an ostrich in the ground, and had to apply a gentle reminder or two with the foot before I could move him, and make him get me some food. He wanted to know why we did not go back to the river at once, as the enemy were so numerous. It was about this time the 7-pounders arrived in camp, the escort having been attacked on the road so severely that one of the guns had to be abandoned, and Lieut. Carrol, who went to hurry them up, had had a very narrow escape from the enemy's horsemen.

The two big guns, on which it was felt the fate of the expedition now depended, were still in the rear, and No. 1 Company under Lieut. M'Clintock (Seaforth Highlanders), which had been defending the camp, also No. 3 Company under Lieut. Burdon, were sent back to aid the two companies acting as escort to these guns, with whom were Lieut. Musters (3rd Hussars), and Lieuts. Gillespie, Margesson, and Day (South Wales Borderers), Lieut. Thorpe (Bedfordshire Regiment), and Capt. Anderson. These guns were, I suppose, about the largest which have ever been wheeled into Africa, and the labour of dragging them across the fields of cultivation, broken up by large lumps of earth, was very great. Little watercourses and stumps of trees formed serious obstacles to them.

The three companies left extended round the camp,

and every one was busy serving out ammunition and filling Maxim-gun belts.

The 7-pounders came into action at once under Lieut. Robinson assisted by Under-Officers Bosher and Halfpenny, principally directed against the flanking parties of cavalry who were working round to the rear, and the moral effect caused by the explosion of their shells must have been very great, though their range of fire was limited to 3000 yards, and they were not very accurate. The enemy, however, did not begin to retire until after the arrival of the 9-pounder Whitworth gun at 4 p.m., when affairs assumed a very different aspect. At this time, there must have been fully from 20,000 to 30,000 of the enemy to the front and the flanks, and this gun opening with great precision at a long range did tremendous execution. Beautifully aimed, the first shell landed in a crowd of the enemy's horse near a village, scattering them in all directions, amidst tremendous cheers from the camp, and some more shells in different directions soon convinced our opponents that it had been a case of "reculer pour mieux sauter." They had dragged out an old cannon from Bida, with which they attempted to retaliate with a great deal of noise but little result. The shell fire was, however, too much for them, and in face of it they gradually drew off to Bida, and as they retired could be seen carrying off some of their dead and wounded, whilst away on each side of the camp parties of horsemen streamed away back to the capital on their tired horses.

The enemy's losses must have been very large, and we heard afterwards that a lucky shell burst right among the Agaie division, allies of the Emir Abu Bekri, Sultan of the Nupes, killing the Agaie general.

His death had the effect of disheartening this portion of the enemy, who left in the night, or early the following morning. It was nearly dusk before the enemy drew off, and, after a fight lasting all day, the camp was now at rest, and everyone sat down to a well-earned meal.

Just as it got dark the 12-pounder arrived, preceded by the buglers, who played the men dragging it and the escort into camp. Great cheering ensued, and at 8 p.m. the gun was aimed by a compass bearing of 10°, which was the direction of the town, and sighted to the highest range, namely, 5400 yards, a shell being then fired, landing as we afterwards heard within the the walls of Bida close to the Markum's palace, a defiance to them and a foretaste of what was to come on the morrow.

It had taken over twelve hours to drag this gun about 10 miles, and the men were all tired and knocked up by the hard work in the sun, the day having been extremely hot.

For an expedition to a point farther than 30 miles from the river it is doubtful whether it would be feasible for a force to take these big guns, as all mobility has to be sacrificed, and so many men have to be detached to escort them. Their effect on the enemy was, however, undeniable, and without them Bida would very probably not have been captured at all.

All the officers collected after dark for the mournful ceremony of burying poor Thomson, whose sad death had cast a gloom over every one. He had been appointed transport officer, no sinecure on this expedition, and had distinguished himself by his ability and hard work.

XVI

SECOND DAY'S FIGHT AT BIDA

THE night of the 26th inst. was spent in the expectation of an attack, notwithstanding which most people slept soundly, tired after the hard fight, and only disturbed by the roar of the rockets, which were fired every two hours. The 12-pounder was also fired again at 11 p.m., and the great shell hurtling through the air in the dead of night must have struck terror into the hearts of the enemy, who were already wondering at strange fiery signs in the sky caused by our rockets. It must be to this fact and the severe handling they had already received that we owed our immunity from a night attack, and lucky it was for us, as most of the sentries were too tired to keep awake, and the safety of the camp depended only on the vigilance of a European, who occasionally went the rounds.

Although dejected by their severe losses, the enemy were still confident of destroying us on the morrow, and voices were heard shouting insulting messages to that effect from the farther side of the ravine. Their spirits had been raised by driving the reconnoitring force back to the ravine.

When morning broke only a few mounted scouts were visible on the ridge, and the force was able to cross the ravine in peace, the big guns being hauled up the other side by ropes.

Hidden by a fold in the ground, and our presence only revealed to the enemy by a cloud of dust, raised by the compact mass of people, a square was now formed of one company in front, two companies each on the flanks, and one company in rear, every man and load of the expedition being inside the square. The carriers were divided into four bodies, two on each side of the square closed up as much as possible, and the 12- and 9-pounders and five smaller guns were drawn in the centre, one company being told off to assist in the dragging of the guns. A deep ditch formed a serious obstacle to these at first, and our movements were very slow and crab-like until every one began to settle down into their positions, and we moved gradually along up the gentle slope towards the ridge, a little to the east of our advance the previous day. Here we came under the fire of the enemy's riflemen, who were posted in the village and clumps of trees to our left, and bullets were soon whistling over the square, which, with its mass of people inside, formed a large target.

This and the unevenness of the ground all combined to create confusion among the carriers, who were so crowded up together, and every now and then one would stumble and fall down after a vain effort to balance his heavy load on his head, and others would be upset by his fall like so many ninepins.

Sir George Goldie's servant fell mortally wounded close to his master's side, whilst, at the same time, Dr. Cargill's horse was shot under him. A soldier in No. 3 Company, on the rear face, who was also desperately wounded, distinguished himself by his

Spartan-like courage in calmly sitting up and probing for the bullet himself. The enemy did not dispute the possession of the ridge this day, but were drawn up on the opposite slope across the stream.

On our approach, our adversaries commenced their old tactics of sending large masses of horsemen round our flanks to surround us and harass the rear, but they were checkmated by our combined movement in square, which was most successfully carried out. The fighting from this point was, in fact, a mere repetition of that of the previous day, and would be tedious to describe in detail.

More of our men had now fallen to the fire from the riflemen in the bushes, which was very harassing and could not be replied to on account of the order regarding the expenditure of ammunition. This had been very considerable on the previous day, and if fighting was to be prolonged there was a danger of running short,— hence the order that the firing was to be very carefully controlled, and to be reserved principally for attacks by cavalry.

Most of the firing, therefore, was done by volleys, at distances of under 400 yards, and by the Maxims. Captain Anderson in his white helmet, on our side of the square, seemed to be a target for the enemy, and though they invariably missed him his vicinity was decidedly dangerous.

The enemy now displayed a certain amount of indecision, and were no doubt wondering what was to be our next move; in truth, it must have been a strange sight to see this little square, covered by a cloud of dust, which was slowly but surely making its way towards the walls of their city, belching forth at times volleys of flame and smoke at the masses of the horse-

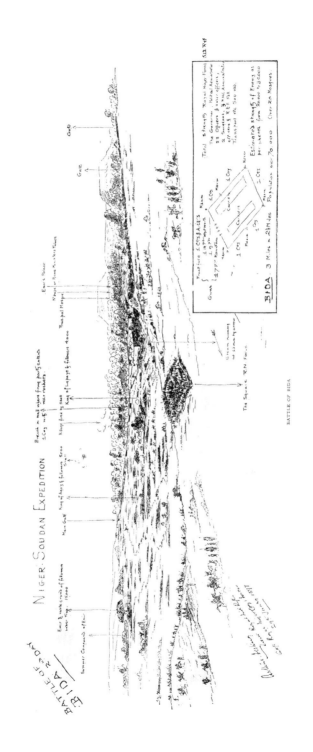

BATTLE OF BIDA

men encircling it. At last we arrived at the top of the undulation, about 2500 yards from the walls of Bida.

A halt was made here, and our opponents were rudely awakened to the power of the Infidel by a shell from one of the big guns, which landed in a village outside the walls, raising a cloud of white dust as it crashed through the mud walls, immediately setting fire to it. The guns, managed by Lieutenant Robinson and Under-Officers Halfpenny and Bosher (the former of whom, unfortunately, received an injury to one of his eyes from the explosion of a cartridge), fired a few more shells, which, assisted by Thorpe's and Margesson's Maxims, cleared the face of the slope opposite, and masses of the enemy retired into the town through the western gate, others drawing off to the high ground to the west. The Emir Abu Bekri who, with a crowd of horse, was standing near a clump of trees not far from the western gate, was wounded in the arm, about this time, as we afterwards found out, which must have still further discouraged the Fulahs. Major Arnold now wheeled the square to the right, and we made our way along the open slope to a point situated 200 yards from the water and on slightly rising ground, forming a capital strategical position, which commanded the town.

Secure here, picked shots kept the enemy's marksmen at a distance; and under cover of a heavy fire from the Maxims, a party of men went down to draw water. The bombardment now commenced in earnest, and shell after shell was sent hurtling into the town, principally directed at the Sultan's palace and enclosures about 2 miles distant. We were only 500 yards from the main wall, where the defenders were now posted and firing at us.

The advantage of having the big guns became apparent when one realised the size of the town, as, with the small force available, it would have been very risky to get involved in hand-to-hand fighting in the maze and network of narrow streets, where the enemy would have derived every advantage from their superior numbers.

Although the enemy might have been driven from the southern portion of the town by the fire from the smaller guns, yet they could have assembled and made a stand in the northern half, and from here issued forth and lain in ambush behind the high walls of the compounds, on which fire made no impression.

The looting propensities of the Hausas were very great, as we had already noticed; and without very careful measures and the strictest discipline, it was possible that the entrance into the town would be followed by the dispersal and melting away of the whole force. It is impossible for anyone who has not seen it, to believe how all military discipline and order is thrown to the winds by an African soldier when he begins to loot. All sense of danger is forgotten, and the only means of bringing him to his senses is to hit him as hard as possible on the head.

About noon, Lieutenants Festing, Gillespie, and Margesson were sent forward to occupy a neighbouring village, already on fire; and from there, covered by a Maxim gun, they advanced to a breach in the main wall, which was surmounted without much difficulty, volleys being fired at a few of the enemy in the vicinity, thus establishing our first footing in the town.

Incendiary rockets were fired in different directions, showing their course by curves of thin white smoke, setting the thatched roofs of this portion of the town on fire, and making it untenable for the enemy; and in the distance thick columns of smoke could be seen rising in the air, results of the shells from the big guns, and a notification to the Emir Abu Bekri and the Nupe army that the white man had conquered.

Thus ended this great fight, which had lasted two days, the most important battle waged in the Western Sudan, and the greatest blow to the slave trade ever dealt in Africa, which has established the prestige of the English power and the Royal Niger Company throughout the Central Sudan, from Bida to the great town of Kano, and on to Lake Chad, making even Rabbah, the conqueror of Wadai, Baghirmi, and Bornu, pause in his onward course, and consider whether it is worth while coming into contact with such a redoubtable opponent. We could see the horsemen drawing off from all sides, and the contest was practically over. Tents were pitched and camp formed close to the ground we then occupied, and what had shortly before been a scene of battle now became a peaceful encampment. Four companies paraded in the afternoon, and marched into the town at different points for about 400 yards, whereupon they extended so as to meet each other, returning then to the main wall, setting fire to and clearing the outskirts.

Lieutenant Tighe was attacked by a man behind a gateway as he entered a compound, but very few of the Fulahs were seen.

Our casualties were extraordinarily small, only seven men being killed and nine wounded, besides Lieutenant Thomson killed. The Nupe riflemen ought to have accounted for more, but as long as the horsemen could be kept out of the square, and the column kept together, few losses were to be feared. On the other hand, a mistaken order, the jamming of a Maxim, or a gap in the square meant the total annihilation of the expedition. Major Arnold has pointed out that "our percentage of losses at Bida was greater than that of the British losses at the historic battle of Plassey, whereon the foundation of the Indian Empire was laid."

It is impossible to estimate the losses of the enemy, but they must have been enormous. The generals of the forces sent to aid the Emir of Bida by the Fulah States of Lapai and Agaie were both killed on the 26th. Prince Lapini, an important chief, was also wounded on that day, and on the 27th, the Emir himself was wounded, and many other minor princes and chiefs were killed and wounded.

Thursday, 28th January, was a day of rest, which was badly wanted; the heat during the two-days' fight having been exceptionally great, even for Equatorial Africa. No signs were to be seen of the enemy, but a few traders came in, also a few villagers, who brought in news of the 7-pounder which the enemy had captured during the first day of the battle. Lieutenant M'Clintock with No. 1 Company was immediately sent out, and succeeded in finding it in a village to the north-west of the town. Reconnaissances were also carried out by other companies east and west, and the Nupe army was reported to be scattered in all directions.

A large number of sheep and goats had been captured, and the smell arising from the slaughtered animals round the camp was so appalling that to escape this and the plague of flies we were obliged to move our tents in the afternoon.

XVII

BIDA

ON the 29th January the whole force marched into the capital, Sir George Goldie taking up his quarters in the Emir's palace, over which the British flag was soon flying; the officers' tents were put up in the market-place outside, under the shade of some lovely trees, and the soldiers and carriers settled themselves down round the square, some of them occupying the houses close to. A company occupied every street abutting on the square, and Maxim guns were placed wherever they could be used in case of a surprise. Bida is a striking place to find in Central Africa, and makes all the more impression on one, after arriving from the delta of the Niger, where the natives are on the lowest scale of civilisation, and a most degraded-looking race with instincts tending to cannibalism. It is situated on slightly rising ground, and watered by two streams, one of which rises only a short way from the walls; these join together in the southern portion of the town, and flow through a beautifully green valley to the east. The main wall must have been erected with great labour, and is about 10 feet in height, with a banquette on the inside to fire from. Broken down in a few instances, it extends round the whole town, and gives access by several large covered gateways.

The main thoroughfares are fairly broad, and lead
from one gate to another, bordered by great enclosures
and compounds, surrounded by lofty walls, excellently
made and often 18 feet in height, a good witness to
the barbaric civilisation existing in these regions under
the Mohammedan religion.   The doorways, high
enough to admit even people on horseback, are in some
cases carved and ornamented.

The walls of the large buildings are very massive,
and very often the roofs of the rooms are arched and
supported on pillars of black clay, which is polished
and looks exactly like stone.   The principal buildings
are those occupied by the princes of the two great
families, the Massaba and Omru, who share between
them the right of occupying the throne.   The Markum,
the head of the Omru family, who was cut off with the
whole of his army by the steamers on the other side of
the Niger, had a large palace in the southern portion
of the town.   The Miaki, or general of the forces,
who was with him, had another, and there was also the
residence of the Ndegi, or Prime Minister, who was
reported to be a most astute old gentleman, and quite
the Bismarck of this part of the world.   In a letter
which the governor received later on from him, he
stated that his slaves had run away with most of his
property, and that he was too infirm to come in, as the
Governor asked him to do.

Last, but not least, we must enumerate the late
Emir's palace, the roofs of which were covered with
corrugated iron, and outside of which lies the slave-
market, where formerly it used to be a common sight
to see 200 slaves exposed of an evening for sale to the
highest bidder.   Unfortunate creatures raided from
various parts of the kingdom, even south of Lokoja in

the Company's territories, they used to be sold here as a source of revenue to the Nupe princes, and transported into the depths of the Sudan. Many came in whilst we were at Bida, and it was a curious sight to watch them having their chains filed off, and their fetters removed by the blacksmith in the market-square.

The entrance to the Emir's palace was covered with a high dome made of bamboos resting on thick walls, and supported at the bottom by short carved wooden pillars. Some tame ostriches and a deer were the sole occupants left in the big outer enclosure, in one of the numerous inner courts of which there is a lovely well of pure water. A few old cannons were lying about near the doorway. The inhabitants, doubtful as to the result of the battle, had begun to remove most of their property, and to leave the town before the bombardment commenced. Yet a large variety of articles were found, including some very good swords, an English general's sword, a claymore, and, curiously enough, a sword belonging to an officer in the 11th Hussars, with a monogram and coronet on it. All loot, as it was found, was supposed to be handed over and placed in the square, where lay heaped up a great pile of different coloured cloths, silks, and an innumerable quantity of brass basins; but of course soldiers and carriers kept whatever they could conceal about them.

Captured in the town, besides, were some cannon, 350 rifles of all imaginable sizes and patterns, 550 barrels of gunpowder, 25,000 cartridges of all sorts, and numerous loads of brass and heterogeneous articles.

A great many books and boards with Arabic writing, also a very tattered old lion skin with a plan and some Arabic characters on it, were found. The latter was just rescued in time, having been appropriated already by the soldiers to sweep the rubbish off the market place. Bida was a great centre of trade, and the people themselves are great workers in leather, and make very good saddles, leather scabbards, and slippers; they are also workers in glass. Indigo forms a valuable article of commerce, and there are numerous dye pits in the town.

Between the main roads there is a network of narrow streets with walls on each side, and there are many mosques, though none of any size and importance.

Whilst at Bida, companies were sent out on reconnaissances in all directions, and no time was lost in making the victory as complete as possible.

On the 30th, I went with two companies out of the northern gate, passing by two curious little hills of red sandstone, to the stream which runs down to the Wanangi Creek, to which boats are able to ascend from the Niger in the rainy season. Several donkeys were captured, and, on returning to the town, the column was headed by about thirty Hausa soldiers mounted on the donkeys. It was very funny to see them all forming line to the front, grinning from ear to ear, as they entered the square, and they elicited roars of laughter from their comrades in camp, who all turned out to see the fun.

Lieutenant Gillespie left in the afternoon with his company for our base on the river, taking the news of the victory, with orders to return as soon as possible, bringing certain supplies, which were needed.

A good many traders and villagers had begun to gain confidence, and were returning to the town and the outskirts, and, on the following day, Sir George Goldie left the town by the northern gate, escorted by two companies for the Zongo camp not far from the main wall. Here were collected all the caravans of traders which had been stopped in their journey southwards by the outbreak of the war. A curious assemblage they were, collected from all parts of the Hausa States and the Sokoto empire. Some came from Kano, and others from Kuka on Lake Chad, the inland sea of this western half of Africa, where the valuable blocks of potash are found. Here, too, were merchants from Tripoli and Benghazi on the Mediterranean, distinguishable from the others by their spotless white garments and red fezzes, and amongst them stood the inevitable Arab, light coloured, and with black, flowing beard, the very picture of a slave-dealer.

In his address the Governor told them that "the Nupe rule was now at an end, and that the Company's aim was to promote trade of all descriptions, and by preventing raids and warfare in this part of the Sudan, to enable them to go from one part of the country to another in peace. He reminded them of the heavy duties and taxes they had been obliged to pay hitherto under the Fulah dominion, and told them he was making arrangements with the Emirs of Zaria and Nasarawa which would enable them to use the shorter route *via* Kano, Zaria, and Kéffi to Lokoja, where they would be able to dispose of their goods without being taxed. This is exactly the same route as that traversed by Mr. Robinson, and described so well by him in his book, *Eight Hundred Miles through the Sudan.* The importance of this trade question and the opening up of the Niger territories will be understood, when it is realised that at present most of the European goods come into the Hausa States from the north, across the great Sahara, several thousand camel loads of goods

15

coming annually into Kano from that direction, besides
quantities of salt, which is in great demand, as it is
found nowhere in Hausaland.

The traders of Kano must have rejoiced at our
victory, as they were thereby freed from paying heavy
taxes to the Emir of Bida.   They were in great dread
at this time of the advance of Rabbah Zobehr.   This
black potentate has been gradually acquiring a large
empire in Central Africa, since the time when he
separated himself with a few followers from the Mahdi
and the dervishes.   Commencing as a slave to Zobehr
Pasha, in Egypt, his has been an extraordinary career,
and he is now a power to be reckoned with in the
advance of European influence into the central Sudan.
Evidently a man of great commanding power and
military skill, he has collected together a large army,
and report has it that he drills his soldiers three times
a day.

To supply the deficiency of gunpowder and rifles, he
has organised a force of bowmen, who make very good
practice, and he has a large body of cavalry.   Starting
from Darfur in 1885, after the surrender of Slatin
Pasha to the Mahdi, his robber bands made themselves a terror to the countries round, and the States
of Baghirmi and Bornu to the south and west of Lake
Chad soon fell into his hands.   His tendency has
always been to push westward, and, according to the
latest reports, he was advancing on Kano, when the
news of the overthrow of the Fulahs at Bida decided
him to retreat.

He has been supposed to be friendly inclined towards
the English, and has always expressed his attachment
and love for his old master, Zobehr Pasha.

His soldiers have sometimes come into conflict with

the dervishes to the eastward, with varying results. Fortunately, the Royal Niger Company has known how to deal with him, and there is no fear of his quarrelling with them.

After the Governor had returned to the town, the two companies under command of Major Cunningham, D.S.O., proceeded on a reconnaissance to the north. along the road which passes out by the Hausa gate. A lovely open country lay spread out before us, across which one could apparently gallop for miles and miles. A few rocky hills stood out on the horizon, and several villages, consisting of a few curious little circular houses, lay scattered about. Many of the inhabitants, now convinced of our peaceable intentions, had returned to their homes, and sat about in little groups watching the soldiers as they passed by. After we had got some distance from the capital, two of the enemy's horsemen came into sight, and, disregarding the shots fired at them, immediately galloped off, pursued by Lieutenant Musters.

It was an exciting chase, and the wild horsemen of the Sudan were no match for him. He had a fast horse, and a seat gained over racecourse and hunting-field soon told; and a Nupe warrior was seen subsiding out of his unwieldy saddle and enormous stirrups under the magnetic influence of a revolver barrel. The horse was a good one, and far the most valuable capture of the two, but now the difficulty was how to secure the pair, and we saw the Nupe making off into some thick grass, as hard as his legs could carry him.

This was the last time poor Musters took any active part in the expedition, and he had to give in at last to the insidious attacks of fever and dysentery. Always cheery and full of go, he was a great loss, and it was

with very sad hearts his brother officers received the
news of his death at the mouth of the Niger, where
he had arrived on his way home, having been invalided
as soon as we returned to the river again.   Fate was
against him, and his strength, already at a very low ebb,
was still further taxed by his having to make a great
part of the journey down to Lokoja in a native canoe,
the steamer in which he was travelling having stranded
on one of the treacherous sandbanks.

A mile or two further on we reached a small hill,
passing on the way through a cloud of locusts, which
quite obscured the atmosphere.   Our commander, can-
tering up to the top, discovered a body of the enemy's
horse in and about a village a short way off.   Signs of
motion were already evident, and there was no time to
be lost.   No. 3 Company went forward at the double,
whilst Lieutenant Musters with his company, and
Margesson with a Maxim, occupied the small hill.
Horsemen could be seen saddling up in haste, and it
was a question whether the Hausas would reach the
village in time.

Lieutenant Tighe, with a section, made a detour to
the right through some trees, and a volley soon rang
out from his men at some of the leading horsemen,
who were escaping in that direction.   The village was
already occupied by the active little Hausas, and a
lucky chance placed Prince Esa, one of the most
important Nupe princes, in our hands, besides twelve
horses, an extremely valuable addition to our stud,
already much reduced by hard marching.

It had been a complete surprise, and if we had only
had a small troop of cavalry the whole party would
have been captured.   The countryside was now covered
by the poor frightened villagers, who were escaping

with whatever they could lay their hands on, and in their flight afforded protection to the horsemen, whom it was no longer possible to fire at.

It was past two o'clock before we reached the walls of Bida, and entered the town with the buglers playing at the head of the column. We had not suspected the importance of our capture, until we noticed the villagers and the few natives who passed prostrating themselves on the ground before our prisoner. He turned out to be the brother of the Markum, head of the Omru family, and was a very fine man; and though fairly dark in colour, a good representative of the Fulah race, to which he belonged. He was lodged in charge of a guard in the Emir's palace, and two of his wives and a personal attendant were allowed to wait on him. He must have been astonished at the good treatment he received, which was very different from what he had expected.

His capture was of great importance, as his mother, widow of the late Sultan Omru, was hereby induced to surrender, and come in with about 200 people, including many of the family.

February the 1st was celebrated in a more peaceful manner, and a gymkhana was held outside the western gate, where a capital racecourse along a sandy track, about five furlongs in length, was laid out and levelled where necessary by a fatigue-party in the morning. The officers' chargers were for the time being transformed into racehorses, but no captured horses were allowed to be ridden. It was amusing to see the crowds of people, soldiers, carriers, and natives trooping out of the town in the afternoon, all anxious to assist at the unaccustomed spectacle. A tent was put up at the place appointed as the grand stand, and to it

even poor Musters insisted on being carried in a
hammock.   It was difficult to believe we had been
fighting so lately over the same ground, and the only
thing to remind one of the presence of an enemy was
the piquet posted on a hill near to give notice of any
threatened attack.

There were three races, the principal being that for
the Bida Cup, value twenty guineas, presented by Sir
George Goldie, with a silver cigarette-case for the
second.

There was a field of twenty-two for this race, which
was run in two heats, and the cup was ultimately
won by Lieutenant Festing on Rifleman IV., Major
Cunningham's Prince of Bida being second.

The race for light-weights under twelve stone was
a splendid race, and resulted in Lieutenant Burdon
beating Major Cunningham by a head, Lieutenant
Carroll on his own horse being third.

The Ndegi Stakes, weight twelve stone and over,
brought out a field of nine.

1st. Lieutenant Vandeleur's Lokitsha, ridden by
Major Cunningham ;

2nd. Lieutenant Bird's Tit Willow.

I received a severe kick on the leg from my own
horse, ungrateful brute, which prevented me from riding,
and I was laid up for the next few days.   The paddock
was no safe place, and our wild steeds, excited by the
racing, were kicking in all directions.

There was a Lloyd-Lindsay competition for officers
of companies, who had to ride a certain distance, fire
six shots with a revolver at a target, and gallop back
again in a certain time.   This was won by No. 1
Company, Lieutenants Bird and M'Clintock.

A race for soldiers, in which they had to carry a

calabash full of water on their heads, occasioned much
amusement among the men; also a race for the native
sergeant-majors, in which they had to catch a goat and
run back with it to the winning-post. The goats were
let loose a certain distance off, and away went the
sergeant-majors after them. It was ludicrous to see
them tumbling over each other in their efforts to catch
hold of the frightened goats, and at last one fleeter
than the rest returned to the winning-post with the goat
in his arms, amidst the shouts of laughter of the natives.

This, the first Bida race-meeting, was a great
success, and was the last event wanting to complete the victory.

The evacuation of the town commenced on the 2nd,
when three companies left with the guns for our old
camp near the ravine. I rode out this day through
the southern, or what is known as the Bomosa Barra
gate, to the scene of the conflict, where there were many
signs left of the destruction wrought by our fire, and
the heavy losses which the enemy must have incurred
by standing up so long before us. The King's tree,
where so many of the enemy were congregated, is not
far from this gate, and is quite a feature of the landscape, affording shade as it does to hundreds of people
under its outstretched branches.

One gets a very good idea of the town from the
high ground near this point, which forms the watershed between two streams, one rising not far from the
western gate; and the reason of the town being so well
supplied with water becomes apparent. Near each of
the main gates there is usually an open space with
shady trees, which is used as a market-place. The
gateways themselves are massive constructions, arched
over with usually a room in the wall at the side.

On returning, I met the Markum's mother riding through the town with a retinue of about 200 people. The Governor had sent some horses for her. She looked a very old woman, and sat huddled up in one of the native saddles, with a man leading the horse. She objected to staying in the town, and took up her residence in one of the villages outside. At Bida the average minimum temperature was 78°, and the maximum 97°, and we were glad to leave it, owing to the heat and the plague of flies and other insects, which was becoming unbearable.

On the 3rd inst. the main body left Bida, and the air was rent by the explosion of gunpowder, signifying the blowing up of the Emir's palace. This nearly proved disastrous to certain gallant officers, who had remained behind to witness it, and the photographer of the party received a severe blow on the arm from one of the fragments. Imagining themselves quite safe, they suddenly saw a volley of stones and rocks coming at them, and turned to run in all directions. Most of the principal buildings belonging to the Nupe princes in the town had been already blown up by detachments on the previous days, and the gunpowder found was utilised for this purpose.

It was under very altered conditions that we marched across our old battlefield; and the long line of porters, natives, and refugees, extended for miles, confident of being no longer in danger of their lives and harassed by the enemy. Hundreds of refugees and slaves were now making their way along the same road to Egbon, where they would be transported across the river, and would be able to settle down in peace.

The 9-pounder had broken down, the wheel having been broken the day before, in dragging it across a small cleft in the ground, and it looked in a very helpless condition lying at the bottom of a ditch. It would have been very awkward if this had happened in the advance, and we should probably have been obliged to abandon it. Great efforts were now being made to get it on, and the seven-pounder carriages were utilised for the purpose, the barrels of the seven-pounders being lashed to strong pieces of wood and carried by porters.

The barrel of the 9-pounder was eventually hoisted on to the 7-pounder carriages, and dragged in this manner to the river with great labour.

The whole force halted at our old camp of Lokitsha for the night, and went on the next day to the creek.

The African porter, with his usual intelligence, decided that after the fall of Bida his work was at an end, and that loads of ammunition and provisions were quite a secondary consideration to his own loot, an enormous pile of usually the most inconceivable rubbish. Great difficulty had been experienced in getting the loads along, and although the number of carriers was known, there were always a number of loads left over in the morning when the men paraded to take them. The creek, however, offered a grand opportunity of discovering the culprits, and each man's load was examined as he arrived, by officers sent on for the purpose, and if consisting of nothing but loot was immediately confiscated.

The climate had already begun to have disastrous results both on officers and men, and several stretchers accompanied the column on the return march. Lieuts. Thorpe, Musters, and Parker, and Captains Hatton and Anderson, took no further part in the operations, and were invalided down river. Numbers of men were suffering, principally from pneumonia, bronchitis, and diarrhœa, and these were also sent to Lokoja.

As we approached the river, the black funnels of the steamers could be seen over the high green grass which extends along the bank, and we were soon back in comparative civilisation again. The booming of the artillery at Bida had been heard distinctly on the steamers 25 miles away, and there had been great excitement on board as they listened to the firing, which continued throughout the two days. A mail had at last arrived, and we received letters and papers from England up to December 10th, 1896.

On arriving at the river, the officers at once took up their quarters on the steamers, and I embarked on the *Empire*, where my spare time was fully occupied in making a plan of Bida and the surrounding country from notes taken there, in which work I was greatly assisted by Pereira, who went round the outer wall and also to the Wanangi Creek. The troops camped on a large open space on the left bank.

XVIII

NIGER POLITICS

MASABA, the founder of the Fulah dynasty in Nupe, was a Sokoto prince related to, but not descended from, Othman dan Fodio, the African Napoleon, who at the commencement of this century created the immense Fulah empire of Sokoto and Gando. Masaba was so deeply indebted to one of his generals, Omru, that he decreed that Omru, though not of royal blood, should succeed him on the throne of Nupe, subject to the assent of Sokoto, but on condition that on Omru's death the throne should return to the Masaba family. Accordingly Meliki a Masaba succeeded Omru and became Emir of Bida, while Muhammed, Omru's eldest son, was given the rank of " Markum," or third in succession to the throne, the heir-apparent always holding the rank of " Sheaba," and the next heir that of " Potum." The Emir Omru had always been very friendly to the Company, but this feeling was not shared by the rulers of the Masaba family who followed him, and, notwithstanding the large subsidy paid him, the Emir Abu Bekri had become defiant and hostile.

During Meliki's reign the rank of heir-apparent or Sheaba died out as successive holders died of poison, one of the disadvantages of having anything to do with the throne in these countries, so that the Potum, Abu Bekri, a Masaba, refused to accept the rank, which was left vacant.

On Meliki's death in 1895, Abu Bekri became Emir or Sultan, Muhammed continuing Markum, while the ranks of Sheaba and Potum have remained unfilled. It had always been understood that the Markum Muhammed would become Emir after Abu Bekri, though the Masaba family have intrigued against him.

Knowing that the Omru family had been strongly opposed to the present war, which was brought about by Abu Bekri and the Masaba family, Sir George Goldie wrote repeatedly to the Markum Muhammed during the expedition to Kabba, to induce him to meet him and discuss terms, but without result, owing to the fear on the part of the Markum of the princes of the Masaba family, who were serving with him.

After the fall of Bida, the political situation looked serious, as the Nupe princes had fled far to the north, and overtures made to the "Ndegi," or Prime Minister, had proved fruitless.

By the capture of Prince Esa, however, the whole Omru family, some forty in number, including the Markum Muhammed's children, were induced to come in and surrender. The Markum's mother, widow of the late Sultan Omru, fell in with the Governor's views, and added a letter of her own to that which Sir George Goldie was sending to the Markum, announcing that the latter held all the family in his hands, and calling upon him to surrender.

Meanwhile the Markum, with the débris of his scattered army, and the Masaba princes in Southern Nupe, was encamped near the south bank of the Niger, unable to cross towards Bida owing to the flotilla under Mr. Wallace, through whom the letters in question were forwarded.

A meeting was arranged for the 5th inst., and on this day the Governor left in his launch for the appointed place at the crossing of Kosoji. The Markum was here, as arranged, with a large body of cavalry and his footmen drawn up on the bank, but it proved very difficult to make him come down to the launch, as he feared being made a prisoner.

However, after repeated assurances, he was induced to come close to the water's edge, where the launch was drawn up.

The scene must have been quite a theatrical one, as on one side of the river stood the "ganagas," or natives, who had been fighting for us, beating their drums and waving their spears, whilst on the other side stood the representatives of the Southern Nupe army.

Everything terminated in a most successful manner, and a treaty was drawn up in English and Arabic, in which the Markum was formally appointed Emir of Bida and Nupe.

TREATY OF KOSOJI.

TREATY made this Fifth day of February 1897 of the Christian Era, and the First day of Ramadán in the year 1314 since the Hegira, between Sir George Goldie for the Royal Niger Company, and Emir Mohammed (son of Omru), the Markum of Bida, for his chiefs and people of Nupe.

1. Abu Bekri, Emir of Nupe, has fled from the country, and is declared to be no longer Emir. As no Schiaba or Potum has been appointed, the Markum is the next successor to the throne, and is now Emir.

2. The new Emir Mohammed recognises that all Nupe is entirely under the power of the Company, and under the British flag. All previous treaties are abrogated.

3. The Company will govern direct that part of Nupe which is to the south-west of the Niger, and such portions of the north-east bank for a distance of 3 miles inland as the Company may from time to time direct.

4. The Emir Mohammed will govern the rest of Nupe, but will conform to such directions in respect of his government as the representatives of the Company may give him from time to time.

(Signed)   GEORGE TAUBMAN GOLDIE.

,,   MOHAMMED (in Arabic).

It was of the utmost importance to remain friends with the Sultan of Sokoto, and to avoid a war with him.

Any blow struck at Nupe and Ilorin was bound to arouse the fanaticism of the whole dominant race of Fulahs and of the higher class of Hausas, who had intermarried with them, besides destroying the revenue, solely of slaves, which the Sokoto empire had hitherto drawn from these provinces.

Sir George Goldie had written to the Sultan of Sokoto at the commencement of the campaign, to inform him of the expedition against Abu Bekri, and the reasons for it. And by this appointment of a Fulah as ruler of Northern Nupe much was done to propitiate him, and he was said to have a liking for the Omru family. The Company, following the example of the East India Company and the Government of India, desired as far as practicable to rule indirectly through native feudatory princes.

The Governor returned on the 5th, very pleased at the results of his negotiations, which had accomplished all he had hoped for, and said the Markum was very submissive, and appeared very grateful at being made Emir.

Preparations were hastened on for the expedition to

Ilorin, which had been finally decided upon, though much doubt was expressed as to whether there would be any fighting. Our forces were considerably reduced, and the expedition which embarked on the 6th February for transport to the new base at Jebba, consisted of 21 Europeans, of whom 15 were officers, and 320 soldiers organised in 5 companies, with 20 gunners and 488 carriers, making a total of 829.

2 seven-pounder mountain guns, and 4 Maxim guns were taken.

The expedition was transported as follows :—

S.W. *Empire*, 4 companies under Major Cunningham, D.S.O.

S.W. *Liberty*, 1 company and horses under Lieutenant Festing.

S.S. *Soudan*, guns, gunners, and carriers.

S.S. *Florence*, executive officers and carriers.

The night before we left, a tornado of rain, rather an unusual event at this time of year, swept over the camp, making it very unpleasant for everyone, especially the officers sleeping on the stern-wheelers.

At night the deck was transformed into a fairyland of mosquito curtains, with which the gale soon played havoc, and the rain penetrated the light sun-deck, coming down in torrents on the beds laid out underneath.

There were ten officers on the steamer, and we all took up our quarters in various corners about the upper deck, which was littered with beds, kit bags, provision boxes, etc.

Mosquito curtains were wanted, more to ward off the malarial mist rising from the water at night than to keep off the mosquitoes. In places there were a certain number of these, and pernicious little sandflies, but nothing to be compared with the mosquitoes on the Upper Nile. The soldiers occupied the lower deck, and always camped on shore during the night; the lighters were lashed to the side.

It was 2 o'clock on the 6th before we got away from Egbon, after saying goodbye to our friends leaving for Lokoja, and as we steamed rapidly away up the river at the head of the flotilla, we had a lovely view looking back towards the Egbon Hills and the Pyramid Peak. It became dark about 6.30 p.m., and we had to draw up alongside the bank at a convenient spot to enable the men to bivouac for the night.

Almost as soon as it got light we were off again, and were soon awaked by the throbbing of the engines and the creaking of the rudder chains; and the lovely cool breeze of the early morning made us draw our blankets closer round us.

The river is about 600 yards broad, though narrower in places, and some of the reaches even remind one of the Thames, though one is soon disabused of this impression by coming across a native village with a crowd of black people yelling and gesticulating on the bank, or by the sight of a big crocodile waddling off a sandbank, disturbed at our approach.

Sometimes we used to pass quite close to the villages on the banks, and it was amusing to watch the natives, who used to run along beside us in a great state of excitement, dancing and cheering vociferously, to show their delight at the defeat of the Fulahs. All the villages had little white flags hung up to show they were on our side.

The navigation at times was very intricate, and we used to tack in all directions to avoid the sandbanks, sunken reefs, and stumps of big trees, which have caused the wrecking of so many steamers on the Niger. Our old pilot, with a glistening row of white teeth, was quite a character, and was continually waving his thin bony hand to point out the direction to the man at the wheel.

Captain Hughes, who had charge of the ship, had the misfortune to fall into the hold, breaking two of his ribs, and sustaining a severe concussion, and was carried up just as we were all sitting down to dinner.

The lower deck was very dimly lighted, and was rather a dangerous place after dark. I heard an unearthly noise going on in the middle of this same night, and on groping my way down found one of the horses had got cast on this deck, and was inextricably mixed up with an enormous anchor and steel cable, from which we had difficulty in releasing him.

The river at Rabba, where the old Nupe capital used to be before the days of Bida, is quite lovely. A rock wall of red and yellow sandstone rises to a height of 40 feet on the left bank, and the water's edge is bordered by brilliant green bushes and yellow flowers, and here even a few graceful palm trees have found a footing, and lean over the water, in which they are prettily reflected.

In the distance an island divides the channel into two, and the right bank is bordered by lovely green meadows, forming a strong contrast to the country beyond, which is withered up by the sun, and covered with a few stunted bushes. Far away lie a line of blue hills behind Jebba, where we arrived at 1 p.m. on the 8th.

There is a large island in mid-stream, on which the Company's station and the native village are situated, but the house used by the officer in charge of the post

16

is on the right bank, at a bend of the river, close to which high hills rise steeply up, and where hartebeest and other antelope are often found.

From here we could see the curious high rock called Baikie's Seat, which is said to be defended from all intruders by swarms of bees, and above which the rapids soon begin forming a barrier to further advance, and closing the navigable portion of the Niger, which is here 400 feet above the level of the sea.

The Niger from its mouth to this point measures about 466 miles, and except for a few months is navigable all the year round, but for a like distance above Jebba there extends a series of rapids and cataracts, making continuous navigation impossible, until one arrives at the calmer water of the Upper Niger commencing at Ansongo, which forms, at high water, a really good water-way, and on which there are boats and launches.

In the previous year Sir George Goldie had visited Bajibo, Leaba, and Bussa, and on his return to Jebba was anxious to journey to Ilorin, with a view to deliver a letter from Her Majesty to the Emir Suliman, and to settle the frontier disputes between Ilorin and Lagos. He, however, received a letter from the Emir entreating him not to come, as he had only lately been put on the throne, and was not sure of the attitude of his generals or, "baloguns." Her Majesty's letter was then forwarded to the Emir by a native Political Agent, but was returned at the instance of the baloguns.

Since that time the attacks on the outposts on the Lagos frontier had continued, and Sir George Goldie decided to march at once to Ilorin. It was still hoped that a peaceful settlement might be attained, and with this object only a small force was taken. There were other reasons also for reducing the numbers of the expedition as much as possible. The dry season was now far advanced, and the difficulty of obtaining water on the road was very great.

Many men who marched in the previous expeditions to Kabba and Bida were sick and footsore, and, if taken, were likely to hamper the force marching to Ilorin, which was now composed of the strongest and soundest men.

Ilorin is a great Mohammedan centre, as Bida also is, and pays tribute to the Sultan of Sokoto, but on all sides it is surrounded by pagan States, with which it has been continually at war.

To the north lies the Bussa country on the west of the Niger, and to the north-west Borgu, visited by Captain Lugard in 1894, a country inhabited by a savage tribe renowned for their skilled bowmen, who have frightened off their enemies hitherto with their deadly poisoned arrows, and have always resisted the Fulah invasion from the north.

After the war with the Jebus, the colony of Lagos extended to the Ibadan country, and the frontier posts were gradually pushed forward, until they came into contact with the Ilorins, who have always been at war with the Ibadan people. Since then the Ilorins had resented any interference, and foolishly closed their doors against any communication with the south, and had by their attacks on the frontier outposts brought on themselves a speedy retribution. The Emir Suliman, who had been recently appointed, was a Fulah, and a very weak man, and although at heart a friend to the English, was completely in the hands of his " baloguns," or generals, namely, Alanamu, Salu, Ajikabi, and Zuheru, who commanded respectively the four divisions of his army. With the army at their backs, these generals were able to settle affairs of State as they pleased, and the Emir, afraid of meeting the same fate as his predecessor, was obliged to conform to their views. Of these baloguns one was a Fulah and the remaining three were Yorubas, representatives of the inhabitants of the country. The army, composed of mercenaries and adventurers from all parts, was usually camped at Otun, ready to repel or make an attack on the Ibadans, their nearest enemies. It was supposed to consist of about a thousand horsemen and five or six times that number of footmen, a much less formidable force than the one we had already encountered at Bida.

The natives and cultivators of the soil are really an entirely different race of people, and, to judge by the behaviour of those we encountered, were quite friendly and peaceably inclined.

It was not with them we had to deal, but their rulers and the army, supported by an overweening confidence in themselves. Many of the inhabitants were slaves, and these were only too glad to welcome us, and seize the opportunity of escaping to their own country.

Two companies started on the march inland on the 9th, with a number of porters carrying food, and with orders to proceed to a place about thirty miles off, where the carriers were to be sent back for more food. The rest of the force remained at Jebba, and paraded in the morning.

Several of the Europeans, including myself, were ill at this time, mainly due to drinking bad water and the insanitary condition of Bida.

XIX

French Occupation of Bussa and Borgu

STARTLING news awaited us at Jebba, of an expedition, believed to be French, and reported to consist of 500 troops and 4 white officers, being on the river Niger between Gombo and Say at a place called Illo. This place Say, situated on the 13th parallel of latitude and on the right or west bank of the Niger, was laid down, as far back as 1890 by treaty, as the boundary between England and France on the Niger. The clause in the important Anglo-French agreement of 5th August 1890, is as follows:—" The Government of Her Britannic Majesty recognises the sphere of influence of France to the south of the Mediterranean possessions, up to a line from Say on the Niger to Barruwa on Lake Chad, drawn in such a manner as to comprise in the sphere of action of the Niger Company all that fairly belongs to the kingdom of Sokoto; the line to be determined by the Commission to be appointed."

It would be natural to suppose that a line drawn roughly at right angles south from Say towards the coast would form the western boundary between the two Powers; and, at the time of the agreement, maps published in France undoubtedly prove that this was considered the case in that country.

Dr. Keltie, writing in 1895, before the recent French

advance to the Niger from Dahome, even says—
" The French cartographers make the western boundary-
line drop directly southward from Say to the Guinea
Coast, completely ignoring Gurma, which is a province
of the Sokoto-Gandu empire, and Borgu, with which
kingdom the Niger Company has treaties.

" It would only be carrying out the arrangement to
draw the line westward from Say to at least the
Greenwich meridian, and thence round the west of
Borgu to the western boundary of the Gold Coast."

By the campaign conducted by General Dodds in
Dahome, and the final overthrow of Behanzin, King
of Dahome, in January 1893, the French acquired
new territory on the West Coast, and the aggressions into the Company's territories have come entirely
from these new possessions in the south, and not from
the Upper Niger and Timbuktu, which they have
occupied from Senegal.

The French in Dahome seem to consider themselves bound by no such rules or boundaries as their
compatriots on the Upper Niger, and the Royal Niger
Company found themselves threatened by this far-
reaching Power from another quarter of the compass, another instance of the persistency with which
the French have endeavoured to obtain a footing on
the navigable waterway of the Niger, or its tributary
the Benuë, at all hazards.

The action of Lieutenant Mizon on the Benuë is
still fresh in the minds of officials in the Niger territories.   Having given every assurance that his expedition was of an entirely peaceful nature, and not
prejudicial to the Company's interest, he proceeded to
establish himself on the banks, and actually to arm the
natives with a number of breech-loading rifles.   This

nearly proved a very serious affair, and hostilities were only avoided by an order at the last minute from the French Government, for him to leave the river at once.

Even if treaties and subsidies paid to native rulers are apparently of no value or importance in the eyes of the French, it is absurd to suppose that, having command of the Lower Niger and with steamers and a large and well-trained force of Hausas at its disposal, the Company's influence does not cover all the navigable waterway of the Niger and Benuë, and a distance of 80 to 100 miles from the furthest point to which launches can ascend. We have seen the ease and celerity with which the force in the present campaign was transferred from one place to another.

Commandant Toutée, in his book *Dahomé, Niger, Touareg*, has been at great pains to lay stress on the navigability of the Niger about Bajibo and Bussa. We do not wish to question this, but it seems all the more reason for asking why the French, recognising British claims to the Lower and navigable Niger, should have entered into the *Hinterland*—belonging, moreover, to the Company by virtue of the treaties with Bussa, or Borgu, of 1885 and 1890, and should have occupied Bussa on the Niger itself.

BRITISH TREATIES IN WEST AFRICA.

(Reprinted from the " Times" of November 12, 1897.)

WE are enabled to publish the following copies of some of the principal treaties, negotiated by the Royal Niger Company in the back country of the British possessions on the West African coast.

The treaties with Sokoto and Gando cover all the territories subject to those States. It will be seen that the treaties of

1894 refer to and confirm previous treaties negotiated with the Emirs of both States.   The dates of the previous treaties were 1885 and 1890, and the Say-Barua line of demarcation fixed by the Anglo-French Agreement of 1890 was determined in consequence of rights acquired by Great Britain under the early treaties.

In the Name of the Most Merciful God.

TREATY made on the 26th day of June 1894, between Abdu, King of the Mussulmans, on the one hand, and Abduramani, who is called Mr. Wallace, on the other hand, for and on behalf of the Royal Niger Company, Chartered and Limited.

1. I, the undersigned, hereby confirm the treaties made between the Sultan Omoru, whom I succeeded, and Thomson and King on behalf of the Royal Niger Company, Chartered and Limited, the latter treaty made on the 15th day of April 1890.   I now renew these treaties.

2. With my own hand I bind myself with Wallace on behalf of the Company, and accept this following treaty made on the 26th day of June 1894.

3. With the view of bettering the condition of my people, and having considered and taken counsel with my chiefs, I give to the Company, and their successors for ever, full power and rights in perpetuity over foreigners in my country, whether travelling or resident, including right of just taxation as they may see fit.   My chiefs are in no way to interfere, and are to recognise no one but the Company.

4. I give to the Company, and their successors for ever, all power in any part of my dominions as to mining rights.

5. The Company bind themselves not to exercise any monopoly of trade.

6. I recognise that the Company receives its power from the Queen of Great Britain, and that they are Her Majesty's representatives to me.   I will not recognise any other white nation, because the Company are my help.

7. I state that Asbon, Adamawa, and Muri are included in my dominion.

8. The Company undertake not to interfere with the customs of the Mussulmans, but to maintain friendly relations.

9. In recognition of the treaties between us, the Company have paid me a subsidy of three thousand (3000) bags as

hitherto annually for the past nine years. They have acted honourably towards me, and as I should desire.

I hereby renew the previous treaties and accept this treaty for myself, for my heirs, and for my successors. No one after me is to alter this treaty. It stands unchangeable for ever.

(Imperial Seal of Sokoto.)

27 June 1894.

We, the undersigned, do hereby declare that the Sultan of Sokoto has this day personally handed to W. Wallace this treaty, in the presence of the undersigned witnesses.

Witness (Sgd.) W. WALLACE.
,,   ,, T. M. TEED.

We, the undersigned, do hereby declare that the Sultan of Sokoto has this day delivered in our presence with his own hand this treaty to W. Wallace, and declared that he made this treaty, with one mind, and will hold to it, and that he gave it with his own hand.

Witness (Sgd.) Q. F. GOMES.
,,   ,, T. F. JOSEPH.
,,   ,, (Copy of Arabic signature.)

I, W. Wallace,* for and on behalf of the Company, do hereby approve and accept the above confirmation of previous treaties and treaty now made, and hereby affix my hand.

* Copy of Mr. Wallace's signature.

In consequence of a French report, to the effect that the British treaty had been superseded by a treaty negotiated on behalf of France by Captain Monteil, the following letter was written to the Company by the Waziri, or Prime Minister, of Sokoto :—

TRANSLATION of Arabic Letter received from the Waziri of Sokoto. Kano, April 27, 1894.

In the name of God the Almighty, through the Prophet, the Great Prophet, from the King of Peace, the one who settles all things, who will always do good, Waziri, Mohommadu Bohariu, to the Queen. Full salutations meeting together. Pure salutations, according as she wants.

After this we saw your messenger, Mr. Wallace. We met him and found him in good health, in peace, in good health.

We saw your paper with the messenger, we saw it and we understood it.   They say in it that we have made a treaty with Monteil.   On account of that we write to you this letter to tell you we made treaty with no one.   There is no treaty made between us and Monteil.   All that Monteil may have said was a lie.   We will make no treaty with any one coming from your parts.   We will make no treaty with any other from the white man's country, except with the Royal Niger Company, Limited. They are the friends of the treaty with the Sarikin Mussiliri and the Waziri.   We gave them power over all foreigners coming from the white man's country, those that are travelling over the land belonging to the Sultan, those that are sitting down.   The Waziri of Sokoto writes this letter to the Queen on the nineteenth day of the moon Shawal.

In the treaty with Gando it will be observed that the Emir distinctly claims Gurma as far as Libtako to be included within his dominions.

(Copy.)

In the Name of the Most Merciful God.

TREATY made on the 4th day of July 1894, between Omoru, Sultan of Gando, on the one hand, and Mr. Wallace on the other hand, for and on behalf of the Royal Niger Company, Chartered and Limited.

1. I, the undersigned, Omoru, Sultan of Gando, hereby confirm the treaties made between the Sultan Maleki, whom I succeeded, and Thomson and King on behalf of the Royal Niger Company, Chartered and Limited—the latter treaty made on the   day of April 1890.   I now confirm these treaties.

2. With my own hand I bind myself with Wallace, on behalf of the Company, and accept this following treaty made on the 4th day of July 1894.

3. With the view of bettering the condition of my people, and having considered and taken counsel with my chiefs, I give to the Company and their successors for ever full power and rights in perpetuity over foreigners in my country, whether travelling or resident, including right of just taxation as they may see fit.   My chiefs are in no way to interfere, and are to recognise no one but the Company.

4. I give to the Company and their successors for ever all power in any part of my dominions as to mining rights.

5. The Company bind themselves not to exercise any monopoly of trade.

6. I recognise that the Company received their power from the Queen of Great Britain, and that they are Her Majesty's representatives to me. I will not recognise any other white nation, because the Company are my help.

7. I state that the country of Ilorin and the country of Gurma are included in my dominions—the latter extending to Libtako.

8. The Company undertake not to interfere with the customs of the Mussulmans, but to maintain friendly relations.

9. In recognition of the treaties between us, the Company have paid me a subsidy of two thousand (2000) bags, as hitherto annually for the past nine years. They have acted honourably towards me, and as I should desire.

I hereby confirm the previous treaties, and accept this treaty for myself, for my heirs, and for my successors. No one after me is to alter this treaty; it stands unchangeable for ever.

(Sgd.)   OMORU   (Copy of Arabic signature.)
4th July 1894.

We, the undersigned, do hereby declare that this treaty was this day read and translated in our presence before the Sultan of Gando, who stated that it was given with his own hand and was approved and accepted by him, and was thereupon handed over by him to Mr. Wallace.

(Sgd.)   W. WALLACE.
 ,,   T. M. TEED.
 ,,   Q. F. GOMES.
 ,,   T. F. JOSEPH.
(Copy of Arabic signature.)

I, W. Wallace,* for and on behalf of the Company, do hereby approve and accept the above confirmation of previous treaties and treaty now made, and hereby affix my hand.

* Copy of Mr. Wallace's signature.

The territory of Borgu, or Bussa, which has been the scene of the late intrusion of expeditions from the French *Hinterland*, lies between the inland frontier of Lagos and the southern frontier of Gando. It is bounded on the east by the river

Niger, and extends on the west to the meridian of Say. It claims independence of Sokoto or Gando, and separate treaties were consequently negotiated in the British interest, first with its principal or ruling Emir, and afterwards with those minor chieftains whose dependence upon the King of Bussa appeared open to any doubt. The first treaty of Bussa, negotiated on January 20, 1890, was among the treaties of which Lord Salisbury and M. Ribot took cognisance in concluding the Anglo-French Agreement of 1890. The position of Bussa, lying due south of Say, on the right bank of the Niger, gives particular significance to the fact that this treaty was included among those which led to the acceptance of the Say-Barua line.

TREATY entered into between the Emir and Chiefs of Bussa (or Borgu) on behalf of themselves and their successors for ever, and the Royal Niger Company, Chartered and Limited, hereinafter called the Company, on behalf of themselves, their successors and assigns.

We, the Emir and Chiefs of Bussa (or Borgu), in council assembled (representing our country, its dependencies and tributaries on both banks of the River Niger, and as far back as our dominion extends, in accordance with our laws and customs) do hereby agree on behalf of ourselves and of our successors for ever—

Firstly, To observe faithfully the agreement entered into between us and the Company (then known as the National African Company, Limited), and dated the 12th day of November 1885.

Secondly, To grant to the Company full and absolute jurisdiction over all foreigners to our territories,—that is to say, over all persons within the territories who are not our native-born subjects. Such jurisdiction shall include the right of protection of such foreigners, of taxation of such foreigners, and of political, criminal, and civil jurisdiction over such foreigners.

Thirdly, That we will not at any time whatever cede any of our territories to any other person or State, or enter into agreement, treaty, or arrangement with any foreign Government, except through and with the consent of the Company, or if the Company should at any time so desire, with the consent of the Government of Her Majesty, the Queen of Great Britain and Ireland and Empress of India.

Fourthly, To place our territories, if and when called upon to do so by the Company, under the protection of the flag of Great Britain.

And we, the Royal Niger Company, on behalf of ourselves, our successors, and our assigns for ever, hereby agree—

Firstly, To admit to the territories of Bussa (or Borgu) any foreigner who may desire to go there, subject to such necessary restrictions as may be necessary in the interests of peace and order.

Secondly, To permit all such foreigners to trade freely, subject to the payment of such taxation as may be necessary for administrative purposes in Bussa (or Borgu), or for the general administration of the Company.

Thirdly, To do our utmost to promote the prosperity and wealth of Bussa (or Borgu), and to develop and open up that country, and to do the utmost in our power to promote peace, order, and good government, and the general progress of civilisation.

Fourthly, To pay to the Emir of Bussa (or Borgu) a yearly sum of fifty bags, native value, in any class of goods, to be taken at the market value of the place where and when the payment is made.

For the Royal Niger Company, Chartered and Limited.

(Sgd.)　Will Lister.

[Signatures of the Emir and Chiefs.]

Dachtra or Dagga	his × mark	Emir of Bussa (or Borgu).
Momo	his × mark	Eldest Son of Emir.
Musa	their ×	Eyusu.
Serikin Riia	× marks.	Chief.

We, the undersigned, are witnesses to the above signatures and marks.

(Arabic signatures.)

I, William Reffle, do here certify that the above has been

faithfully interpreted to the Emir and Chiefs of Bussa (or Borgu), and understood by them in every sense.

(Sgd.)   W. REFFLE.

Done in triplicate at Bussa this 20th day of January 1890.

The following treaties of Kishi, in the Yoruba country, and of Keioma or Kiama, and of Nikki, in Borgu, with the important declaration of Ilesha, in which the people acknowledge dependence upon Nikki, and confirm Captain Lugard's account of the negotiation of the treaty of November 10, are given in the order of their date.   It will be observed with regard to all these treaties, that, far from being carelessly negotiated, they are in every case accompanied by the attestation of the interpreters in whose presence the negotiations were conducted.

TREATY made on the 13th day of October 1894, between Folawiyo, King of Kishi (Yoruba), and his Chiefs, on the one hand, and the Royal Niger Company, Chartered and Limited, for themselves and their assigns, for ever, hereinafter called "The Company," on the other hand.

1. We, the undersigned King and Chiefs of Kishi (Yoruba), with the view of bettering the condition of our country and people, do this day cede to The Company, including as above their assigns, for ever, the whole of our territory, but The Company shall pay private landowners a reasonable amount for any portion of land that The Company may require from time to time.

2. We thereby give to The Company and their assigns, for ever, full jurisdiction of every kind, and we pledge ourselves not to enter into any war with other tribes without the sanction of The Company.

3. We give to The Company and their assigns, for ever, the sole right to mine in any portion of our territory.

4. We bind ourselves not to have any intercourse as representing our tribe or State, on tribal or State affairs, with any person or persons other than The Company, who are hereby recognised as the authorised Government of our territories; but this provision shall not be interpreted as authorising any monopoly of trade, direct or indirect, by The Company or others, nor any restriction of private or commercial intercourse

with any person or persons, subject, however, to such administrative measures as may be taken by The Company in the interests of commerce and of order.

5. In consideration of the foregoing, The Company bind themselves not to interfere with any of the native laws or customs of the country, consistently with the maintenance of order and good government, and the progress of civilisation.

6. The Company bind themselves to protect, as far as practicable, the said King and Chiefs from the attacks of any neighbouring aggressive tribes.

7. In consideration of the above, The Company have this day paid the said King and Chiefs of Kiski (Yoruba) a donation, receipt of which is hereby acknowledged.

This treaty having been interpreted to us, the above-mentioned King and Chiefs of Kishi (Yoruba), we hereby approve and accept it for ourselves and for our people, and in testimony of this, having no knowledge of writing, do affix our marks below it.

× FOLAWIYO.

× OKIMFALU.

× AGORO.

× BALE.

We, the undersigned witnesses, do hereby solemnly declare that the King and Chiefs whose names are placed opposite their respective marks, have in our presence affixed their marks of their own free will and consent, and that Capt. F. D. Lugard, on behalf of The Company, has in our presence affixed his signature.   (Sgd.)   T. A. REYNOLDS.
                                                  „   GUY N. MOTTRAM.

I, Capt. F. D. Lugard, for and on behalf of The Company, do hereby approve and accept the above treaty, and hereby affix my hand.   (Sgd.) F. D. LUGARD, Capt. Cmdg. Borgu Expd.

Declaration by Interpreter.

I, T. F. Joseph, native of Sierra Leone, do hereby solemnly declare that I am well acquainted with the Yoruba language, and that on the 13th day of October 1894, I truly and faithfully explained the above treaty to all the native signatories, and that they understood its meaning.

[Signature or mark of interpreter]   (Sgd.) T. F. JOSEPH.
Witnesses to the above   (Sgd.)   GUY N. MOTTRAM.
   mark or signature,   „   T. A. REYNOLDS.

Done in triplicate at Kishi (Yoruba) this 13th day of October 1894.

TREATY made on the 22nd day of October 1894, between
Mousa Pobida, King of Keioma, Borgu, on the one hand,
and The Royal Niger Company, Chartered and Limited, for
themselves and their assigns, for ever, hereinafter called
" The Company," on the other hand.

1. I, the undersigned Musa Pobiba, King of Keioma,
Borgu, with the view of bettering the condition of my country
and people, hereby give to The Company and their assigns, for
ever, full criminal and civil jurisdiction of every kind over all
foreigners to my country, including the rights of protection
and taxation, and I pledge myself and my successors not
to exercise any jurisdiction whatever over such foreigners
without the sanction of The Company.

2. I bind myself not to have any intercourse as representing
my tribe or State, on tribal or State affairs, with any foreigner
or foreign government other than The Company ; but this
provision shall not be interpreted as authorising any monopoly
of trade, direct or indirect, by The Company or others, nor any
restriction of private or commercial intercourse with any
person or persons ; subject, however, to such administrative
measures as may be taken by The Company, as a Government,
in the interests of order and of commerce.

3. I recognise that The Company, as a Government,
represents Her Majesty, the Queen of Great Britain and
Ireland, and I accept the protection of the British ;[1] but I
understand that such protection against the attacks of neighbouring aggressive tribes can only be afforded as far as
practicable.

4. I give to The Company and their assigns, for ever, the
sole right to mine or dispose of mining rights in any portion of
territory.

5. In consideration of the foregoing, The Company bind
themselves not to interfere with any of the native laws or
customs of the country, consistently with the maintenance of
order and good government, and the progress of civilisation.

6. As a pledge of their good faith, The Company have this
day paid the said King Musa Pobida, of Keioma Borgu, a
donation, receipt of which is hereby acknowledged.

This treaty having been interpreted to me, the above-

---

[1] And I engage not to fly the flag of any other nation.

mentioned King and Chiefs of Keioma, I hereby approve and accept it for myself and for my successors for ever.

[Attestation.]

[Signature of Native Ruler.]
× Mousa Pobida.
× Yankpan.
× Nawogigaginawo.

(Sgd.) Guy N. Mottram }
    „   Tom A. Reynolds } Witness to all signatures.

I, Capt. Lugard, for and on behalf of The Company, do hereby approve and accept the above Treaty, and hereby affix my hand.

(Sgd.) F. D. Lugard, Capt. Comdg. Borgu Exped.

Declaration by Interpreter.

I, T. F. Joseph, native of Sierra Leone, do hereby solemnly declare that I am well acquainted with the Hausa language, and that on the 19th day of October, 1894, I truly and faithfully explained the above Treaty to the said King Musa Pobida, and that he understands its meaning.

[Signature or mark of interpreter.]
(Sgd.) T. F. Joseph.

Witness to the above
interpreter's mark or signature,

(Sgd.) Guy N. Mottram.
    „   Tom A. Reynolds.

Done in triplicate at Keioma Borgu, this 22nd day of October, 1894.

Treaty made on the 10th day of November, 1894, between The King of Nikki (which is the capital of Borgu) on the one hand, and the Royal Niger Company, Chartered and Limited, for themselves and their assigns, for ever, hereinafter called " The Company," on the other hand.

1. I, Lafia (also called Absalamu, son of Wurukura), King of Nikki and of all Borgu country, with the view of bettering the condition of my country and people, hereby give to The Company and their assigns, for ever, full criminal and civil jurisdiction of every kind over all Foreigners to my country, including the rights of protection and taxation, and I pledge myself and my successors not to exercise any jurisdiction whatever over such Foreigners without the sanction of The Company.

17

2. I bind myself not to have any intercourse, as representing my tribe or state, on tribal or state affairs, with any Foreigner or Foreign Government other than the Company; but this provision shall not be interpreted as authorising any monopoly of trade, direct or indirect, by The Company or others, nor any restriction of private or commercial intercourse with any person or persons; subject, however, to such administrative measures as may be taken by The Company, as a Government, in the interests of order and of commerce.

3. I recognise that The Company, as a Government, represents Her Majesty the Queen of Great Britain and Ireland, and I accept the protection of the British flag; but I understand that such protection against the attacks of neighbouring aggressive tribes can only be afforded as far as practicable.

4. I give to The Company and their assigns, for ever, the sole right to mine or dispose of mining rights in any portion of my territory.

5. In consideration of the foregoing, The Company bind themselves not to interfere with any of the native laws or customs of the country, consistently with the maintenance of order and good government, and the progress of civilisation.

6. As a pledge of their good faith, The Company have this day paid the said Lafia, King of Nikki and Borgu, a donation, receipt of which is hereby acknowledged.

This Treaty having been interpreted to us (the representatives deputed to act for him by the above-mentioned Lafia, King of Nikki and of Borgu), we hereby approve and accept it for the King and for his successors for ever.

[Signature of Native Ruler.]
Arabic signatures of
THE LEMAN.
THE SIRKIN POWA.
THE NAIMIN.

[Attestation.]

(Sgd.) T. A. REYNOLDS ⎱ Witness to
   „ GUY N. MOTTRAM ⎰ all signatures.

I, Captain F. D. Lugard, for and on behalf of The Company, do hereby approve and accept the above Treaty, and hereby affix my hand.

(Sgd.) F. D. LUGARD, Capt. Comdg. Borgu Exped.

I certify and solemnly declare that I was sent to the King Lafia by Capt. Lugard, to carry to him a present from the

Company, and that at that interview, in accordance with my instructions, I asked the King myself, in the presence of various chiefs and people, whether he had himself deputed the Leman, and Sirkin Powa, and Naimin, to act for him in the matter of this Treaty, and that he thrice declared to me that he had done so. (Sgd.) T. F. JOSEPH.

Witnesses

(Sgd.) T. A. REYNOLDS.

„ GUY N. MOTTRAM.

Declaration by Interpreter.

I, T. F. Joseph, native of Sierra Leone, do hereby solemnly declare that I am well acquainted with the Hausa language, and that on the 10th day of November, 1894, I truly and faithfully explained the above Treaty to the representatives deputed by the said Lafia, and that they understand its meaning.

[Signature or mark of interpreter] (Sgd.) T. F. JOSEPH.

Witness to the above

interpreter's mark or signature.

(Sgd.) T. A. REYNOLDS.

„ GUY N. MOTTRAM.

Done in triplicate at Nikki Borgu, this 10th day of November 1894.

The King, being blind and also having a superstitious dread of personally meeting any European, has deputed the Leman and the Sirkin Powa to be his representatives and proxies and to sign the Treaty on his behalf. In the presence of these and other important men the Treaty has been translated word by word and fully explained in Hausa—many understanding that language—and retranslated again sentence by sentence into Borgu dialect.

(Sgd.) F. D. LUGARD, Capt. Comdg. Borgu Exped.

WE, the undersigned, who are five of the principal Chiefs of Ilesha, a town of Borgu subservient to Nikki, do hereby testify as follows in token whereof we have affixed our marks as evidence :—

Whereas the King of Ilesha is an exceedingly old man, at present indisposed in health ; and whereas it is also contrary to the etiquette of Borgu that a vassal Chief should do otherwise than follow in the minutest detail the procedure of his Suzerain King; and whereas the King of Nikki, under whose jurisdiction the town is, did not in person see Captain Lugard, owing to the fact of his age and blindness, and other causes; and whereas we fear that if the King of Ilesha should see Captain Lugard, as he is personally anxious to do, it may cause offence to the King of Nikki, as bearing the construction that the said King of Ilesha was arrogating to himself an honour greater than his Suzerain King, the aforesaid King of Nikki—

We therefore, having been deputed by the King, have this day held a council or palaver with the said Captain Lugard; We on our part acting for and in the name of the King, Chiefs, and people of Ilesha, and the said Captain F. D. Lugard, acting solely on behalf of the Royal Niger Company, Chartered and Limited—

I. We have assured Captain Lugard that whatsoever treaty, agreement, or contract has been entered into between himself, on behalf of the Royal Niger Company, on the one part, and the King of Nikki, on the other part, is binding on us in every minutest detail; for if the King of Nikki ordered us to eat sand, we should eat it, and in every way we acknowledge him our King.

II. We have heard from Captain Lugard the main provisions of the treaty made between the Royal Niger Company and the King of Nikki, viz., that the King of Borgu cedes absolutely to the Company all jurisdiction, civil and criminal, over foreigners who are settled or may hereafter settle in Borgu, including the right of protection, taxation, etc., over such foreigners: That the King of Borgu is now in treaty alliance with the Royal Niger Company, and his country has become part of the Government of the Niger Territories under the aforesaid Company: That the Company, little by little as they may be able, and as the country is opened up and settled and civilised, will afford their protection to the King of Borgu, and assist him in any just war undertaken with their consent and approval: That the Company claim no monopoly of trade, and will not interfere with native laws and customs, except in the interests of trade, or at the dictates of humanity: That the King of Borgu undertakes to make no other treaty, accept no flag with any people or foreigners other than the Royal Niger Company, and that he cedes to the said Company all mining rights and concessions in Borgu, absolutely and solely.

III. And we, the undersigned, do gladly subscribe to the above conditions, and any others which may have been entered into on behalf of all Borgu by the King of Nikki; and we are pleased with the outline of the treaty, as explained to us, in the hope that it will promote peace, trade, and prosperity in the country; and in this assent we act for and on behalf of the King, Chiefs, and people of Ilesha and district.

IV. We state, moreover, that no European has to our knowledge ever before visited Ilesha, nor have we ever made any treaty or agreement with any European; and in the future, as stated in the treaty, we undertake to make no treaty or agreement whatsoever with any European or foreigners, other than the Royal Niger Company.

In witness whereof, we do hereby subscribe our signatures or our marks. Each Chief has held the pen before his name was written in token of assent.

Witness to all signatures,

(Sgd.)	T. A. REYNOLDS.	TAKU	×
„	GUY N. MOTTRAM.	SAMARE	×
		SARE	×
		KOM	×
		TABE	×

Signed by me, F. D. Lugard, on behalf of the Royal Niger Company, this Twenty-fourth day of November 1894 (eighteen ninety-four).

(Sgd.)   F. D. LUGARD, Capt. Commanding Borgu Expedition.

I, Captain F. D. Lugard, do hereby testify that I have this day held a council with the Chiefs of Ilesha, who, for the reason assigned in the document hereto attached, have met together to act in this matter on behalf of the King, Chiefs, and people of the town and district of Ilesha; and that whereas they do assure me, in the strongest manner possible (strengthened and enforced by many native similes), that they are wholly and entirely bound by any treaty engagements entered into by the King of Borgu who resides at Nikki, and who is already in treaty alliance with the Royal Niger Company;—I have therefore embodied this declaration in the attached document, which has been very carefully translated to them and assented to (the pen being handled by each in token of assent to signature), by each Chief in my presence. I have, moreover, explained to them carefully and fully, to the best of my ability, the main provisions of the treaty made with the King of Borgu at Nikki, to all of which they gladly assented.

(Sgd.)   F. D. LUGARD, Captain Commanding
Borgu Expedition.

22nd November, 1894.

I, G. N. Mottram, do hereby testify that I was present at the conference between Captain Lugard (acting for the Royal Niger Company) and the Chiefs of Ilesha; that I heard the five Chiefs declare, in the strongest possible manner, that they and their King were entirely under the King of Borgu at Nikki, and absolutely bound by all treaty engagements entered into by him;—that they all assented gladly to the provisions of that treaty, which were fully explained in simple English by Captain Lugard, and translated sentence by sentence (apparently accurately and in closest detail) by Mr. Joseph, and that the only reason why the conference was not held in the presence of the King was (as stated by his messenger and the Chiefs present) his old age, sickness, and the Borgu etiquette, which forbade him to initiate any other procedure than that followed at Nikki.

(Sgd.)   GUY N. MOTTRAM.

I, T. F. Joseph, do certify that I have fully and literally translated all that Captain Lugard said at the conference, on the subject of the treaty with Borgu, to the Chiefs of Ilesha, and have also faithfully and literally translated their replies. I also certify that I have faithfully and literally translated to them all that is contained in the attached document, and that they have fully understood the same. I am thoroughly conversant with the Haussa language, and spoke in that dialect, many present, including several of the Chiefs, being able to speak Haussa. To those who could not understand Haussa each sentence was translated into Borgu by their own Haussa-speaking people.

(Sgd.)   T. F. JOSEPH.

Commandant Toutée says (p. 124): "Je voyais journellement des barques conduites par des Baribas et chargées à couler, descendre ou remonter le fleuve, elles allaient jusqu'à des dépôts où arrivaient les navires à vapeur."

This ought surely to have been enough to convince him that he was in the English sphere of influence; and yet, without further inquiry or misgiving, a fort is built and called Fort d'Arenberg. It is impossible for France to effectively occupy with military posts the whole of her vast possessions comprised between the Mediterranean, the Niger, and the Atlantic, which is known as the French Sudan, and there is no necessity for her doing so. Her occupation—where it exists—of the immense territory claimed by her is so far purely military, involving an expenditure of about half a million sterling.[1]

Our occupation of the Niger territories is, on the other hand, principally a commercial one, and trade there follows the flag, which it certainly does not in the French Sudan. To quote from Lord Salisbury's speech at the Guildhall, 9th November 1897: " The objects which we have in our view are strictly business objects. We wish to extend the commerce, the trade, the industry, and the civilisation of mankind. We wish to throw open as many markets as possible, to bring as many consumers and producers into contact as possible; to throw open the great natural highways, the great waterways of this great continent. We wish that trade should pursue its unchecked and unhindered course upon the Niger, the Nile, and the Zambesi."

Regarding effective occupation, it was laid down at the Berlin Conference that occupations on the *coast* of Africa, in order to be valid, must be effective, and any new occupation on the *coast* must be formally notified to the Signatory Powers for the purpose of enabling them, if need be, to make good any claim of their own.

[1] J. S. Keltie, *The Partition of Africa*, p. 293.

Article 35 of the General Act restricts to possessions on the *coasts* of Africa the obligation to ensure the establishment of authority sufficient to protect existing rights. A curious point is that the refusal of the Powers to extend the principle of " effective occupation " to the *interior* was solely due to the representations of the French plenipotentiary, Baron de Courcel.

Sir George Goldie, in the *New Review*, June 1897, says : " The principle for which Baron de Courcel thus successfully contended was, in my humble opinion, imperative in the interests of Europe, and of France in particular.   The early effective occupation of the vast African continent, with three times the area of Europe, being impracticable, the necessity of effective occupation to validate treaty rights would have destroyed the foundations of the principle of spheres of influence, but for which a general European war could hardly have been averted.   As regards France, that Power had in 1885, and still has to-day, within her spheres of influence a larger unoccupied area in the interior of Africa than any other colonising nation.   To-day, as in 1885, France is the power which can least afford to throw over the principle propounded by her in Berlin, and agreed to by the fourteen Signatory States.   Her existing rights behind the British colonies of the Gambia, Sierra Leone, and the Gold Coast have been entirely based on treaties with native potentates.   On this ground she has successfully relied in all the West African arrangements made during the last ten years with the British Government."

The only demarcation possible between the two Powers is a line cutting the river, and it is difficult to understand of what use it was fixing this point at Say, if expeditions from the south are to strike the river below it, and seize any place they find unoccupied ; and it would be a parallel case if the British colonies on the West Coast were to send expeditions into the *Hinterland* belonging to the French, who have there so effectually blocked all farther extension on our part.

A few days after the first rumour was received of the French being at Illo, the news was confirmed in a decisive manner by the arrival of messengers at Ilorin, with a letter from the King of Bussa informing Sir George Goldie that the expedition had descended along the river bank from Illo to Bussa, and had now occupied the capital, and asking urgently for assistance.

At this time the Bussa country was actually under the protection of the Royal Niger Company, and garrisons were occupying Fort Goldie, $27\frac{1}{2}$ miles up the Niger from Jebba, and another place called Leaba, 30 miles farther north. The king had expressed a wish that the capital should not be occupied by soldiers, owing to the difficulties always arising about the women, and it was in accordance with this wish that Bajibo and Leaba were selected as military posts in the Bussa country.

Bussa itself is 320 miles from Say by the river. To arrive there the French marched due north from Dahome, passing within a stone's - throw of Nikki, where Captain Lugard, specially sent out, made a treaty the year before, and through a country ruled over by native chiefs who are in constant touch with and subsidised by the Company. It was then necessary to march eastward, and they eventually struck the river at Illo, from which they descended to Bussa. All this time every available soldier and European in the Niger territories was engaged in the operations against the states of Nupe and Ilorin. Even then, at the close of the Bida expedition, and on hearing of the French at Illo, it would have been possible to postpone the march to Ilorin and take possession of Bussa with the excellently organised and already well-tried force, had not Sir George Goldie on leaving England pledged himself to abstain from any operations north of Jebba, so as to avoid prejudicing negotiations between the English and French Governments.

The French took a most unfair advantage of this pledge.   It is only too plain that these aggressions on their part must some day lead to an unfortunate collision between their troops and those in the Niger territories, much the same as occurred in 1892 behind Sierra Leone when the English forces engaged in fighting the Sofas were attacked at dawn by an enemy which proved to be French native troops; and white officers, besides many of the black soldiers, were killed on both sides before the conflict could be stopped.

If Bussa formed part of the *Hinterland* of Dahome, there might be some reason for their eagerness to obtain it; but, as will be seen from the map, it is right away in the *Hinterland* of the colony of Lagos and the Royal Niger Company, which, with the Niger Coast Protectorate, will no doubt at a future date be welded together as one great English possession under the same administration.   The meridian of Say agrees with the frontier between Lagos and the French possessions in Dahome, which was arranged previously in 1889, but which was carefully delimited in 1896 from the coast to the 9th parallel of latitude —a distance of 170 miles, following for the last few miles the Ocpara River.

Mr. Fowler, who was a member of the British Com-

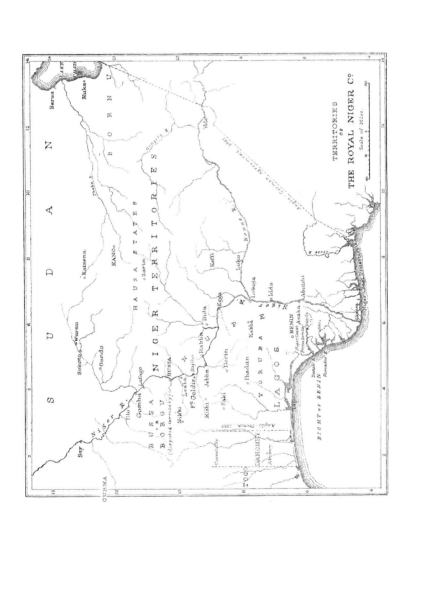

TERRITORIES
OF
THE ROYAL NIGER C°.

Scale of Miles

mission to settle the frontier, says: "The frontier up to the 9th parallel is so clearly defined that it is quite impossible for any French officer or expedition to have crossed into the Lagos *Hinterland* without intending to do so." The 9th parallel does not form a boundary of any sort, and it only happens to be the limit to which the frontier has as yet been accurately delimited. Yet the French expeditions, on reaching the corner formed by the two lines, seem to think they have a right to go where they please, and, as a rule, wheel directly to the right, if they have not done so before, into the country from which Lagos—an English colony long before the conquest of Dahome was even thought of—draws its trade.

The present Lagos-Dahome frontier, if continued, as no doubt was the intention, passing west of Nikki, would strike the Niger a little north of the 12th parallel and 60 miles south of Say. It will be seen that the debatable territory is in the shape of a triangle, contained by the Middle Niger, the meridian of Say, and the 9th parallel. It can in no case be called *Hinterland* belonging to any French possession, and if surrendered to France will simply form a wedge extending into the side of our fine, and up to the present compact, possessions in the area of Africa watered by the Niger and Benuë Rivers.

XX

ILORIN EXPEDITION

ON 10th February we started on our march south, along the route traversed by Mr. Fowler in his survey. Making a short march the first day, on the next we reached a village called Bodi Sadu, which forms a regular sort of custom-house for taking toll from the traders who pass along the road. Tighe, who was with the advance-guard, heard a low growl in the grass close to the camping-ground, and saw a lion trotting off through the bush.

The country was frightfully burnt-up and dry at this time of the year, and the difficulties of marching were considerable. A sandy path led through low trees and bushes, and across at times open spaces covered with dried-up grass, and the aspect of the country during the first part of the march was very similar to the waterless plateau called the Haud in Somaliland, over which I had travelled in 1894. The camp at Bodi Sadu was pitched just beyond a small native village, on the stony slope leading down to the watercourse, where still a few little pools of water were to be found. The stony ground reflected the burning rays of the sun, and three officers, including Dr. Craster, were affected by the intense heat during the day.

All food had to be carried, and the water in some

places was very bad. On the third day, beyond an important village called Lanwa, the only water we could get to drink was unfit even to wash in, and very soon clogged all the filters brought to bear on it.

At first we travelled due south, close to a range of hills which was on our right, whilst on the other side lay the wooded valley in which runs the river Osin, flowing into the Niger not far from Jebba. Several dry watercourses were crossed, and on the 12th we camped at a small stream called the Orere. The country improves vastly as one enters it and ascends on to the high ground, and there are some very fine trees—acacia trees with red fruit, and baobab, also a species of poplar. The villages are often surrounded by rubber trees and small banana groves,—the houses themselves being untidy and tumble-down looking, and very different from the neat huts in the Nupe country. In the centre of the village there was usually an open space with some fine shady trees, which formed the market-place. The natives were all clothed in varying shades of blue cloth, native-dyed, and were ugly and unprepossessing.

The first large village we came to was Lanwa, which was thronged with natives, who appeared friendly, and brought in milk.

We were delayed for one and a half hours here owing to the water question, and eventually camped 3½ miles farther on, at about 1 p.m.

On the 14th February we arrived at the Arebi River, now in the dry season only a river in name, and even the pools of water had to be searched for. This was one of the most enjoyable marches I have made in Africa. Starting about sunrise, in the cool of the morning, we passed through a lovely country more

like an English park than anything else, up and down
gentle hills where there was no thick undergrowth to
hinder us, and sometimes close to high rocks, near which
a small village was usually planted as if for protection.
The front of the column halted at a large village
called Illaga, or Ladogba, at 8.30, to allow the rear
of the column to close up, and for the usual rest. A
small stream bordered by banana groves ran past the
village and made the valley look green and flourishing.
At our camp at the Arebi River we were already
1100 feet above the sea, having ascended 700 feet
from the Niger at Jebba.

Two messengers arrived from the Emir in the
afternoon, and great interest was excited as to whether
it was to be peace or war.

The Governor had written to the Emir already, to
say that as the latter did not wish the force to enter
Ilorin he would meet him at 5 p.m. on the following
day at the river Asa, outside the town. He now
learnt that the attitude of the Ilorin army was very
hostile, and that the Emir would be probably forced
by the leading baloguns to join in an attack on the
expedition. This was no doubt the reason why
orders were issued at night for the surprise-lights and
wire to be placed round the camp, and for rockets to
be fired at intervals.

The sun was not yet up, and the light was still
dim and uncertain when we started on our march on
the 15th instant, with Nos. 3 and 5 Companies forming
the advance-guard with the Governor.

As we went on along the road to Ilorin the country
began to assume more and more of a park-like appearance. As it was, on approaching Bida, the tangled
bush and undergrowth gave place to rolling plains

dotted about with fine trees of all sorts, and we passed little villages hidden away in banana groves. At the first few villages we passed the natives remained at their doors, and everything seemed perfectly peaceful; but as we went on, and came down the gentle slope towards the Oyon River, several events combined to rouse our suspicions. Men on the road ran out of the way on our approach, disregarding the shouts of our guide to come nearer. Natives could be seen peering at us from behind trees and houses at a safe distance, and beyond, near the banks of the river, there seemed to be a large number of mounted men, conspicuous in their white tobes.

No shot had yet been fired, and it was hard to believe the Ilorins were really going to oppose us, after receiving the news of the victory at Bida over a much more powerful State—the most important Sultanate in the kingdom of Sokoto.

We were still marching along in single file, but at 8.15 a.m. matters had become so threatening that the head of the column halted, and Major Arnold ordered square to be formed on No. 5 Company, with which were Captain Sangster and Lieutenant Pereira.

A half company of No. 3 Company, Lieutenants Burdon and Tighe, which with No. 5 Company had constituted the advance - guard, formed up on each flank as part of the side faces. The column was well closed up, and square was formed very rapidly as the successive detachments arrived and were put into their places, the carriers being herded up in the centre.

Sir George Goldie used the utmost forbearance before giving the word to fire, and every possible chance had been given for peaceful negotiations, when it became evident that, if the square was to be saved, fire must be opened at once. A body of 300 to 400 horsemen, who had collected unperceived behind us, and followed up the rear - guard, were now charging through the thin burnt-up grass, which, though no obstacle to their movements, had effectually concealed their approach. This force, which must have been commanded by one of the four " baloguns," or generals of the Ilorin army, was evidently carrying out a preconceived plan of attacking us, in conjunction with three other large bodies of the enemy's cavalry in our front and on the flanks, who had up to that time kept hidden away as much as possible, and with whom were all the footmen.

The action was brought on precipitately by this body of cavalry, and there can be no doubt that the intention was to draw us on in column of route to the Oyon River, where the main body of the enemy was posted, and then to fall upon us from all sides.

Forming square upset all their arrangements, and in the contest which ensued they showed a lamentable disregard of the deadly effect of modern firearms. One could not but admire the daring courage these fanatical Fulah horsemen displayed in galloping up close to the square, which they did at the opening of the fight, in the face of a serried line of fixed bayonets and the very muzzles of rifle barrels.

They waited too long, and lost their opportunity. If the charge had been made whilst the square was still unformed and the carriers were hastening up from the rear, the result would have been disastrous.

Lieutenant Gillespie with his company, and Lieutenant Margesson with a Maxim, who formed the rear-guard, had only just time to form up on the rear face of the square when they saw this large body of the enemy's horse coming down on them. As no

FULAH HORSEMEN CHARGING

order had yet been given, they reserved their fire till the very last minute; and so close were the enemy, that the leader, a little in front of the rest, was heard exhorting his men to charge into the square, which at that time had several gaps in it, and was greeted by jeers and shouts from the Hausa soldiers.

In another moment the order to fire was given, a deadly volley rang out, and the leader fell out of the saddle a lifeless corpse, and paid the penalty for his rash act, with several of his followers and horses. The remainder swerved round both flanks of the square, receiving a deadly fire from both faces at a distance of only about 50 to 100 yards. It was an exciting time for those on the front face, and, looking back, one could see glimpses of horses falling and men reeling in the saddles, through little openings in the dense cloud of smoke overhanging the square. When this lifted, the Ilorin horsemen were seen flying in all directions, leaning down at full gallop to escape the iron hail which was pursuing them: poor dead and wounded horses were lying about round the square, and the peaceful countryside was transformed into a scene of battle and destruction.

Few troops would have behaved as coolly as the Hausas did under the circumstances, and there is no doubt that they had derived an incalculable benefit from the fighting at Bida; they had learnt to rely on themselves and their white officers; to feel and know the power firearms and discipline gave them over undisciplined masses; and, finally, they were proud of themselves and their achievements. No one could have shown greater *sang froid* in what were really rather exciting circumstances.

The generalship of our opponents was bad, and
18

nowhere was this more evident than in our immediate front, where down in the hollow by the Oyon River was drawn up the main body of the enemy, offering a splendid target to the big guns and the Maxims. The main attack, however, at first, after the cavalry action in the rear, came from the right front, where one of the baloguns was posted with his corps in some rather thick grass and bushes. He advanced them from here, and made a demonstration on our right flank, covered by a very ill-directed fire from his riflemen. Lieutenant M'Clintock with his company, and Bird with his Maxim, who completed this face of the square with the half company of No. 3 already in position, opened a very heavy fire on them, and soon drove them back to a safer distance.

Firing became general after this, and Lieutenants Neale and Day with their Maxims also did considerable execution on the enemy, who were holding a small village and the surrounding bushes to the left front.

After the fire had cleared the ground in the immediate vicinity, Major Arnold ordered the square to advance. Whether owing to the previous practice in marching in square before Bida, or the small size of it —only 80 yards in length and less in breadth, which will give an idea of the smallness of the forces engaged on our side—the square advanced at a great pace, $2\frac{1}{2}$ to 3 miles an hour, with the carriers and guns in the centre.

Two halts were made, and Captain Sangster with No. 5 Company had a great deal to do in clearing the way for the advance. The Maxims on the front face also opened fire with great effect. Masses of the enemy, noticeable in their white garments, could be still seen pouring down the road from Ilorin, evidently intending to dispute the passage of the river Oyon, where, behind the crossing, two large brown rocks covered with boulders and stunted bushes rose up about 100 yards in rear of it, offering splendid cover for the enemy's riflemen.

The two 7-pounders, under the direction of Under-Officer Bosher, now opened fire, aimed on the enemy's reserves, drawn up on the high ground south of the stream. Shrapnel shells with percussion fuses were used, and must have sadly disturbed our opponents. Two common shells were also fired, bursting right among them.

A second advance was made to within 400 yards of the river, and fire was again opened, which had the effect of driving the enemy right back to the top of the ridge opposite and away from the river. It was now 10.30 a.m, and the fight had lasted two hours. Camp was formed here, it being considered too late to fight our way to Ilorin and capture the town in the same day.

Major Cunningham with Nos. 1 and 5 Companies advanced to force the passage of the river, which was still held by a few of the enemy's skirmishers. It was a pretty sight, and we from camp were able to watch all that went on. One good volley rang out from No. 5, which was drawn up in line on our side of the river, and No. 1 crossed and formed up on the other side. The two companies then advanced in line to the right of the road, Lieutenant Bird with his Maxim marching along the road to the left of the line.

Large masses of the enemy could be seen in the trees and bushes near the crest awaiting their approach, and it was at first feared that, concealed by the

wooded fringe on the high ground, they would surprise the reconnoitring force.   The 7-pounders opened
fire over the heads of the advanced companies at
2000 yards, and several shells burst right among the
trees, from which the enemy were seen retreating in
haste.

The Maxim also opened fire on some of the enemy
slowly retiring along the road; little spurts of dust
showed the shots were a little underneath, and with a
little more elevation it made very good practice.   After
their forces had been driven over the crest, Major
Cunningham changed direction to the right, and made
for the village in this direction recently occupied, and
from which a few Ilorins were seen departing in haste.
A detour was then made round to the right, and the
force returned to camp at 11.30.   Our casualties were
very small, and it is difficult to understand why the
Ilorins did not make better use of the numbers of
breech-loading rifles, amongst which there were even
some curious magazine rifles, or of the quantity of
ammunition which they possessed, and which was
afterwards captured in the town.

Lieutenant Carroll was wounded in the mouth by a
slug.   Lieutenant Festing's horse was shot, and a
headman of carriers was wounded.   The latter had
been very warlike, and was the amusement of the
whole camp.   He was a little, grey-haired old man, in
charge of a company of carriers, and had been used to
strut about with a great air of bravado, saying, "If
you give me one hundred men, I send them all to
hell!"

The enemy's losses were heavy.   Curiously enough,
one of the horsemen who was killed in the first charge
was recognised as one of the Emir's two messengers the

day before. These two men had probably been the cause of the Ilorins' determination to fight us, as, on their return to the capital from our camp, they had brought in news how small the expedition was. To a casual observer in the afternoon the force would have appeared even smaller than it really was. Soldiers were hidden away under trees and shelters, to escape the fierce rays of the sun. Some of the carriers were probably foraging or bargaining in the villages near. Maxim guns with coverings on would very likely have escaped their attention, and even the 7-pounders with their short barrels were not very imposing-looking guns.

A piquet was posted on the rocks near the river in the afternoon, and Lieutenant Pereira was stationed here with a Maxim gun. Several shots were exchanged with the enemy, who were apparently still defiant, and brought out some old cannon from the town to fire upon us with. It is said that a projectile of some sort was seen moving along the ground like a rabbit.

Soon after the day ended and darkness had set in, the moon was seen rising over the trees, and, by the time the bugle sounded at 9 p.m., and the troops fell in at their posts before lying down to rest, it was a lovely moonlight night, such as one can only see in a tropical country, and very unfavourable for a night attack, for which the Ilorins were noted. Every precaution had been taken to guard against one. The strands of wire were fastened on pickets round the square, and the surprise-lights were attached to trees and posts around. The corners of the square were thrown back somewhat, so as to lessen the space to be guarded, and from now onwards rockets were fired regularly during the night. These rushing fiery comets must have appeared something supernatural to the Ilorins, suddenly expanding into a number of shining stars, and then falling rapidly to the ground.

It was a weird evening, and all around us appeared a circle of fires lit by the enemy, which, however, did not interfere with us at all, as the grass round the camp had been burnt. Cannons were also fired, and drums beaten to frighten us. They were awfully mistaken in their ideas of our tactics, and confident that we were going to retire the next day: men came down and shouted to the piquet on the rocks, that they would follow us back to Jebba and drive the remnant of us into the river. A certain amount of firing went on from the piquet at the crossing of the Oyon River, which was under a native corporal, and did very good work in this responsible position. Objects coming over the sand in the moonlight made a very good target for the soldiers posted in the rocks. About 11 p.m., after a fusilade from the rocks, a wounded Ilorin was brought in on a stretcher, who, on being interrogated, said he and some others had been sent out to look for one of the chiefs who was missing. It is nearly certain that this was the leader of the charge early in the day, as he was very richly dressed, and his horse was covered with fine trappings.

Soon after midnight there was an alarm, and the force stood to arms, with the exception of an officer in charge of a Maxim gun, who slept peacefully through the turmoil.

Réveillé sounded at 4.30 sharp the next morning, 16th February, one of the coldest we had yet experienced, the thermometer standing at 58° Fahr., which is very low in this climate, and we went shivering to breakfast in the fading moonlight.

Tents were struck, and as soon as it was light two

companies moved down and crossed the river, quite shallow at this time of year and running in a sandy bed, and halted on the farther side, where square was to be formed.

The carriers came trooping across with their loads, and by 6.30 a.m. everyone was in position. The bugle sounding a " G " was the signal for Maxim guns to be dismounted, and for all loads to be taken up preparatory to moving off. Major Arnold then sounded the advance, and the square moved steadily on, led by Lieut. M'Clintock with No. 1 Company, with its left resting on the road, and a Maxim gun on each flank.

A white mist at this early hour of the morning veiled all our movements from the enemy, and we moved on unseen towards the summit of the ridge, about a mile and a half distant. The ground, ploughed into ridges for cultivation, made marching difficult, and every now and then a porter would collapse with his load, but still the general advance was excellent. A small scouting party of Ilorins retired calmly and unconcernedly before us, only 200 yards distant, and the drumming and blowing of horns now commenced along their position, which seemed to extend round our left flank. The mist began to lift, and glimpses of horsemen and footmen became more distinct. Fire was opened on us, and the square halted. The Maxim guns at the corners were immediately mounted, and opened fire with great rapidity, together with one of the 7-pounders, which had been dragged along the road. Although the target was an uncertain one, owing to the light, yet the effect was instantaneous, and a general retreat commenced on all sides. It was only possible to fire the Maxim by having someone at a little distance off to watch the first two or three shots, and then, after the proper elevation and direction had been obtained, to clamp it tight and continue firing. Almost from the first the black powder and the stillness of the air caused a dense cloud of smoke to overhang the gun.

The enemy were massed together more than they had been the day before, and in this manner the guns did tremendous execution. They really worked wonders in this campaign, and there were no jams except one or two caused by cartridges, which were easily remedied. Mr. Maxim personally superintended the sending out of the six new Maxim guns and the ammunition for them, and Lieutenant Margesson, who had been trained at the factory, inspected them and took them to pieces periodically. If used much in one day, it was only necessary to clean them out thoroughly when opportunity offered; and of course water was a necessity, and was always carried by one of the gun detachment in the water-carrier for the purpose.

The Maxim guns were used during the expedition much the same as artillery, and the Hausa soldiers really formed an escort to these guns, and rarely fired, except at short ranges, to keep off cavalry.

If a carriage could be devised whereby the gun could be carried for a certain distance by two or three men, mounted and ready for action, it would be invaluable. During the retirement in square at Bida, it was found impossible to carry the gun mounted, owing to its being so unwieldy, and there was always a danger of being rushed before the gun got into action.

The Ilorins were demoralised, and only once more did they stand—on the top of the ridge in front of Ilorin. Here a big tree with a village formed the centre of their position, and the latter, surrounded by a good mud wall and full of trees, offered a splendid position for their riflemen, with a good line of retreat, but was, strange to say, unoccupied.

The rattle of the Maxims again filled the air, accompanied by the booming of the 7-pounder, and the sheets of lead which must have poured over them from these deadly guns completed the disaster, and a *sauve qui peut* ensued. Their leaders were heard exhorting them to remain firm; but it was no good, and little groups of horse were seen galloping about all over the country, and masses flying along the road to Ilorin.

We advanced over the ridge, passing close to the left of the village, which formed the centre of their position, and which was set on fire. Marks of their camp fires could be seen on all sides, and they had occupied this ridge the night before.

After passing through some clumps of trees, we came in sight of the town, which lies on the farther side of the Aza River, evidently covering an enormous extent of ground, but not nearly so fine in appearance as Bida. On all sides lay an open plain, broken here and there by a small village and some cultivation, and perhaps two or three isolated palm trees, and to the north the great Sobi rock formed a prominent feature of the landscape.

We bore slightly to the right, and at 8.15 halted on the slope, still keeping the old square formation. Away to the left the Ilorin horsemen were streaming through one of the gates into the town, and their pace was still further accelerated by some shots from the Maxim at about 1400 yards.

Soon after, a white flag was hoisted up near one of the gateways, and firing ceased. Sir George Goldie rode forward, escorted by a company, to within a few hundred yards of the town, and waited here a long time for anyone to come out. His interpreter, Esa, one of the finest blacks I have ever seen, and looking very picturesque in his big Nupe straw hat, flowing garments, and red leather riding-boots, rode up close to the walls, and at last induced two men to come out.

These turned out to be Hausa traders, and it appeared the flag had been hung out by the Hausa people outside their own quarter, and was in no wise a sign of submission on the part of the Emir. However, the men were sent back with an ultimatum to the Emir, that if no answer was received in two hours, the bombardment would commence, and the walls of his palace would be brought down over his head.

In the meantime crowds of people could be seen moving across the open space in the town to the right, where there seemed to be a break in the main wall. Most of these were heavily laden, and were evidently carrying their goods and chattels away.

No answer being received, the force moved off in a southerly direction for a mile and a half to a better position on some rising ground, only 400 yards from the walls. There was little to be feared now from their cavalry, and the square proceeded to unfold itself into a long serpentine line, as companies and transport companies alternately filed out in column of route, and marched parallel to the wall to the new position, affording a curious spectacle to the defenders in the town, who up to that time had only seen us in square, which gave a very small idea of our numbers. We passed several gardens, irrigated by little streams running into the Aza River, and amongst other vegetables were onions, radishes, and potatoes, so that we looked forward to having a good dinner.

The only explanation of the stupidity of the Ilorins in thus refusing to avail themselves of our many efforts at negotiation, is that the chiefs and the Emir were at complete variance with one another, and that they could not believe till the last minute that we should enter the town with such a small force.

Posted on the rising ground, the little battery consisting of the two 7-pounders opened fire on the town. There was only a very limited amount of ammunition left, and great care was necessary that no shell should be wasted. The first shell was fired at the exterme range, about 3000 yards in a westerly direction, and the next one at 2500 yards, and so on, the range being reduced after each discharge until it came down to 1000 yards, where the high thatched roof of the Emir's palace, standing out by itself among a clump of dark green trees, formed a good target. Common shell and double shell were used, and most of these effectually set fire to something where they exploded. A few shells burst prematurely very high up, forming little white clouds in the air, owing to the fuses being affected by the great heat. Although quite harmless, the moral effect of these explosions in mid-air, and seen from all parts of the town, must have been considerable. Detachments went forward to the wall to fire incendiary rockets, a few shots being fired at them by the defenders, and soon the ill-fated capital was in flames in several places. The fire, fanned by the strong Harmattan wind that was blowing, spread with great rapidity, little pieces of lighted thatch being carried from roof to roof.

The Hausa colony had now taken refuge with us

with their belongings, and amongst them the soldiers recognised many of their own relations, — fathers, mothers, brothers, and sisters,—the scene in rear of the position where they were all collected being a very strange one, and a perfect babel of sounds went up from it. These Hausas, most of them peaceful traders, had wished to join us before, but had been forcibly prevented from leaving the town.

It was after midday, and soldiers and carriers were all busily engaged preparing savoury dishes from the numerous sheep and goats which they had looted from villages quite close. Two or three captured horses were brought in by enterprising looters, and one of them, Mr. Watt's syce, armed with a long spear and with a big straw hat, rode round and round the camp, acting the buffoon, to the immense delight of all the blacks, some of whom followed him round shouting and cheering. One of the buglers also rode in on a nice horse, very pleased with himself, and proceeded to swagger round the camp. It was an intensely hot day, and three tents were put up behind the position for officers to lunch in, from where we could watch the curious scene that was going on. On joining my Maxim-gun detachment after lunch, I found my corporal in charge. Osman Kano had apparently discovered most of his own family, and introduced me with great glee to his father, mother, and other relations, whom· he had packed away in a corner, where they had erected a temporary shelter with cloths and sticks against the sun. They had come from the north a long way to trade in Ilorin, and had been about four weeks in the town, from which they had barely escaped with their lives, owing to the hostility of the inhabitants.

In the afternoon, to our astonishment, we saw what

looked like a white woman walking up the slope towards the camp, with very scanty garments on. A certain amount of excitement was created among the officers, who went out to see her arrive, but she turned out to be an albino, and her absolute repulsiveness soon put everyone to flight.

A great deal of the northern and the southern portion of the town had been set on fire by shells, and the bombardment ceased. The two little 7-pounder mountain-guns had only just lasted out long enough to do what was required of them, and the carriages of both of them were broken. If further resistance had been encountered, it would have been a serious matter.

Several of our wounded adversaries were brought into camp and treated by Surgeons Craster and Cargill, who accompanied this expedition. The enemy's losses in the two days' fighting were severe. From information afterwards obtained, it is certain that over 200 horsemen alone were killed, and the proportion of footmen to cavalry was apparently about six to one.

At 3.30 p.m., all resistance being at an end, Sir George Goldie marched into the town at the head of the column, preceded by the buglers. Entering by the Hausa gate, we marched along an avenue about ten yards wide, bordered by a neat fence, and then, winding between still smoking walls and thatched roofs, we reached a large open space with shady trees in front of the Emir's enclosure.

The first thing we noticed on entering the square was the gruesome spectacle of the corpse of some malefactor, or, as was asserted by some people, a Hausa, who had probably been executed with untold cruelties, and exposed on a heap of stones, with his legs and arms hacked off as a warning to others.

The destruction of the palace—rather a misnomer for this collection of rude stone buildings—was indeed complete, and the market-place, where we pitched our tents, was still filled with the smoke and smell of burning. The archway forming the main entrance had not yet fallen in, and, stepping quickly over the hot stones, I entered the inner court, from which again several small enclosures led to a large open grass space within the outer walls of the palace, where the Governor afterwards took up his quarters. The walls were very massive, and little harm had been done to them by the fire.

The force, reduced as it was in numbers of both officers and men, had crushed a power which at one time it was said would require many black troops, and even a white battalion, to do.

A curious episode was the fact of the "fall in" for the guard being sounded that evening in the market-place of Ilorin by an ex-bugler of the Lagos Constabulary, a few hours previously a slave in the same town, and still with the chains on his legs.

Everyone soon settled down and made themselves comfortable after the hard day's work in the sun; and it was curious to think that, only fourteen days before, we had been occupying a similar market-place in Bida.

XXI

Ilorin

O N the morning after the entry into Ilorin, detachments were sent out in all directions to stop any further looting and burning, with orders, if possible, to get into communication with the chief inhabitants, to reassure them and persuade them to return to the town.

This was no easy task, and the destructive effect of the shells in this enormous town had been very complete; the northern portion, which is more a suburb of the main town, and where a new gateway and outer wall had been lately erected, escaped being set on fire, and the line of houses within half a mile of the western and north-western *enceinte* were also intact, including a large enclosure belonging to one of the four baloguns. I started off this day with Major Cunningham, Pereira, and twenty men to the western gate, and we inspected the balogun's house *en route*. A covered-in gateway, with a heavy wooden door (made out of three planks), about 9 feet in height, admitted one to a courtyard about 40 yards broad, round which the dwelling-houses were situated. The walls were capitally made, but the whole effect was marred by the untidily - thatched roofs. There were little compartments, with low roofs with raised ledges, probably used to sleep on. The occupants had evidently left in great haste, and things were scattered about pell-mell in all directions ; on the walls were fastened a few gaudy advertisements and pictures obtained from Lagos, and the floor was littered with papers and rubbish of all sorts. Amongst the papers were a number of letters and Hausa documents in Arabic writing. Through a door in the further wall one entered into an inner yard, where a lame horse was tethered, and round it there were more houses, probably for slaves and attendants. There was a curious little pair of miniature leg-irons, such as are used for manacling slaves, fastened in the floor at the main gateway, and it was reported to be a fetish of some kind to ward off the evil spirit.

On nearing the western gate, we passed through some grass fields and banana plantations, where we could see some of the inhabitants mowing. After a great deal of talking and shouting, one or two of them approached nearer, and then others gained confidence and came out behind houses around, until we had quite a respectable gathering. They were told to go and inform their friends that they would not be molested, that the fighting was all over, and they could return to the town.

We discovered several of the carriers hard at work in the furthest outskirts looting, utterly regardless, as usual, of their lives, and the morning was spent hunting them back to camp. They had, perforce, to drop some of their enormous loads when pursued, and preferred this to being captured and beaten.

I collected as many data as possible for making a map of the town, and the next day went out again with Lieutenant Margesson, and twenty men as an escort, when we worked round the southern portion, afterwards making our way to the northern gate.

The town is 9 miles in circumference, and except on the north-east, surrounded by a dilapidated mud wall. From the many gateways, well-used roads lead in all directions across the open grass country outside the town, towards the south to Ogbomosho and Lagos.

To the south, the houses become more detached, and a large extent of meadow-land is enclosed within the outer wall.

Magnificent baobab trees, affording splendid shade, adorn the open spaces in the town. The water supply at this time of year is not first-rate, and there are only some evil-smelling stagnant pools of water at a few of the cross-roads, in addition to the limited number of wells in the town itself, and the water is mostly drawn from the river Aza outside.

Crowds of people were trooping back into the town, and we stopped at one of the farthest gates to watch the continual stream of women, children, etc., returning. I took three or four photographs of them, which unfortunately, like so many others, turned out failures.

On reaching the northern gate, known as the Bodi Osenoagwa, we found we were close to the high Sobi rock, and the ground sloped steeply down to a stream between, which flowed into the Aza River.

A few palm trees bordered the stream, otherwise the country was entirely open. This gateway was really a very fine one, and the walls on each side were from 12 to 15 feet thick. A rich trader named Doda had a large compound out in this direction.

Although Ilorin is a great Mohammedan town, the mosques, though numerous, are small and insignificant.

The Ilorins are a Yoruba-speaking people, and it is interesting to record that, according to Captain Mockler Ferryman, a desperate fight occurred in 1840, over

19

exactly the same ground where we fought, between the
Fulahs, who were in possession of the town, and the
Yorubas, aided by a small contingent of Borgus. The
latter were gaining the victory after a prolonged contest,
when their leader fell, and the pagans, losing heart
owing to his death, were eventually utterly routed.

The Emir and his baloguns had fled to the villages
far and wide, and were in a sorry plight, as only 30
miles to the south lay the Ibadan country and the Lagos
frontier, over which they had no mercy to expect; and
to the west the pagan tribes, in the direction of Borgu,
would have been only too glad to take advantage of
the defeat of their long-standing enemies. Sir George
Goldie, who had been in communication with the
Emir, was able to induce him to come in, and surrender himself with the four baloguns, on the 18th
inst. It was a great piece of diplomacy, and solved
the difficult problem of leaving an established government behind instead of the utter chaos which would
have ensued, if the column had been obliged to march
out and leave the town without one. Even if the old
Yoruba dynasty had been reinstated, as it was before
the Fulah conquest, a strong garrison would have had
to be left behind to hold the town and disperse the
bands of Fulahs. If no settlement had been come to
we should probably have had to remain in Ilorin all
through the wet season from April to October, not a
bright prospect; and one must be thankful that the
Emir and his baloguns showed such confidence as to
surrender themselves. They came in about 1 p.m.
with a few followers, to make their peace with the
Governor. Mounted on their small horses, covered
with picturesque saddle-cloths and head-collars, they
presented a curious appearance, and the Emir himself

looked an extraordinary object, with his head wrapped up in several folds of white cloth, forming a great bunch behind the back of his head, and completely covering his face with the exception of his eyes and nose, the whole crowned by an enormous native straw hat, such as is worn in this country. They were mostly dressed in plain white robes, according to the Fulah custom. The Dogali, or Lord High Executioner, a most villainous looking individual, wore a green robe, perhaps a badge of his office.

On being taken to the Governor they threw themselves on their knees before him, and showed the most utter submission.

During the interview, and the parade of the troops which followed, they were very nervous and apprehensive of what might happen to them. The troops were drawn up in the square, where the British flag was flying, and they sat down on a mat laid out near the table, close to which the guns were drawn up, so as to make as much show as possible. Cunningham also donned a red tunic for the occasion, which, with a white helmet, formed a dazzling combination in comparison with our much-worn khaki uniforms, and the natives must have thought him a very big man indeed.

The treaty was read out to the Emir, and was as follows:—

TREATY OF ILORIN.

This Treaty is made on the 18th February 1897 of the Christian Era, and the 15th day of Ramadán, in the year 1314 since the Hegira. The Treaty is between Sir George Goldie, Governor for the Royal Niger Company, and the Emir Suliman, son of the former Emir Alihiu, for his chiefs and people for ever.

1. The Company will recognise Suliman as Emir of Ilorin.

2. The Emir Suliman recognises that Ilorin is entirely under the protection and power of the Company.

3. He will obey all such directions in respect of his Government as the Company may give him from time to time.

4. The Emir Suliman agrees to make no war without the consent of the Company, and to accept such frontier line between Ilorin and Lagos as the Company may decide.

5. The Emir Suliman agrees to take every step in his power to prevent the further introduction of gin and rum into his country from Lagos, and to destroy all the gin and rum that may be found in his country.

6. All previous Treaties are abrogated, but Ilorin remains under the protection of Her Majesty, the Queen of Great Britain and Ireland, and Empress of India.

7. I, Suliman, Emir of Ilorin, hereby accept this Treaty, and I, George Taubman Goldie, Governor of the Royal Niger Company, also hereby accept it.

(Signed)   SULIMAN (in Arabic).

,,   GEORGE TAUBMAN GOLDIE.

We, the undersigned, declare that the Emir of Ilorin, Suliman, has in our presence declared, through two interpreters, that he has perused and understands the Hausa (Arabic) copy of this Treaty, and that he has had the English copy fully explained to him.

We declare also, that the Governor, Sir George Goldie, and the Emir Suliman, duly affixed their signatures to all the copies in our presence, this 18th February, 1897.

(Signed)   G. CUNNINGHAM, Major, Derby Regiment.

,,   W. D. BIRD, Lieut., 2nd, The Queen's Regiment.

,,   C. F. S. VANDELEUR, Lieut., Scots Guards.

,,   A M'CLINTOCK, Lieut., Seaforth Highlanders.

After the ceremony the Emir had another private interview with the Governor, in which a great many important matters were discussed, and then retired grateful and glad at having got so easily out of the desperate and hopeless situation, into which he and his baloguns had reduced themselves. It was interesting to hear their account of the fight; and they allowed to losing 200 horsemen during the contest on the 15th

and 16th. The Maxim guns impressed them more than
the 7-pounders, and they admit to having a particular
dread of the guns with the handles.

Everything having been arranged satisfactorily, in
accordance with the celerity which characterised these
operations throughout, the force marched out of Ilorin
the next day, 19th February, at daybreak, only sixty-
three hours after entering the town at the close of the
bombardment. As soon as everyone had cleared out of
the square, the captured gunpowder was blown up, and a
loud explosion rent the air.

I was with the rear-guard this day, and after passing
out of the town through the Hausa gate, the road was at
first blocked by crowds of Hausa people — traders,
refugees, and slaves, carrying their goods in baskets on
their heads, and on donkeys—who intended to accompany the column.   Numbers of slaves had come into the
camp at Ilorin to have their chains knocked off their
legs.

We camped at the Arebi River, after an extremely
hot march, the thermometer registering 97° F. in the
shade, during the middle of the day ; one halt was made
at the Oyon River, where it was interesting to see the
crowds of people streaming by on their way to the
Niger.   Some of the loads carried by them were
enormous, and must have weighed fully eighty to
one hundred lb. At every few hundred yards little
groups of men and women were sitting under shady
trees to rest themselves on the journey, their loads
lying on the ground near them. Owing to the knowledge
gained of the road, and the watering places, the
return march of 52 miles was much quicker, and we
reached Jebba in four days. Thousands of people must
have accompanied us, and several recruits were obtained

on the way—men who had been brought as slaves to Ilorin from the interior of Hausaland, and who now found relations and friends amongst the successful soldiery.

On his way back the Governor received the following amusing letter from the newly reappointed Emir of Ilorin.

" I thank you very much for recognising me as a king—may God recognise you as the Governor of the Queen !

" I wish you to know that all the slaves in the town, belonging to me and my people, ran away with your men, and I am afraid they will not come back again to their masters. I therefore beseech you, in the name of God, to send back these people to me, if you please, when my messengers are coming back ; I hold your feet. There are robbers in the town raiding and molesting the people ; I want you to give me permission to judge them as before, if you please."

Mr. Wallace and the steamers were waiting for us at Jebba, having been engaged in important work on the river ; a few Nupe chiefs who still held out had been crushed, and a large portion of the Markum's followers and soldiers had been transferred from the southern to the northern bank at Kosoji (Kusagi).

Some of the Hausa people who had come with us were ferried over in canoes to the northern bank to return to their homes, others were offered a free passage down to Lokoja, where a new settlement was to be formed about 6 miles further down the river, and close to the spot selected by the ill-fated government expedition of 1841. Curiously enough, although the middle of the dry season, the sky was nearly always dull and overcast at Jebba, and we had several small

ROYAL NIGER CONSTABULARY

showers of rain. Fortunately, the night before we left, there was a clear sky, and I was able to take observations.

We started away at 6 a.m. sharp on the 23rd, in advance of the other steamers, and at noon reached Kosoji, where we stopped for the Governor's interview with the Emir of Lafiagi, another small State on the south side of the river. As the stern-wheeler swung round, it was seen, too late, that the impetus must carry it and the barge filled with soldiers into the bank where all the canoes were lying. Some natives jumped into their canoes quickly, and succeeded in getting out of the way, but the remaining canoes were gradually forced together, and then a dreadful crunching noise ensued as the ill-fated canoes were rapidly transformed into a sort of collapsible berthon boat.

A small guard of honour was landed from the steamers, and the Emir with a large escort of horsemen, arrived about two o'clock ; the latter charged up to where the Governor was sitting, at full gallop, and then reined up their horses on their haunches in a cloud of dust, waving their spears and swords. It was a very pretty sight, and they repeated it twice, some of them colliding and falling off. Like the similar custom in Somaliland and elsewhere, it is a form of salutation and greeting.

The Emir, who was a wizened-looking old man, did not join in this part of the proceedings, and indeed had great difficulty in sitting on his horse at all. He arrived with a great noise of drums and horns, and sat down with his followers in front of the Governor. He was informed of the overthrow of Bida and Ilorin, and exhorted to remain as he had always done, a good friend to the Company, and finally, a fresh treaty was concluded.

While the flotilla now continued the journey to Lokoja, Sir George Goldie returned up river to Fort Goldie, opposite Bajibo, to await an answer from the commander of the French force at Bussa.

The journey down river was a most delightful one, and quite an exciting experience was jumping the sandbanks ; and the stern-wheeler I was on proved so good at this, that it soon distanced the remainder of the fleet, who were lying inert, like crocodiles on the treacherous banks of sand, having to drag themselves off by an iron cable.

On the 24th we passed Egga, an important station of the Royal Niger Company, situated at the bend of the river, quite a fine looking place with rows of warehouses covered with corrugated iron.

On the 24th Major Arnold passed us in the *Bornu*, a fast launch, to try and reach Lokoja that evening, but ran with tremendous force on to a sandbank, from which there was great difficulty in getting off. We reached Lokoja early on the 24th, where it seemed strange to find oneself again after the numerous exciting events which had been crowded together in the last two months. There was naturally great excitement at the return of the troops, and crowds assembled on the banks to see them march up to the barracks. All the wives came down to see their husbands return, and affectionate greetings took place, the former taking charge of their husbands' superfluous luggage and bundles of loot, as the latter marched up through the town, headed by the drums and pipes. People here had received little news of what was going on, and at one time a report that the expedition had been cut up before Bida, and that the Nupes were advancing south on Lokoja, caused a general exodus from the town.

It was on our way down river that we first heard the sad news of the massacre at Benin, which had occurred in the previous month, long after the news had been received in England. At first, hopes were entertained that some use might be made of our force, mobilised and organised as it was with water and land transport; and I understand Sir George Goldie telegraphed as soon as possible, offering the services of the expedition, but it was too late. As we steamed down the Niger we received our long-delayed mails, and curiously enough heard almost on three consecutive days of the massacre, the subsequent expedition to Benin, and capture of the town, events which occupied fully seven or eight weeks, but on the Middle Niger, only a few hundred miles away, were brought within the compass of three days.

We remained at Lokoja four days, and Cunningham and I had leave to go away and shoot, so started in a canoe with our tents and six soldiers, to a place about 6 miles below Lokoja, where we camped.

There were a very few kobus kob and hartebeest about, and we only succeeded in killing one of the former.

Sir George Goldie arrived at Lokoja in his launch, the *Zaria*, on the 1st of March, and in the afternoon met the officers of the expedition, to whom he communicated a telegram of congratulation sent by the Prime Minister ; and the kind message was received with great gratification by everyone, and it was a pleasure to all to know that their efforts had been appreciated at home.

XXII

Patani Expedition

PREPARATIONS for the expedition against the Patani tribe were hastened on. The tribe—which occupied an important position close to the junction of the Forcados branch with the river Niger—had been giving a good deal of trouble of late, and the king's son and chiefs had been already warned several times to desist from the slave raids, which they had been carrying on in the vicinity of their country. In the afternoon of the 2nd March a force of 200 men under Major Arnold, with ten officers, five Maxim guns, four 7-pounders, and two Maxim - Nordenfeldts, embarked on the *Empire* for transport down river.

Idda was reached about midday on the 3rd, and a halt was made here to allow the king to come down to see the Governor ; after a great deal of delay, messages were sent to the effect that the king was frightened by the number of soldiers, and would not come to the river side; and the Governor, escorted by a company, marched up to the village, about 2 miles distant, to interview the king himself. On arriving there he was nowhere to be found, and had fled into the bush. The natives assumed rather a threatening attitude, and the Governor sent a message to the king, that he would have to pay a fine of so many measures of rubber within two months, or else a force would be sent against him.

A good many natives were hanging about among the trees and houses with guns and bows and arrows—which in this country are poisoned with strophantus juice—and the few who were induced to come near had the audacity to have their bows strung and two arrows ready in their hand. The journey down river was resumed on the 4th inst., and the campaign was successfully brought to a close by the submission of the Patanis, who had been already somewhat disconcerted by the news of the victories on the Upper Niger, and whose hearts now failed at the show of force brought against them. Hostages were rendered for their good behaviour in the future, and this truculent tribe may be now considered to have given in to the influence of civilisation, and no more trouble is expected from them in the future.

We stayed at Abutshi on the 5th, one of the Company's principal stations on the Niger, and I went on shore to see the coffee plantations which were started about three years ago. A fairly good crop was obtained last year, but it is a great expense watering the young trees in the dry season.

It was here we first heard the sad news of poor Musters' death on board the mail steamer at Forcados.

Captain Rennie (late 93rd Highlanders) had also died of fever at Asaba, whilst we were away on the expedition.

Steaming on rapidly it seemed like a dream to find oneself again on the mail steamer *Loanda*, which was luckily waiting for us at Forcados. Sir George Goldie and Mr. Wallace followed later in the *Croft* (the Niger Company's steamer).

It was hard to believe that the whole campaign, consisting of a series of different expeditions from different bases on the Niger waterway, had been brought to a successful conclusion in exactly two months from the date on which the force marched out of Lokoja; and the operations had been throughout a triumph of organisation and strategic skill, which counterbalanced the disadvantage of being in a great minority, and the absence of white troops.

That such a success was attained by force of arms, was only made possible by the intimate knowledge of the language and customs of the inhabitants and their rulers possessed by white officials of the Company, who have spent years in this country, such as Mr. Wallace C.M.G., Messrs. Watts and Drew, and by the large staff of educated coloured officials, of whom the Company has made use of to an extent unknown in either British or foreign colonies in West Africa.

The Governor, before leaving Asaba, issued a proclamation, to the effect that the legal status of slavery was abolished in all the Company's possessions.

We were all delighted when the monotonous and deafening noise of the crane ceased on the 8th, as the last of the cargo was hoisted on board, and we at last steamed away from the inhospitable feverish delta of the Niger.

We anchored outside the bar at Lagos for a few hours on the 9th and reached Accra and the Gold Coast on the 11th, where I landed with the Governor, Sir W. Maxwell, and also saw General Sir Francis Scott. Small columns were then being sent out beyond Ashanti in all directions, to try and occupy some of the *Hinterland* which was being so rapidly parcelled out by French and German expeditions.

After a dreary and uneventful voyage along the coast Sir G. Goldie, Pereira, and I landed at Dakar, the French port, to wait for the Messageries steamer S.S. *Brésil*, from Rio Janeiro to Lisbon. Our hopes of going by the railway to St. Louis were, however, spoiled by the *Brésil* being due a very few hours before we could return from St. Louis ; the train only running in the daytime.

An unpleasant experience at Lisbon, was being forced to land in small boats in a rather rough sea on the Lisbon side of the Tagus, whilst our luggage was put in quarantine for thirty-six hours on the other side. I returned to England overland, *viâ* Paris, where I was proud to receive the news, that in the annual awards of the Royal Geographical Society I had been awarded the Murchison Grant for work done in 1894–97.

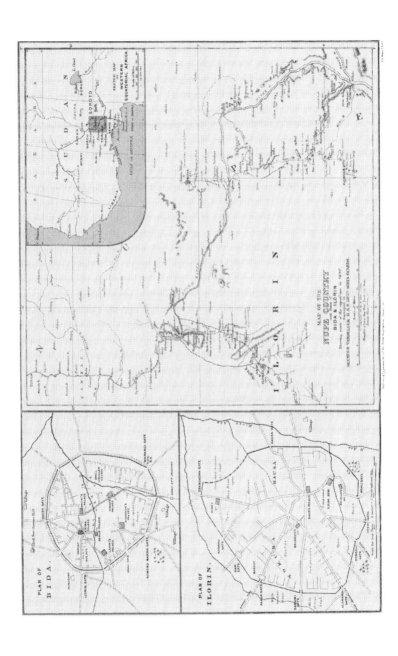

MAP OF THE
NUFE COUNTRY
with the
BIDA & ILORIN
Shewing route of the expedition in 1897.
SEYMOUR VANDELEUR, D.S.O. 1ST SCOTS GUARDS.

PLAN OF
BIDA.

PLAN OF
ILORIN.

INSET MAP
WESTERN
EQUATORIAL AFRICA

APPENDIX I

METEOROLOGICAL OBSERVATIONS TAKEN DURING EXPEDITIONS IN UGANDA AND UNYORO

Day.	Hour.	Place.	Thermometer in Shade.	Maximum Thermometer.	Minimum Thermometer.	Aneroid.	Remarks.
			Fahr.	Fahr.	Fahr.	Inches.	
1894. Dec. 18	3 p.m.	Ntebi Hill	78°	...	...	25.2	Altitude, 4201 ft.
,, 19	6 ,,	Lake shore	67°	...	...	25.5	
,, 20	3 ,,	Taba Camp, Uganda	82°	...	60°	25.32	
,, 20	9.30 ,,	2nd camp on road to Singo	76°	...	...	25.32	
,, 21	5 ,,	3rd ,, ,,	83°.5	...	...	25.15	
,, 22	2 ,,	Fort Raymond, Singo	76°	...	...	25.28	
,, 23	3 ,,	Kamatumbi Camp	82°	...	...	25.05	
,, 24	3 ,,	Kiatabya Camp	79°	...	...	25.28	
,, 25	3 ,,	Nsala Camp	83°	...	...	24.8	
,, 26	3 ,,	Mkandwa Camp	81°	...	...	25.5	
,, 27	6.30 a.m.	,, ,,	60°	...	...	25.55	
,, 27	3 p.m.	Buniga Camp	90°	...	...	25.37	
,, 28	3 ,,	Ntuti Camp	87°	91°	63°	25.65	
,, 28	7 a.m.	At edge of escarpment	...	...	...	24.97	
,, 28	7.40 ,,	In plain	...°	...	...	26.62	
,, 29	6 ,,	Ntuti Camp	67°	...	...	25.76	

Day.	Hour.	Place.	Thermometer in Shade.	Maximum Thermometer.	Minimum Thermometer.	Aneroid.	Remarks.
			Fahr.	Fahr.	Fahr.	Inches.	
1894. Dec. 29	3 p.m.	Kaduma Fort	87°	...	...	25.78	
,, 30	6 a.m.	,, ,,	67°	...	...	25.92	
,, 30	3 p.m.	Camp 2 miles from Baranwa Hill	83°	...	...	25.84	
,, 31	3 ,,	Baranwa Fort	90°	...	...	25.81	
1895. Jan. 1	4 ,,	Fort Hoima	87°	...	...	25.72	Altitude, 3820 ft.
,, 3	4 ,,	,, ,,	85°	93° (In tent.)	60°	25.85	
,, 4	3 ,,	,, ,,	83°	90°	61°	25.85	
,, 5	3 ,,	,, ,,	85°	93°	60°	25.85	
,, 6	4 ,,	,, ,,	83°	96°	59°	25.83	
,, 7	3 ,,	Fort Kitanwa	85°	...	...	25.91	Major Cunningham's aneroid read 25.85 in.
,, 7	7 ,,	Fort Kibero	80°	...	...	27.35	Major Cunningham's aneroid read 27.3 in.
,, 8	3 ,,	Wadelai	87°	95°	70°	27.36	Altitude, 2113 ft.
,, 11	4 ,,	2nd camp above Dufile	90°	...	...	27.36	
,, 16	7 a.m.	Mgerenin	71°	...	...	27.45	
,, 20	7 ,,	Wadelai	...	...	...	27.47	
,, 21	4.30 p.m.		89°.5	...	...	27.34	Major Cunningham's aneroid read 27.37 in.
,, 24	7 ,,	Lukwai's	71°	...	...	27.38	Major Cunningham's aneroid read 27.4 in.
,, 25	7 a.m.	,,	...	...	...	27.46	

	2 p.m.		Temp.	(In verandah of house.)		Barometer	Altitude, 2113 ft.
Jan. 25	2 p.m.	Fort Kibero	...	...	...	27.35	Altitude, 2113 ft.
Feb. 9	...	Fort Hoima	...	83°	64°	...	
,, 10	...	,,	...	...	64°	...	
,, 12	...	Misriandura (Babadongo's)	...	...	...	25.97	3820 ,,
,, 12	...	Top of Msaga Nkasi	...	...	...	25.3	3820 ,,
,, 15	...	Fort Hoima	...	86°	64°	...	
,, 16	...	,,	...	82°	64°	...	
,, 22	7 a.m.	Kivari	...	...	...	25.75	
,, 23	7 ,,	,,	...	...	...	25.8	
,, 24	7 ,,	River Katagurakwa	...	...	...	25.9	
Mar. 1	4.30 p.m.	Kajumbura Is. (Victoria Nile)	...	...	...	26.15	
,, 3	4.30 ,,	Kajumbura Is. (Victoria Nile)	72°	...	...	26.15	
,, 5	7 ,,	Kalianongo	81°	...	...	25.95	,, 3820 ,,
,, 6	4.30 ,,	Mtunzi	75°	...	65°	25.8	
,, 7	4.30 ,,	Mashudi	75°	...	...	25.75	
,, 8	4.30 ,,	Camp in Busindi	77°	...	64°	25.76	
,, 9	5 ,,	Usuju	80°	...	62°	25.75	
,, 10	5 ,,	Kibugumia Hill	81°	...	...	25.65	
,, 11	4 ,,	Lendui	...	...	...	25.0	
,, 12	...	Fort Hoima	68°	89°	64°	25.69	
,, 13	...	,,	...	81°	64°	...	Rain in evening.
,, 14	5.30 ,,	,,	75°	83°	62°	25.85	Heavy rain in afternoon.
,, 15	...	,,	...	84°	61°	...	,, ,,
,, 16	4 ,,	,,	...	87°	66°	25.75	,, ,,
,, 17	...	,,	...	87°	65°	...	
,, 18	...	,,	...	...	...	...	Little rain.

Day.	Hour.	Place.	Thermometer in Shade. Fahr.	Maximum Thermometer. Fahr.	Minimum Thermometer. Fahr.	Aneroid. Inches.	Remarks.
1895. Mar. 19	...	Fort Hoima	...	80°.5	64°	...	
,, 20	4 p.m.	,,	80°	85°.5	59°	25.81	Rain night and afternoon.
,, 21	4 ,,	,,	74°	80°.5	62°	25.88	
,, 22	...	,,	...	82°.5	62°	...	
,, 23	4 ,,	,,	80°	83°	57°	25.85	
,, 24	4 ,,	,,	68°	82°	64°	25.9	Rain in afternoon.
,, 25	4 ,,	,,	82°	85°	60°	25.85	
,, 26	4 ,,	,,	86°	89°	63°	25.8	
,, 27	4 ,,	,,	77°	79°.5	61°	25.78	Heavy rain in morning.
,, 28	4 ,,	,,	80°	83°.5	63°.5	25.79	
,, 29	4 ,,	,,	75°	77°	64°	25.9	Rainy.
,, 30	4 ,,	,,	75°	83°.5	61°	25.85	
,, 31	4 ,,	,,	75°	85°	65°	25.82	Heavy rain in afternoon.
April 1	...	,,	...	83°.5	63°	...	
,, 2	5 ,,	,,	78°	83°.5	61°.5	25.85	
,, 3	4 ,,	,,	80°.5	88°	63°.5	25.81	,, ,,
,, 4	...	,,	...	87°	64°	...	
,, 5	4 ,,	,,	72°	82°	65°	25.82	,, ,,
,, 6	5.30	,,	74°	78°.5	64°	25.85	Little rain in afternoon.
,, 7	5 ,,	,,	72°	83°	64°	25.84	
,, 8	5 ,,	,,	68°	82°	59°	25.89	
,, 9	4 ,,	Lendui ,,	78°	83°	61°	25.85	
,, 10	4 ,,	Kibugumia	79°	...	...	25.51	
,, 11	4 ,,	,,	71°	...	...	25.67	Heavy rain.

Date	Time	Place				Aneroid	Rain.
April 12	4 p.m.	Kibana . . .	76°	...	...	25.75	
,, 13	4 ,,	River Katagurakwa	81°	...	...	25.85	
,, 14	4 ,,	Chagwe . .	80°	...	...	26.02	} Heavy rain in afternoon.
,, 15	4 ,,	Fort Mruli . .	80°	...	...	26.15	Altitude, 3510 ft.
,, 18	4 ,,	,, ,, . .	79°	...	...	26.1	Rain in morning.
,, 19	4 ,,	,, ,, . .	87°	...	...	26.09	
,, 20	4.30 ,,	,, ,, . .	70°	...	...	26.15	
,, 24	4.30 ,,	Camp on right bank of Nile, off Mruli	77°	...	...	26.12	
,, 26	4 ,,	Camp off Magia Hill	85°	...	...	26.08	
,, 28	4 ,,	,, ,, ,,	82°	...	...	26.11	
,, 29	5 ,,	Kitao . . .	75°	...	...	26.15	
May 1	4 ,,	Kosoka . . .	82°.5	90°.5 (In tent.)	65° (In tent.)	26.12	Rain at night.
,, 4	4 ,,	Kitongo in Wakedi .	...	...	...	26.12	Major Cunningham's aneroid read 26.06 in.
,, 5	4 ,,	Niambari . .	82°.5	...	...	26.08	
,, 6	9 a.m.	,, . .	78°	86°	61°	26.18	
,, 6	4 p.m.	,, . .	72°.5	...	...	26.09	Stormy in afternoon.
,, 7	4 ,,	Foweira . .	71°.5	...	...	26.08	Altitude, 3470 ft.
,, 8	4 ,, noon	,, . .	81°.5	87° (In tent.)	64°	26.2	
,, 8	4 p.m.	,, . .	82°	...	...	26.09	
,, 8	6 ,,	,, . .	75°.5	...	...	26.11	Little rain in afternoon.
,, 8	8.30 ,, noon	,, . .	69°	87°.5	65°	26.2	Thermom. in tent, 84°
,, 9	2 p.m.	,, . .	79°.5	...	...	26.2	,, ,, 87°
,, 9	4 ,,	,, . .	82°.5	...	...	26.15	,, ,, 82°.5
,, 9	6 ,,	,, . .	77°.5	...	...	26.12	,, ,, 71°
,, 9		,, . .	67°	...	...	26.15	

Day.	Hour.	Place.	Thermometer in Shade. Fahr.	Maximum Thermometer. Fahr.	Minimum Thermometer. Fahr.	Aneroid. Inches.	Remarks.
1895 May 9	8 p.m.	Foweira	66°	...	...	26.25	Thermom. in tent, 67°.5
,, 9	10 ,,	,,	69°	...	...	26.28	,, ,, 69°
,, 9	midnight	,,	...	...	...	26.27	,, ,, 67°
,, 10	6 a.m.	,,	66°	(Under screen.)	66°	26.23	
,, 10	8 ,,	,,	74°	84°.5	...	26.26	
,, 10	10 ,,	,,	77°	...	...	26.29	,, ,, 79°
,, 10	noon	,,	...	...	...	26.23	,, ,, 85°
,, 10	2 p.m.	,,	82°	...	...	26.16	,, ,, 80°
,, 11	4 ,,	,,	76°	...	...	26.16	,, ,, 86°
,, 12	4 ,,	,,	71°	82°	64°	26.15	Little rain.
,, 13	5 ,,	,,	83°	85°	63°	26.14	Heavy rain in afternoon.
,, 14	4 ,,	,,	81°	84°	62°	26.11	Little rain in afternoon.
,, 15	4 ,,	,,	83°	84°	61°	26.12	
,, 16	4 ,,	,,	84°.5	86°.5	61°	26.09	
,, 17	4 ,,	,,	81°.5	87°	61°.5	26.07	
,, 18	4 ,,	1st camp from Foweira	82°.5	86°	63°	26.10	
,, 19	4 ,,	Kirunguru Camp	76°	...	63°	26.07	4 feet above river
,, 20	4 ,,	Dwempindu	83°	...	...	25.87	
,, 21	5 ,,	Kigia	81°	...	...	25.90	
,, 22	4 ,,	2nd camp south of Kaduku Hill	...	...	...	26.01	
,, 23	5.40 ,,	Busindi	79°	...	...	25.93	Rain in afternoon.
,, 23	4 ,,	,,	68°.5	...	...	25.90	
,, 24		,,	83°.5	...	...	25.89	

Date	Hour	Station	Temp.	(Under screen.)		Bar.	Remarks
May 25	4 p.m.	Busindi	81°	86°	59°.5	25.89	Altitude of Mt. Fumbi, 4640 ft.
,, 25	10 a.m.	Base of Mount Fumbi	...	...	...	25.89	
,, 25	11 ,,	Top	...	...	...	25.20	Altitude, 3878 ft.
,, 26	4 p.m.	Fort Masindi, site of	76°	76°	62°.5	25.82	
,, 27	4 ,,	,,	71°	82°	62°.5	25.85	
,, 28	4 ,,	,,	73°	85°.5	57°.5	25.85	
,, 29	4 ,,	,,	80°	83°	59°	25.8	
,, 30	4 ,,	,,	81°.5	85°	61°	25.8	
,, 31	4 ,,	,,	79°	85°	64°	25.77	
June 1	4 ,,	,,	79°.5	84°	63°	25.8	
,, 2	4 ,,	,,	81°	...	...	25.8	
,, 3	5 ,,	Kibugumia Camp	69°	...	...	25.73	Heavy rain.
,, 4	4 ,,	Lendui	72°	...	...	25.7	Rain in afternoon.
,, 5	4 ,,	Fort Hoima	72°	77°	62°	25.92	Altitude, 3820 ft.
,, 6	4 ,,	,,	73°	84°	61°	25.95	Little rain.
,, 7	4 ,,	,,	69°.5	82°	63°	25.9	,, ,,
,, 8	4 ,,	,,	75°	...	61°	25.9	
,, 9	4 ,,	,,	78°	...	...	25.9	
,, 10	4 ,,	,,	71°	...	63°	25.9	
,, 11	4 ,,	,,	75°	...	64°	25.9	
,, 12	4 ,,	,,	74°	...	60°	25.9	
,, 13	4 ,,	,,	80°	...	60°	25.89	
,, 14	...	Chikakule's	77°	...	...	25.9	
,, 17	4 ,,	Mwenda's	72°	...	...	25.92	
,, 18	4 ,,	Masuba	70°	...	...	25.91	
,, 20	4 ,,	Bianja	78°	...	...	25.85	Altitude, 3733 ft.
,, 21	5 ,,		72°	...	...	27.89	
,, 22	5 ,,		71°	...	...	25.06	

Day.	Hour.	Place.	Thermometer in Shade.	Maximum Thermometer.	Minimum Thermometer.	Aneroid.	Remarks.
			Fahr.	Fahr.	Fahr.	Inches.	
1895. June 23	4 p.m.	Fort Nakabimba	75°	...	55°	25.1	Altitude, 4582 ft.
,, 24	4 ,,	Bawanga ,,	69°.5	...	59°	25.18	
,, 25	4 ,,	Bawanga ,,	73°	...	57°	25.05	
,, 26	4 ,,	Bnzaga	73°	...	58°	25.33	Little rain in afternoon.
,, 27	4 ,,	Kisimba	76°	...	58°	25.6	
,, 28	...	Mwenda's	...	...	58°	...	
,, 29	4 ,,	Chikakule's	79°	...	58°	25.85	Altitude, 3733 ft.
,, 30	4 ,,	Msaga Nkasi	78°	...	...	25.77	
July 2	4 ,,	Fort Hoima	79°	...	...	25.85	
,, 4	4 ,,	,, ,,	78°.5	...	...	25.85	,, 3820 ,,
,, 7	4 ,,	,, ,,	79°	...	...	25.85	
,, 8	4 ,,	,, ,,	80°	...	...	25.82	
,, 9	4 ,,	,, ,,	80°.5	...	...	25.82	
,, 10	4 ,,	Fort Kibero	76°	...	...	27.37	,, 2113 ,,
,, 11	4.30 ,,	,, ,,	83°	...	...	27.15	
,, 13	4 ,,	Mahagi (Mswa)	77°	...	...	27.37	
,, 14	4 ,,	Mahagi	77°	...	...	25.86	
,, 17	4 ,,	Fort Hoima	77°	...	...	25.89	,, 3820 ,,
,, 18	4 ,,	,, ,,	77°	...	...	25.85	
,, 20	4 ,,	,, ,,	51°	...	49°	...	
,, 21	6 a.m.	,, ,,	82°	...	...	...	
,, 21	noon	,, ,,	84°	...	...	...	
,, 21	3 p.m.	,, ,,	81°	...	...	25.85	
,, 21	4 ,,	,, ,,	73°	...	...	...	
,, 21	6 ,,	,, ,,					

Date	Time	Locality	Temp. (in shade)	Temp.	Barometer	Remarks
July 22	6 a.m.	Fort Hoima	53°	52°	...	
,, 22	noon	,,	84°	...	25.85	
,, 22	4 p.m.	,,	78°	...	...	
,, 23	noon	,,	82°	52°.5	25.88	
,, 23	2 p.m.	,,	84°	...	...	
,, 23	4 ,,	,,	82°	53°	25.89	
,, 24	noon	,,	83°	...	25.87	
,, 24	2 p.m.	,,	84°	53°	25.99	
,, 24	4 ,,	,,	82°	...	...	
,, 25	noon	,,	75°	...	25.97	
,, 25	4 p.m.	,,	78°	56°	...	
,, 26	4 ,,	,,	76°.5	...	26.0	
,, 27	noon	,,	78°	54°	...	
,, 27	2 p.m.	,,	80°	...	25.95	
,, 27	4 ,,	,,	78°	56°	25.95	
,, 28	noon	,,	74°	59°	25.92	
,, 28	2 p.m.	,,	78°	...	...	
,, 28	4 ,,	,,	74°	57°.5	25.95	
,, 29	2	,,	84°	...	25.91	
,, 29	4	,,	80°	59°	...	
,, 30	2	,,	84°	58°	...	Heavy rain in afternoon.
,, 30	4	,,	80°	60°	...	
,, 31	2	,,	83°	...	...	
,, 31	4	,,	79°	...	...	
Aug. 1	4	,,	78°	...	...	
,, 1	4	,,	78°	...	...	
,, 2	4	,,	71°	...	...	
,, 3	noon	,,	70°	...	...	Heavy rain in morning.
,, 3	2 p.m.	,,	71°	...	...	Rainy.
,, 3	4 ,,	,,	70°	...	25.98	

Day.	Hour.	Place.	Thermometer in Shade.	Maximum Thermometer.	Minimum Thermometer.	Aneroid.	Remarks.
1895. Aug. 4	noon	Fort Hoima	Fahr. 78°	Fahr. …	Fahr. 62°	Inches. …	
,, 4	2 p.m.	,,	72°	…	…	…	
,, 4	4 ,,	,,	71°	…	…	25.97	
,, 5	noon	,,	78°	…	55°	…	
,, 5	2 p.m.	,,	79°	…	…	25.91	
,, 6	4 ,,	,,	78°	…	…	…	
,, 6	noon	,,	81°	…	60°.5	25.91	
,, 6	2 p.m.	,,	72°	…	…	…	
,, 7	4 ,,	,,	73°.5	…	…	25.91	
,, 7	2 ,,	,,	76°	…	59°.5	…	
,, 8	4 ,,	,,	73°	…	…	25.96	
,, 8	noon	,,	75°	…	63°	…	
,, 9	2 p.m.	,,	69°	…	…	…	
,, 9	noon	,,	67°	…	56°	…	
,, 9	2 p.m.	,,	72°	…	…	25.95	
,, 10	4 ,,	,,	71°	…	56°	25.9	
,, 12	2 ,,	Fort Masindi	79°	…	…	…	Altitude, 3878 ft.
,, 13	4.30 ,,	,, ,,	70°	…	…	…	,, ,, 3470 ,,
,, 14	4.30 ,,	Pakano	66°	…	…	…	Heavy rain at night.
,, 15	4 ,,	Kimena	81°	…	…	…	Altitude, 3936 ft.
,, 16	4 ,,	Pamanji	77°	…	…	…	Rainy.
,, 17	4 ,,	Paniatoli	77°	…	…	…	
,, 19	4 ,,	Kidopo	70°	…	…	…	
,,	4 ,,	Victoria Nile	70°	…	…	…	Rain at night.
,, 22	4.30 ,,	Kosh	80°.5	…	…	…	

Date	Time	Place				Temp.		Temp.	Remarks
Aug. 26	4 p.m.	Kibega	…	…	…	80°	…	…	Heavy rain.
,, 27	4.30 ,,	Lal	…	…	…	69°	…	…	Rain in evening.
,, 28	5 ,,	Kimena	…	…	…	70°	…	…	Rain afternoon and night.
,, 29	4 ,,	Pakano	…	…	…	83°.5	…	…	Heavy rain in afternoon.
Sept. 3	4 ,,	Fort Hoima	…	…	…	69°	…	…	
,, 4	noon	,, ,,	…	…	57°	79°	…	…	
,, 5	4 p.m.	,, ,,	…	…	…	71°	…	…	Little rain in afternoon.
,, 6	noon	,, ,,	…	…	58°	84°	…	…	
,, 7	4 p.m.	,, ,,	…	…	…	74°	…	…	
,, 8	4 ,,	,, ,,	…	…	59°	78°	…	…	
,, 9	2 ,,	,, ,,	…	…	58°	85°	…	…	
,, 17	4 ,,	Kikingo	…	…	…	68°	…	…	
,, 19	6 ,,	Chikunika	…	…	…	77°	…	…	Rain at night.
,, 21	4.30 ,,	Kiambogo	…	…	…	79°	…	…	Little rain in morning.
,, 22	4.30 ,,	Katagala	…	…	…	70°	…	…	
,, 28	4 ,,	Kampala	…	…	…	79°	…	…	
Oct. 1	4 ,,	Ntebi (Victoria Nyanza)	…	…	…	73°, 77°	…	…	Altitude, 3820 ft.

METEOROLOGICAL OBSERVATIONS TAKEN DURING NANDI EXPEDITION

Day.	Hour.	Place.	Thermometer in Shade.	Maximum Thermometer.	Minimum Thermometer.	Aneroid.	Remarks.
			Fahr.	Fahr.	Fahr.	Inches.	
1895. Oct. 26	4 p.m.	Sio Bay	80°	...	...	25.78	Altitude, 4421 ft.
Nov. 2	4 ,,	Mumiäs	80°	...	...	25.22	
,, 3	4 ,,	,,	82°	...	...	25.25	
,, 4	4 ,,	Camp on Lusumo River	76°.5	...	...	25.04	
,, 5	4 ,,	Camp near Kikelelwas Forest	80°	...	...	24.73	
,, 6	4 ,,	Kabras	77°	...	...	24.68	
,, 7	4 ,,	Near Kamobir Hill	77°	...	...	24.52	,, 5464 ,,
,, 8	4 ,,	Camp on escarpment	70°	...	...	23.56	,, 5260 ,,
,, 9	4 ,,	Samwiti	71°.5	...	...	23.22	
,, 10	4 ,,	Kimong	66°.5	...	...	23.02	,, 6627 ,,
,, 11	4.30 ,,	Alagabiet	72°	...	...	23.21	,, 6872 ,,
,, 12	10 a.m.	,,	68°	...	54°	23.32	
,, 12	noon	,,	64°	...	...	23.25	
,, 12	2 p.m.	,,	64°	...	...	23.24	
,, 12	4 ,,	,,	62°	...	...	23.26	Rain in afternoon.
,, 12	6 ,,	,,	61°	...	...	23.27	
,, 12	8 ,,	,,	61°	...	...	23.3	
,, 12	10 ,,	,,	57°	...	...	23.3	
,, 13	4 ,,	Samwiti	62°	...	52°	23.22	Little rain in afternoon.
,, 15	4 ,,	Kakobis	70°	...	...	23.3	

Date	Hour	Station	Temp.		Temp.		Bar.	Remarks
Nov. 16	10 a.m.	Kakobis	69°	...	56°	...	...	Altitude, 6531 ft.
,, 16	noon	,,	75°	...	...	...	...	
,, 16	2 p.m.	,,	72°.5	...	...	...	23.32	
,, 16	4 ,,	,,	72°	...	...	...	23.2	
,, 17	4 ,,	Kiture	68°	...	55°	...	22.82	{ Altitude, 6650 ft. / Rain early in day.
,, 18	4.30 ,,	Teito	69°	...	54°	...	...	Altitude, 7119 ft.
,, 19	2 ,,	,,	79°	...	...	...	23.42	
,, 19	4.30 ,,	,,	72°	...	...	...	...	
,, 20	2 ,,	Mitete	79°	...	...	...	23.74	,, 6039 ,,
,, 20	4 ,,	,,	69°	...	...	...	...	
,, 21	4 ,,	1st camp on Mau escarpment	60°.5	...	58°	...	...	,, 8898 ,,
,, 22	4 ,,	2nd camp on Mau escarpment	53°	...	49°	...	...	{ Cold and wet. / Altitude, 9122 ft.
,, 23	8 ,,	Campi ya Mwiba	56°	...	...	...	22.92	Altitude, 7645 ft.
,, 27	5 ,,	Camp on hills	56°	...	...	...	24.19	{ Altitude, 6945 ,, / Rain in afternoon.
,, 28	4.30 ,,	Camp near R. Emboga	68°	...	...	...	24.34	{ Altitude, 5437 ft. / Rain in afternoon.
,, 29	4.30 ,,	,, Endubo Mt.	63°	...	...	...	25.5	
,, 30	4.30 ,,	Sendege's Plain	66°.5	...	...	...	25.02	Altitude, 3990 ft.
Dec. 1	4 ,,	Pangwa	69°	...	...	...	23.28	{ Altitude, 4425 ,, / Rain in afternoon.
,, 2	4 ,,	Chibonyai	61°	...	...	...	23.4	Altitude, 6545 ft.
,, 3	4 ,,	Kwakiminu	70°	...	...	...	23.73	,, 6445 ,,
,, 4	4 ,,	Kavaren	69°	...	...	...	24.29	,, 5998 ,,
,, 5	4 ,,	Runye	72°	...	...	...	24.69	,, 5310 ,,
,, 6	4 ,,	Chovyika	69°	...	...	...	24.69	,, 4900 ,,
,, 7	4 ,,	Siyonso	71°	...	...	...	24.68	,, 4800 ,,

Day.	Hour.	Place.	Thermometer in Shade. Fahr.	Maximum Thermometer. Fahr.	Minimum Thermometer. Fahr.	Aneroid. Inches.	Remarks.
1895. Dec. 8	4 p.m.	Siyonso	67°	...	...	24.83	
,, 9	4 ,,	Mumiäs	70°	...	...	25.13	Altitude, 4421 ft.
,, 12	4 ,,	,,	71°	...	...	25.17	
,, 13	4 ,,	Kabras	82°	...	...	25.13	
,, 16	4 ,,	Near Samwiti	79°	...	...	24.24	,, 5464 ,,
,, 17	4 ,,	Near Kimonde R.	69°	...	...	23.02	,, 6835 ,,
,, 18	4.30 ,,	Koboi	...	...	...	23.3	
,, 20	4 ,,	Near Chibonyai	69°	...	52°	23.19	,, 6627 ,,
,, 21	4 ,,	Moran	64°	...	...	23.42	
,, 22	5 ,,	,,	64°	...	52°.5	23.33	{ Altitude, 6348 ,,
,, 23	10.30 a.m.	,,	74°	...	53°	23.36	{ Little rain.
,, 23	2 p.m.	,,	76°	...	...	23.3	
,, 23	4 ,,	,,	71°.5	...	...	23.32	Altitude, 6455 ,,
,, 23	6 ,,	Near Moraba Peak	64°	...	...	23.35	
,, 23	10 p.m.	,,	59°	...	...	23.35	
,, 24	10 a.m.	,,	74°.5	...	54°	23.63	
,, 24	noon	,,	77°	...	...	23.6	
,, 24	2 p.m.	,,	78°	...	...	23.53	
,, 24	4 ,,	,,	78°	...	...	23.52	,, 6212 ,,
,, 24	6 ,,	,,	66°	...	...	23.54	
,, 25	8 a.m.	,,	69°	...	54°	23.63	
,, 25	10 ,,	,,	78°	...	...	23.62	
,, 25	noon	,,	81°	...	...	23.54	
,, 25	2 p.m.	,,	82°	...	...	23.52	

Dec. 25	4 „	Near Moraba Peak ·	75°	...	...	...	23.53	Altitude, 5645 ft.
„ 25	6 „	„ ·	65°	...	...	...	23.55	„ 4969 „
„ 26	4 „	Near Kevillat Peak ·	80°	...	...	...	23.98	„ 5428 „
„ 27	4 „	Tiriki ·	79°	...	...	64°	24.62	„ 4942 „
„ 28	4 „	Near Marugwa Peak ·	80°	...	...	55°	24.23	
„ 29	4 „	Near Chubugumo ·	83°	...	...	...	24.64	
„ 30	5.45 a.m.	...	46°	...	...	45°	...	
„ 30	4.30 p.m.	Mumias ·	79°	...	...	...	24.82	„ 4421 „
„ 31	4 „	...	83°	...	...	55°	25.25	
1896.								
Jan. 4	4 „	„, Camp, right bank of Moia	77°	...	...	...	25.22	
„ 5	4 „	Ntebi ·	80°	...	...	...	25.22	
Feb. 10	4.30 p.m.	Lake shore (Victoria Nyanza)	78°	...	...	...	...	
„ 10	4.30 „		77°	...	...	...	...	

APPENDIX II

LIST OF ASTRONOMICAL OBSERVATIONS IN UGANDA, UNYORO, AND ON THE UPPER NILE

TABLE OF LATITUDE AND HEIGHTS

	Latitude North.			Heights.
	°	′	″	Feet.
Buniga Camp	0	54	36	...
Kaduma Fort	1	5	56	...
Baranwa ,, ...	1	14	14	...
Hoima ,, ...	1	26	56	3820
Kibero ,, ...	1	41	1	2113
Mahagi	2	6	28	...
East bank of Nile near Amat . .	2	26	30	...
Wadelai old Fort (left bank) . .	2	43	11	...
Dufile ,, ,, . .	3	34	21	...
Lukwia	1	58	21	...
Kangara	1	32	28	...
Kajumbura Island	1	51	10	...
Kilianongo	1	51	45	...
Kibugumia	1	34	33	...
Kisoga Camp	1	39	8	...
Mruli	1	39	3	3510
Lukungu	1	39	27	...
Kitao	1	50	36	...
Niambari	2	0	26	...
Foweira, near old station . . .	2	11	14	3470
Kirunguru	2	1	2	...
Dwempindu	1	54	42	...
Kigia	1	48	47	...
Masindi Fort	1	41	5	3878
Raymond	0	22	41	...
Mwenda's	1	4	15	3733
Nakabimba Fort	0	38	24	4582
Kimena		...		3470
Paniatoli	2	5	44	3636
Bajan	2	14	57	...
Kibega	2	8	52	...
Kijange	1	36	37	...
Kikingo	1	32	15	...
Chikunika	1	16	56	...
Kalagala	0	39	7	...

TABLE OF LATITUDE AND HEIGHTS.—*continued.*

	Latitude North.			Heights.
	°	′	″	Feet.
Ntebi.		...		3820
Mumiās	0	20	6	4421
Kikelelwas (near)	0	21	12	...
Kamobir Hill	0	22	32	...
Samwiti	0	18	36	6627
Kimong	0	25	26	6872
Alagabiet Mountain	0	24	49	7128
Kiture	0	10	48	6650
Teito.		...		7119
Mitete	0	0	41	6039
Olmasidi	0	15	7	...
Sendege's Plain		...		3990
Paugwa		...		4425
Chibonyai		...		6545
Kwakiminu		...		6445
Kavaren		...		5998
Runye		...		5310
Siyonso		...		4800
Kabras		...		5464
Moran	0	0	13	6455
Moraba Peak		...		6212
Kevillat ,,		...		5800
Tiriki	0	1	19	4969
Marugwa Peak	0	1	30	5428
Chubugumo	0	8	37	4946

MERIDIAN DISTANCES

Longitude of Hoima, 31° 21′ 15″ E.

					°	′	″
Kaduma Fort, east of Hoima			interval 4 days	.	0	7	45
Mruli Fort (first observation) east of Hoima		,,	6 ,,	.	0	42	15[1]
Kivari (Unyoro)	,,	,,	,, 4 ,,	.	0	22	45
Kibana (Unyoro)	,,	,,	,, 3 ,,	.	0	19	0
Mruli Fort (second observation) ,,		,,	,, 9 ,,	.	0	43	15[1]
Niambari, east of Mruli	.	.	,, 6 ,,	.	0	17	30[1]
Foweira, west of Niambari	.	.	,, 3 ,,	.	0	1	15[1]
Dwempindu, west of Foweira	.	.	,, 3 ,,	.	0	14	45
Wadelai Fort, east of Hoima	.	.	,, 5 ,,	.	0	6	45[1]
Dufile Fort, east of Hoima	.	.	,, 9 ,,	.	0	40	45
Kibero, west of Hoima	.	.	,, 2 ,,	.	0	5	45

[1] Rate of watch determined at both places.

APPENDIX III

LIST OF ASTRONOMICAL OBSERVATIONS IN THE NIGER TERRITORIES

Place.	Latitude.				Longitude.			
	°	′	″		°	′	″	
Lokoja	7	48	22	N.	6	42	30	E.
					(Assumed longitude on which other observations depend.)			
Jakura (camp 1½ miles E. of) .	7	59	56	,,	6	31	7.5	,,
Akpara	8	4	49	,,		...		
Pati Sura (camp near) . .	8	5	34	,,	6	11	46	,,
Kabba Town	7	50	17.5	,,	6	3	22	,,
Ferafi (camp 2 miles N. of) .	8	13	30	,,		...		
Kosobeji	8	30	44.5	,,	6	4	58	,,
Egbom	8	45	28	,,	5	58	11	,,
Bida (1st camp) . . .	9	3	35.5	,,		...		
Bida (2nd camp outside Sultan's palace)	9	5	17	,,	5	58	34	,,
Jebba (camp 2¾ miles S. of) .	9	5	3	,,		...		
Bodi Sadu	8	55	52	,,	4	47	42	,,
Ilorin (outside Emir's palace) .	8	29	36	,,	4	32	42	,,
Arebi River (camp) . .	8	34	42	,,	4	40	39	,,
Lanwa Ilorin	8	44	32	,,		...		
Jebba (S. side of river at bend)	9	7	54	,,	4	47	53	,,

PRINTED BY MORRISON AND GIBB LIMITED, EDINBURGH

A CATALOGUE OF BOOKS AND ANNOUNCEMENTS OF METHUEN AND COMPANY PUBLISHERS : LONDON 36 ESSEX STREET W.C.

CONTENTS

NOVEMBER 1897

MESSRS. METHUEN'S
ANNOUNCEMENTS

Poetry

SHAKESPEARE'S POEMS. Edited, with an Introduction and Notes, by GEORGE WYNDHAM, M.P. *Crown 8vo. Buckram. 6s.*

This is a volume of the sonnets and lesser poems of Shakespeare, and is prefaced with an elaborate Introduction by Mr. Wyndham.

ENGLISH LYRICS. Selected and Edited by W. E. HENLEY. *Crown 8vo. Buckram. 6s.*

Also 15 copies on Japanese paper. *Demy 8vo. £2, 2s. net.*

Few announcements will be more welcome to lovers of English verse than the one that Mr. Henley is bringing together into one book the finest lyrics in our language.

NURSERY RHYMES. With many Coloured Pictures. By F. D. BEDFORD. *Small 4to. 5s.*

This book has many beautiful designs in colour to illustrate the old rhymes.

THE ODYSSEY OF HOMER. A Translation by J. G. CORDERY. *Crown 8vo. 7s. 6d.*

Travel and Adventure

BRITISH CENTRAL AFRICA. By Sir H. H. JOHNSTON, K.C.B. With nearly Two Hundred Illustrations, and Six Maps. *Crown 4to. 30s. net.*

CONTENTS.—(1) The History of Nyasaland and British Central Africa generally. (2) A detailed description of the races and languages of British Central Africa. (3) Chapters on the European settlers and missionaries; the Fauna, the Flora, minerals, and scenery. (4) A chapter on the prospects of the country.

WITH THE GREEKS IN THESSALY. By W. KINNAIRD ROSE, Reuter's Correspondent. With Plans and 23 Illustrations. *Crown 8vo. 6s.*

A history of the operations in Thessaly by one whose brilliant despatches from the seat of war attracted universal attention.

THE BENIN MASSACRE. By CAPTAIN BOISRAGON. With Portrait and Map. *Crown 8vo. 3s. 6d.*

This volume is written by one of the two survivors who escaped the terrible massacre in Benin at the beginning of this year. The author relates in detail his adventures and his extraordinary escape, and adds a description of the country and of the events which led up to the outbreak.

FROM TONKIN TO INDIA. By PRINCE HENRI OF ORLEANS. Translated by HAMLEY BENT, M.A. With 80 Illustrations and a Map. *Crown 4to.* 25s.

The travels of Prince Henri in 1895 from China to the valley of the Bramaputra covered a distance of 2100 miles, of whith 1600 was through absolutely unexplored country. No fewer than seventeen ranges of mountains were crossed at altitudes of from 11,000 to 13,000 feet. The journey was made memorable by the discovery of the sources of the Irrawaddy. To the physical difficulties of the journey were added dangers from the attacks of savage tribes. The book deals with many of the burning political problems of the East, and it will be found a most important contribution to the literature of adventure and discovery.

THREE YEARS IN SAVAGE AFRICA. By LIONEL DECLE. With an Introduction by H. M. STANLEY, M.P. With 100 Illustrations and 5 Maps. *Demy 8vo.* 21s.

Few Europeans have had the same opportunity of studying the barbarous parts of Africa as Mr. Decle. Starting from the Cape, he visited in succession Bechuanaland, the Zambesi, Matabeleland and Mashonaland, the Portuguese settlement on the Zambesi, Nyasaland, Ujiji, the headquarters of the Arabs, German East Africa, Uganda (where he saw fighting in company with the late Major 'Roddy' Owen), and British East Africa. In his book he relates his experiences, his minute observations of native habits and customs, and his views as to the work done in Africa by the various European Governments, whose operations he was able to study. The whole journey extended over 7000 miles, and occupied exactly three years.

WITH THE MOUNTED INFANTRY IN MASHONA-LAND. By Lieut.-Colonel ALDERSON. With numerous Illustrations and Plans. *Demy 8vo.* 12s. 6d.

This is an account of the military operations in Mashonaland by the officer who commanded the troops in that district during the late rebellion. Besides its interest as a story of warfare, it will have a peculiar value as an account of the services of mounted infantry by one of the chief authorities on the subject.

THE HILL OF THE GRACES: OR, THE GREAT STONE TEMPLES OF TRIPOLI. By H. S. COWPER, F.S.A. With Maps, Plans, and 75 Illustrations. *Demy 8vo.* 10s. 6d.

A record of two journeys through Tripoli in 1895 and 1896. The book treats of a remarkable series of megalithic temples which have hitherto been uninvestigated, and contains a large amount of new geographical and archæological matter.

ADVENTURE AND EXPLORATION IN AFRICA. By Captain A. ST. H. GIBBONS, F.R.G.S. With Illustrations by C. WHYMPER, and Maps. *Demy 8vo.* 21s.

This is an account of travel and adventure among the Marotse and contiguous tribes, with a description of their customs, characteristics, and history, together with the author's experiences in hunting big game. The illustrations are by Mr. Charles Whymper, and from photographs. There is a map by the author of the hitherto unexplored regions lying between the Zambezi and Kafukwi rivers and from 18° to 15° S. lat.

History and Biography

A HISTORY OF EGYPT, FROM THE EARLIEST TIMES TO THE PRESENT DAY. Edited by W. M. FLINDERS PETRIE, D.C.L., LL.D., Professor of Egyptology at University College. *Fully Illustrated. In Six Volumes. Crown 8vo. 6s. each.*

VOL. V. ROMAN EGYPT. By J. G. MILNE.

THE DECLINE AND FALL OF THE ROMAN EMPIRE. By EDWARD GIBBON. A New Edition, edited with Notes, Appendices, and Maps by J. B. BURY, M.A., Fellow of Trinity College, Dublin. *In Seven Volumes. Demy 8vo, gilt top. 8s. 6d. each. Crown 8vo. 6s. each. Vol. IV.*

THE LETTERS OF VICTOR HUGO. Translated from the French by F. CLARKE, M.A. *In Two Volumes. Demy 8vo. 10s. 6d. each. Vol. II.* 1835-72.
This is the second volume of one of the most interesting and important collection of letters ever published in France. The correspondence dates from Victor Hugo's boyhood to his death, and none of the letters have been published before.

A HISTORY OF THE GREAT NORTHERN RAILWAY, 1845-95. By C. H. GRINLING. With Maps and Illustrations. *Demy 8vo. 10s. 6d.*
A record of Railway enterprise and development in Northern England, containing much matter hitherto unpublished. It appeals both to the general reader and to those specially interested in railway construction and management.

A HISTORY OF BRITISH COLONIAL POLICY. By H. E. EGERTON, M.A. *Demy 8vo. 12s. 6d.*
This book deals with British Colonial policy historically from the beginnings of English colonisation down to the present day. The subject has been treated by itself, and it has thus been possible within a reasonable compass to deal with a mass of authority which must otherwise be sought in the State papers. The volume is divided into five parts :—(1) The Period of Beginnings, 1497-1650; (2) Trade Ascendancy, 1651-1830; (3) The Granting of Responsible Government, 1831-1860; (4) *Laissez Aller*, 1861-1885; (5) Greater Britain.

A HISTORY OF ANARCHISM. By E. V. ZENKER. Translated from the German. *Demy 8vo. 10s. 6d.*
A critical study and history, as well as a powerful and trenchant criticism, of the Anarchist movement in Europe. The book has aroused considerable attention on the Continent.

THE LIFE OF ERNEST RENAN By MADAME DARMES-TETER. With Portrait. *Crown 8vo. 6s.*
A biography of Renan by one of his most intimate friends.

A LIFE OF DONNE. By AUGUSTUS JESSOPP, D.D. With Portrait. *Crown 8vo. 3s. 6d.*
This is a new volume of the 'Leaders of Religion' series, from the learned and witty pen of the Rector of Scarning, who has been able to embody the results of much research.

OLD HARROW DAYS. By J. G. COTTON MINCHIN. *Crown 8vo. 5s.*

A volume of reminiscences which will be interesting to old Harrovians and to many of the general public.

Theology

A PRIMER OF THE BIBLE. By Prof. W. H. BENNETT. *Crown 8vo. 2s. 6d.*

This Primer sketches the history of the books which make up the Bible, in the light of recent criticism. It gives an account of their character, origin, and composition, as far as possible in chronological order, with special reference to their relations to one another, and to the history of Israel and the Church. The formation of the Canon is illustrated by chapters on the Apocrypha (Old and New Testament); and there is a brief notice of the history of the Bible since the close of the Canon.

LIGHT AND LEAVEN : HISTORICAL AND SOCIAL SERMONS. By the Rev. H. HENSLEY HENSON, M.A., Fellow of All Souls', Incumbent of St. Mary's Hospital, Ilford. *Crown 8vo. 6s.*

Devotional Series

THE CONFESSIONS OF ST. AUGUSTINE. Newly Translated, with an Introduction, by C. BIGG, D.D., late Student of Christ Church. With a Frontispiece. *18mo. 1s. 6d.*

This little book is the first volume of a new Devotional Series, printed in clear type, and published at a very low price.

This volume contains the nine books of the 'Confessions' which are suitable for devotional purposes. The name of the Editor is a sufficient guarantee of the excellence of the edition.

THE HOLY SACRIFICE. By F. WESTON, M.A., Curate of St. Matthew's, Westminster. *18mo. 1s.*

A small volume of devotions at the Holy Communion.

Naval and Military

A HISTORY OF THE ART OF WAR. By C. W. OMAN, M.A., Fellow of All Souls', Oxford. *Demy 8vo. Illustrated. 21s.*

Vol. II. MEDIÆVAL WARFARE.

Mr. Oman is engaged on a History of the Art of War, of which the above, though covering the middle period from the fall of the Roman Empire to the general use of gunpowder in Western Europe, is the first instalment. The first battle dealt with will be Adrianople (378) and the last Navarette (1367). There will appear later a volume dealing with the Art of War among the Ancients, and another covering the 15th, 16th, and 17th centuries.

The book will deal mainly with tactics and strategy, fortifications and siegecraft, but subsidiary chapters will give some account of the development of arms and armour, and of the various forms of military organization known to the Middle Ages.

A SHORT HISTORY OF THE ROYAL NAVY, FROM
EARLY TIMES TO THE PRESENT DAY. By DAVID HANNAY.
Illustrated. 2 *Vols*. *Demy 8vo*. *7s. 6d. each*. Vol. I.

This book aims at giving an account not only of the fighting we have done at sea,
but of the growth of the service, of the part the Navy has played in the development of the Empire, and of its inner life.

THE STORY OF THE BRITISH ARMY. By Lieut.-Colonel
COOPER KING, of the Staff College, Camberley. Illustrated. *Demy
8vo*. *7s. 6d.*

This volume aims at describing the nature of the different armies that have been
formed in Great Britain, and how from the early and feudal levies the present
standing army came to be. The changes in tactics, uniform, and armament are
briefly touched upon, and the campaigns in which the army has shared have
been so far followed as to explain the part played by British regiments in them.

General Literature

THE OLD ENGLISH HOME. By S. BARING-GOULD.
With numerous Plans and Illustrations. *Crown 8vo*. *7s. 6d.*

This book, like Mr. Baring-Gould's well-known 'Old Country Life,' describes the
life and environment of an old English family.

OXFORD AND ITS COLLEGES. By J. WELLS, M.A.,
Fellow and Tutor of Wadham College. Illustrated by E. H. NEW.
Fcap. 8vo. *3s*. *Leather*. *4s*.

This is a guide—chiefly historical—to the Colleges of Oxford. It contains numerous
illustrations.

VOCES ACADEMICÆ. By C. GRANT ROBERTSON, M.A.,
Fellow of All Souls', Oxford. *With a Frontispiece*. *Fcap. 8vo*.
3s. 6d.

This is a volume of light satirical dialogues and should be read by all who are interested in the life of Oxford.

A PRIMER OF WORDSWORTH. By LAURIE MAGNUS.
Crown 8vo. *2s. 6d.*

This volume is uniform with the Primers of Tennyson and Burns, and contains a
concise biography of the poet, a critical appreciation of his work in detail, and a
bibliography.

NEO-MALTHUSIANISM. By R. USSHER, M.A. *Cr. 8vo*. *6s.*

This book deals with a very delicate but most important matter, namely, the volun-
tary limitation of the family, and how such action affects morality, the individual,
and the nation.

PRIMÆVAL SCENES. By H. N. HUTCHINSON, B.A., F.G.S.,
Author of 'Extinct Monsters,' 'Creatures of Other Days,' 'Pre-
historic Man and Beast,' etc. With numerous Illustrations drawn
by JOHN HASSALL and FRED. V. BURRIDGE. *4to*. *6s.*

A set of twenty drawings, with short text to each, to illustrate the humorous aspects
of pre-historic times. They are carefully planned by the author so as to be
scientifically and archæologically correct and at the same time amusing.

THE WALLYPUG IN LONDON. By G. E. FARROW,
Author of 'The Wallypug of Why.' With numerous Illustrations.
Crown 8vo. 3s. 6d.
An extravaganza for children, written with great charm and vivacity.

RAILWAY NATIONALIZATION. By CLEMENT EDWARDS.
Crown 8vo. 2s. 6d. [*Social Questions Series.*

Sport

SPORTING AND ATHLETIC RECORDS. By H. MORGAN
BROWNE. *Crown 8vo. 1s. paper ; 2s. cloth.*
This book gives, in a clear and complete form, accurate records of the best perform-
ances in all important branches of Sport. It is an attempt, never yet made, to
present all-important sporting records in a systematic way.

THE GOLFING PILGRIM. By HORACE G HUTCHINSON.
Crown 8vo. 6s.
This book, by a famous golfer, contains the following sketches lightly and humorously
written :—The Prologue—The Pilgrim at the Shrine—Mecca out of Season—The
Pilgrim at Home—The Pilgrim Abroad—The Life of the Links—A Tragedy by
the Way—Scraps from the Scrip—The Golfer in Art—Early Pilgrims in the West
—An Interesting Relic.

Educational

EVAGRIUS. Edited by PROFESSOR LÉON PARMENTIER of
Liége and M. BIDEZ of Gand. *Demy 8vo. 7s. 6d.*
[*Byzantine Texts.*

THE ODES AND EPODES OF HORACE. Translated by
A. D. GODLEY, M.A., Fellow of Magdalen College, Oxford.
Crown 8vo. buckram. 2s.

ORNAMENTAL DESIGN FOR WOVEN FABRICS. By
C. STEPHENSON, of The Technical College, Bradford, and
F. SUDDARDS, of The Yorkshire College, Leeds. With 65 full-page
plates, and numerous designs and diagrams in the text. *Demy 8vo.
7s. 6d.*
The aim of this book is to supply, in a systematic and practical form, information on
the subject of Decorative Design as applied to Woven Fabrics, and is primarily
intended to meet the requirements of students in Textile and Art Schools, or of
designers actively engaged in the weaving industry. Its wealth of illustration is
a marked feature of the book.

ESSENTIALS OF COMMERCIAL EDUCATION. By
E. E. WHITFIELD, M.A. *Crown 8vo. 1s. 6d.*
A guide to Commercial Education and Examinations.

PASSAGES FOR UNSEEN TRANSLATION. By E. C. MARCHANT, M.A., Fellow of Peterhouse, Cambridge; and A. M. COOK, M.A., late Scholar of Wadham College, Oxford: Assistant Masters at St. Paul's School. *Crown 8vo.* 3s. 6d.

This book contains Two Hundred Latin and Two Hundred Greek Passages, and has been very carefully compiled to meet the wants of V. and VI. Form Boys at Public Schools. It is also well adapted for the use of Honour men at the Universities.

EXERCISES IN LATIN ACCIDENCE. By S. E. WINBOLT, Assistant Master in Christ's Hospital. *Crown 8vo.* 1s. 6d.

An elementary book adapted for Lower Forms to accompany the shorter Latin primer.

NOTES ON GREEK AND LATIN SYNTAX. By G. BUCKLAND GREEN, M.A., Assistant Master at the Edinburgh Academy, late Fellow of St. John's College, Oxon. *Cr. 8vo.* 3s. 6d.

Notes and explanations on the chief difficulties of Greek and Latin Syntax, with numerous passages for exercise.

A DIGEST OF DEDUCTIVE LOGIC. By JOHNSON BARKER, B.A. *Crown 8vo.* 2s. 6d.

A short introduction to logic for students preparing for examinations.

TEST CARDS IN EUCLID AND ALGEBRA. By D. S. CALDERWOOD, Headmaster of the Normal School, Edinburgh. In a Packet of 40, with Answers. 1s.

A set of cards for advanced pupils in elementary schools.

HOW TO MAKE A DRESS. By J. A. E. WOOD. Illustrated. *Crown 8vo.* 1s. 6d.

A text-book for students preparing for the City and Guilds examination, based on the syllabus. The diagrams are numerous.

Fiction

LOCHINVAR. By S. R. CROCKETT, Author of 'The Raiders,' etc. Illustrated by FRANK RICHARDS. *Crown 8vo.* 6s.

BYEWAYS. By ROBERT HICHENS. Author of 'Flames,' etc. *Crown 8vo.* 6s.

THE MUTABLE MANY. By ROBERT BARR, Author of 'In the Midst of Alarms,' 'A Woman Intervenes,' etc. *Crown 8vo.* 6s.

THE LADY'S WALK. By Mrs. OLIPHANT. *Crown 8vo.* 6s.

A new book by this lamented author, somewhat in the style of her 'Beleagured City.'

TRAITS AND CONFIDENCES. By The Hon. EMILY LAW-
LESS, Author of ' Hurrish,' ' Maelcho,' etc. *Crown 8vo.* 6s.

BLADYS. By S. BARING GOULD, Author of 'The Broom
Squire,' etc. Illustrated by F. H. TOWNSEND. *Crown 8vo.* 6s.
A Romance of the last century.

THE POMP OF THE LAVILETTES. By GILBERT PARKER,
Author of ' The Seats of the Mighty,' etc. *Crown 8vo.* 3s. 6d.

A DAUGHTER OF STRIFE. By JANE HELEN FINDLATER,
Author of ' The Green Graves of Balgowrie.' *Crown 8vo.* 6s.
A story of 1710.

OVER THE HILLS. By MARY FINDLATER. *Crown 8vo.* 6s.
A novel by a sister of J. H. Findlater, the author of ' The Green Graves of Balgowrie.'

A CREEL OF IRISH STORIES. By JANE BARLOW, Author
of ' Irish Idylls.' *Crown 8vo.* 6s.

THE CLASH OF ARMS. By J. BLOUNDELLE BURTON,
Author of ' In the Day of Adversity.' *Crown 8vo.* 6s.

A PASSIONATE PILGRIM. By PERCY WHITE, Author of
' Mr. Bailey-Martin.' *Crown 8vo.* 6s.

SECRETARY TO BAYNE, M.P. By W. PETT RIDGE.
Crown 8vo. 6s.

THE BUILDERS. By J. S. FLETCHER, Author of 'When
Charles I. was King.' *Crown 8vo.* 6s.

JOSIAH'S WIFE. By NORMA LORIMER. *Crown 8vo.* 6s.

BY STROKE OF SWORD. By ANDREW BALFOUR. Illustrated by W. CUBITT COOKE. *Crown 8vo.* 6s.
A romance of the time of Elizabeth

THE SINGER OF MARLY. By I. HOOPER. Illustrated
by W. CUBITT COOKE. *Crown 8vo.* 6s.
A romance of adventure.

KIRKHAM'S FIND. By MARY GAUNT, Author of 'The
Moving Finger.' *Crown 8vo.* 6s.

THE FALL OF THE SPARROW. By M. C. BALFOUR.
Crown 8vo. 6s.

SCOTTISH BORDER LIFE. By JAMES C. DIBDIN. *Crown
8vo.* 3s. 6d.

A 2

MESSRS. METHUEN'S
PUBLICATIONS

———◆———

Poetry

RUDYARD KIPLING'S NEW POEMS

Rudyard Kipling. THE SEVEN SEAS. By RUDYARD
KIPLING. *Third Edition. Crown 8vo. Buckram, gilt top.* 6s.
'The new poems of Mr. Rudyard Kipling have all the spirit and swing of their pre-
decessors. Patriotism is the solid concrete foundation on which Mr. Kipling has
built the whole of his work.'—*Times.*
'Full of passionate patriotism and the Imperial spirit.'—*Yorkshire Post.*
'The Empire has found a singer; it is no depreciation of the songs to say that states-
men may have, one way or other, to take account of them.'—*Manchester
Guardian.*
'Animated through and through with indubitable genius.'—*Daily Telegraph.*
'Packed with inspiration, with humour, with pathos.'—*Daily Chronicle.*
'All the pride of empire, all the intoxication of power, all the ardour, the energy,
the masterful strength and the wonderful endurance and death-scorning pluck
which are the very bone and fibre and marrow of the British character are here.'
—*Daily Mail.*

Rudyard Kipling. BARRACK-ROOM BALLADS; And
Other Verses. By RUDYARD KIPLING. *Twelfth Edition. Crown
8vo.* 6s.
'Mr. Kipling's verse is strong, vivid, full of character. . . . Unmistakable genius
rings in every line.'—*Times.*
The ballads teem with imagination, they palpitate with emotion. We read them
with laughter and tears; the metres throb in our pulses, the cunningly ordered
words tingle with life; and if this be not poetry, what is?'—*Pall Mall Gazette.*

'Q.' POEMS AND BALLADS. By "Q.," Author of 'Green
Bays,' etc. *Crown 8vo. Buckram.* 3s. 6d.
'This work has just the faint, ineffable touch and glow that make poetry. 'Q.' has
the true romantic spirit.'—*Speaker.*

"Q." GREEN BAYS: Verses and Parodies. By "Q.," Author
of 'Dead Man's Rock,' etc. *Second Edition. Crown 8vo.* 3s. 6d.
'The verses display a rare and versatile gift of parody, great command of metre, and
a very pretty turn of humour.'—*Times.*

E. Mackay. A SONG OF THE SEA. By ERIC MACKAY,
Author of 'The Love Letters of a Violinist.' *Second Edition.
Fcap. 8vo.* 5s.
'Everywhere Mr. Mackay displays himself the master of a style marked by all the
characteristics of the best rhetoric. He has a keen sense of rhythm and of general
balance; his verse is excellently sonorous.'—*Globe.*

Ibsen. BRAND. A Drama by HENRIK IBSEN. Translated by
WILLIAM WILSON. *Second Edition. Crown 8vo. 3s. 6d.*

'The greatest world-poem of the nineteenth century next to "Faust." It is in
the same set with "Agamemnon," with "Lear," with the literature that we now
instinctively regard as high and holy.'—*Daily Chronicle.*

"A. G." VERSES TO ORDER. By "A. G." *Cr. 8vo. 2s. 6d.
net.*

A small volume of verse by a writer whose initials are well known to Oxford men.
'A capital specimen of light academic poetry. These verses are very bright and
engaging, easy and sufficiently witty.'—*St. James's Gazette.*

Belles Lettres, Anthologies, etc.

R. L. Stevenson. VAILIMA LETTERS. By ROBERT LOUIS
STEVENSON. With an Etched Portrait by WILLIAM STRANG, and
other Illustrations. *Second Edition. Crown 8vo. Buckram. 7s. 6d.*

'Few publications have in our time been more eagerly awaited than these "Vailima
Letters," giving the first fruits of the correspondence of Robert Louis Stevenson.
But, high as the tide of expectation has run, no reader can possibly be disappointed
in the result.'—*St. James's Gazette.*

Henley and Whibley. A BOOK OF ENGLISH PROSE.
Collected by W. E. HENLEY and CHARLES WHIBLEY. *Crown 8vo. 6s.*

'A unique volume of extracts—an art gallery of early prose.'—*Birmingham Post.*
'An admirable companion to Mr. Henley's "Lyra Heroica."'—*Saturday Review.*
'Quite delightful. A greater treat for those not well acquainted with pre-Restoration
prose could not be imagined.'—*Athenæum.*

H. C. Beeching. LYRA SACRA : An Anthology of Sacred Verse.
Edited by H. C. BEECHING, M.A. *Crown 8vo. Buckram. 6s.*

'A charming selection, which maintains a lofty standard of excellence.'—*Times.*

"Q." THE GOLDEN POMP : A Procession of English Lyrics
from Surrey to Shirley, arranged by A. T. QUILLER COUCH. *Crown
8vo. Buckram. 6s.*

'A delightful volume : a really golden "Pomp."'—*Spectator.*

W. B. Yeats. AN ANTHOLOGY OF IRISH VERSE.
Edited by W. B. YEATS. *Crown 8vo. 3s. 6d.*

'An attractive and catholic selection.'—*Times.*

G. W. Steevens. MONOLOGUES OF THE DEAD. By
G. W. STEEVENS. *Foolscap 8vo. 3s. 6d.*

A series of Soliloquies in which famous men of antiquity—Julius Cæsar, Nero,
Alcibiades, etc., attempt to express themselves in the modes of thought and
language of to-day.
The effect is sometimes splendid, sometimes bizarre, but always amazingly clever
—*Pall Mall Gazette.*

Victor Hugo. THE LETTERS OF VICTOR HUGO. Translated from the French by F. CLARKE, M.A. *In Two Volumes. Demy 8vo.* 10s. 6d. *each.* Vol. I. 1815-35.

This is the first volume of one of the most interesting and important collection of letters ever published in France. The correspondence dates from Victor Hugo's boyhood to his death, and none of the letters have been published before. The arrangement is chiefly chronological, but where there is an interesting set of letters to one person these are arranged together. The first volume contains, among others, (1) Letters to his father; (2) to his young wife; (2) to his confessor, Lamennais; a very important set of about fifty letters to Sainte-Beuve; (5) letters about his early books and plays.

'A charming and vivid picture of a man whose egotism never marred his natural kindness, and whose vanity did not impair his greatness.'—*Standard.*

C. H. Pearson. ESSAYS AND CRITICAL REVIEWS. By C. H. PEARSON, M.A., Author of 'National Life and Character.' Edited, with a Biographical Sketch, by H. A. STRONG, M.A., LL.D. With a Portrait. *Demy 8vo.* 10s. 6d.

'Remarkable for careful handling, breadth of view, and knowledge.'—*Scotsman.*
'Charming essays.'—*Spectator.*

W. M. Dixon. A PRIMER OF TENNYSON. By W. M. DIXON, M.A., Professor of English Literature at Mason College. *Crown 8vo.* 2s. 6d.

'Much sound and well-expressed criticism and acute literary judgments. The bibliography is a boon.'—*Speaker.*

W. A. Craigie. A PRIMER OF BURNS. By W. A. CRAIGIE. *Crown 8vo.* 2s. 6d.

This book is planned on a method similar to the 'Primer of Tennyson.' It has also a glossary.
'A valuable addition to the literature of the poet.'—*Times.*
'An excellent short account.'—*Pall Mall Gazette.*
'An admirable introduction.'—*Globe.*

Sterne. THE LIFE AND OPINIONS OF TRISTRAM SHANDY. By LAWRENCE STERNE. With an Introduction by CHARLES WHIBLEY, and a Portrait. *2 vols.* 7s.

'Very dainty volumes are these; the paper, type, and light-green binding are all very agreeable to the eye. *Simplex munditiis* is the phrase that might be applied to them.'—*Globe.*

Congreve. THE COMEDIES OF WILLIAM CONGREVE. With an Introduction by G. S. STREET, and a Portrait. *2 vols.* 7s.

'The volumes are strongly bound in green buckram, are of a convenient size, and pleasant to look upon, so that whether on the shelf, or on the table, or in the hand the possessor is thoroughly content with them.'—*Guardian.*

Morier. THE ADVENTURES OF HAJJI BABA OF ISPAHAN. By JAMES MORIER. With an Introduction by E. G. BROWNE, M.A., and a Portrait. *2 vols.* 7s.

Walton. THE LIVES OF DONNE, WOTTON, HOOKER, HERBERT, AND SANDERSON. By IZAAK WALTON. With an Introduction by VERNON BLACKBURN, and a Portrait. 3s. 6d.

Johnson. THE LIVES OF THE ENGLISH POETS. By SAMUEL JOHNSON, LL.D. With an Introduction by J. H. MILLAR, and a Portrait. *3 vols. 10s. 6d.*

Burns. THE POEMS OF ROBERT BURNS. Edited by ANDREW LANG and W. A. CRAIGIE. With Portrait. *Demy 8vo, gilt top. 6s.*

This edition contains a carefully collated Text, numerous Notes, critical and textual, a critical and biographical Introduction, and a Glossary.

'Among the editions in one volume, Mr. Andrew Lang's will take the place of authority.'—*Times.*

F. Langbridge. BALLADS OF THE BRAVE: Poems of Chivalry, Enterprise, Courage, and Constancy. Edited, with Notes, by Rev. F. LANGBRIDGE. *Crown 8vo. Buckram. 3s. 6d. School Edition. 2s. 6d.*

'A very happy conception happily carried out. These "Ballads of the Brave" are intended to suit the real tastes of boys, and will suit the taste of the great majority.' —*Spectator.* 'The book is full of splendid things.'—*World.*

Illustrated Books

Jane Barlow. THE BATTLE OF THE FROGS AND MICE, translated by JANE BARLOW, Author of 'Irish Idylls,' and pictured by F. D. BEDFORD. *Small 4to. 6s. net.*

S. Baring Gould. A BOOK OF FAIRY TALES retold by S. BARING GOULD. With numerous illustrations and initial letters by ARTHUR J. GASKIN. *Second Edition. Crown 8vo. Buckram. 6s.*

'Mr. Baring Gould is deserving of gratitude, in re-writing in honest, simple style the old stories that delighted the childhood of "our fathers and grandfathers." As to the form of the book, and the printing, which is by Messrs. Constable, it were difficult to commend overmuch.—*Saturday Review.*

S. Baring Gould. OLD ENGLISH FAIRY TALES. Collected and edited by S. BARING GOULD. With Numerous Illustrations by F. D. BEDFORD. *Second Edition. Crown 8vo. Buckram. 6s.*

'A charming volume, which children will be sure to appreciate. The stories have been selected with great ingenuity from various old ballads and folk-tales, and, having been somewhat altered and readjusted, now stand forth, clothed in Mr. Baring Gould's delightful English, to enchant youthful readers.'—*Guardian.*

S. Baring Gould. A BOOK OF NURSERY SONGS AND RHYMES. Edited by S. BARING GOULD, and Illustrated by the Birmingham Art School. *Buckram, gilt top. Crown 8vo. 6s.*

'The volume is very complete in its way, as it contains nursery songs to the number of 77, game-rhymes, and jingles. To the student we commend the sensible introduction, and the explanatory notes. The volume is superbly printed on soft, thick paper, which it is a pleasure to touch; and the borders and pictures are among the very best specimens we have seen of the Gaskin school.'—*Birmingham Gazette.*

H. C. Beeching. A BOOK OF CHRISTMAS VERSE. Edited by H. C. BEECHING, M.A., and Illustrated by WALTER CRANE. *Crown 8vo, gilt top.* 5s.

A collection of the best verse inspired by the birth of Christ from the Middle Ages to the present day. A distinction of the book is the large number of poems it contains by modern authors, a few of which are here printed for the first time.

‘An anthology which, from its unity of aim and high poetic excellence, has a better right to exist than most of its fellows.’—*Guardian.*

History

Gibbon. THE DECLINE AND FALL OF THE ROMAN EMPIRE. By EDWARD GIBBON. A New Edition, Edited with Notes, Appendices, and Maps, by J. B. BURY, M.A., Fellow of Trinity College, Dublin. *In Seven Volumes. Demy 8vo. Gilt top.* 8s. 6d. each. *Also crown 8vo.* 6s. each. *Vols. I., II., and III.*

‘The time has certainly arrived for a new edition of Gibbon's great work. . . . Professor Bury is the right man to undertake this task. His learning is amazing, both in extent and accuracy. The book is issued in a handy form, and at a moderate price, and it is admirably printed.’—*Times.*

‘The edition is edited as a classic should be edited, removing nothing, yet indicating the value of the text, and bringing it up to date. It promises to be of the utmost value, and will be a welcome addition to many libraries.’—*Scotsman.*

‘This edition, so far as one may judge from the first instalment, is a marvel of erudition and critical skill, and it is the very minimum of praise to predict that the seven volumes of it will supersede Dean Milman's as the standard edition of our great historical classic.’—*Glasgow Herald.*

‘The beau-ideal Gibbon has arrived at last.’—*Sketch.*

‘At last there is an adequate modern edition of Gibbon. . . . The best edition the nineteenth century could produce.’—*Manchester Guardian.*

Flinders Petrie. A HISTORY OF EGYPT, FROM THE EARLIEST TIMES TO THE PRESENT DAY. Edited by W. M. FLINDERS PETRIE, D.C.L., LL.D., Professor of Egyptology at University College. *Fully Illustrated. In Six Volumes. Crown 8vo.* 6s. each.

> Vol. I. PREHISTORIC TIMES TO XVI. DYNASTY. W. M. F. Petrie. *Third Edition.*

> Vol. II. THE XVIITH AND XVIIITH DYNASTIES. W. M. F. Petrie. *Second Edition.*

‘A history written in the spirit of scientific precision so worthily represented by Dr. Petrie and his school cannot but promote sound and accurate study, and supply a vacant place in the English literature of Egyptology.’—*Times.*

Flinders Petrie. EGYPTIAN TALES. Edited by W. M. FLINDERS PETRIE. Illustrated by TRISTRAM ELLIS. *In Two Volumes. Crown 8vo.* 3s. 6d. each.

‘A valuable addition to the literature of comparative folk-lore. The drawings are really illustrations in the literal sense of the word.’—*Globe.*

‘It has a scientific value to the student of history and archæology.’—*Scotsman.*

‘Invaluable as a picture of life in Palestine and Egypt.’—*Daily News.*

Flinders Petrie. EGYPTIAN DECORATIVE ART. By
W. M. FLINDERS PETRIE, D.C.L. With 120 Illustrations. *Crown
8vo. 3s. 6d.*

'Professor Flinders Petrie is not only a profound Egyptologist, but an accomplished
student of comparative archæology. In these lectures, delivered at the Royal
Institution, he displays both qualifications with rare skill in elucidating the
development of decorative art in Egypt, and in tracing its influence on the
art of other countries.'—*Times.*

S. Baring Gould. THE TRAGEDY OF THE CÆSARS.
The Emperors of the Julian and Claudian Lines. With numerous
Illustrations from Busts, Gems, Cameos, etc. By S. BARING GOULD,
Author of ' Mehalah,' etc. *Fourth Edition. Royal 8vo. 15s.*

' A most splendid and fascinating book on a subject of undying interest. The great
feature of the book is the use the author has made of the existing portraits of the
Caesars, and the admirable critical subtlety he has exhibited in dealing with this
line of research. It is brilliantly written, and the illustrations are supplied on a
scale of profuse magnificence.'—*Daily Chronicle.*
' The volumes will in no sense disappoint the general reader. Indeed, in their way,
there is nothing in any sense so good in English. . . . Mr. Baring Gould has
presented his narrative in such a way as not to make one dull page.'—*Athenæum.*

H. de B. Gibbins. INDUSTRY IN ENGLAND : HISTORI-
CAL OUTLINES. By H. DE B. GIBBINS, M.A., D.Litt. With
5 Maps. *Second Edition. Demy 8vo. 10s. 6d.*

This book is written with the view of affording a clear view of the main facts of
English Social and Industrial History placed in due perspective. Beginning
with prehistoric times, it passes in review the growth and advance of industry
up to the nineteenth century, showing its gradual development and progress.
The book is illustrated by Maps, Diagrams, and Tables.

A. Clark. THE COLLEGES OF OXFORD : Their History
and their Traditions. By Members of the University. Edited by A.
CLARK, M.A., Fellow and Tutor of Lincoln College. *8vo. 12s. 6d.*

' A work which will certainly be appealed to for many years as the standard book on
the Colleges of Oxford.'—*Athenæum.*

Perrens. THE HISTORY OF FLORENCE FROM 1434
TO 1492. By F. T. PERRENS. Translated by HANNAH LYNCH.
8vo. 12s. 6d.

A history of Florence under the domination of Cosimo, Piero, and Lorenzo de
Medicis.
' This is a standard book by an honest and intelligent historian, who has deserved
well of all who are interested in Italian history.'—*Manchester Guardian.*

J. Wells. A SHORT HISTORY OF ROME. By J. WELLS,
M.A., Fellow and Tutor of Wadham Coll., Oxford. With 4 Maps.
Crown 8vo. 3s. 6d.

This book is intended for the Middle and Upper Forms of Public Schools and for
Pass Students at the Universities. It contains copious Tables, etc.
' An original work written on an original plan, and with uncommon freshness and
vigour.'—*Speaker.*

E. L. S. Horsburgh. THE CAMPAIGN OF WATERLOO. By E. L. S. HORSBURGH, B.A. *With Plans. Crown 8vo.* 5*s.*

'A brilliant essay—simple, sound, and thorough.'—*Daily Chronicle.*
'A study, the most concise, the most lucid, the most critical that has been produced.
—*Birmingham Mercury,*

H. B. George. BATTLES OF ENGLISH HISTORY. By H. B. GEORGE, M.A., Fellow of New College, Oxford. *With numerous Plans. Third Edition. Crown 8vo.* 6*s.*

'Mr. George has undertaken a very useful task—that of making military affairs intelligible and instructive to non-military readers—and has executed it with laudable intelligence and industry, and with a large measure of success.'—*Times.*

O. Browning. A SHORT HISTORY OF MEDIÆVAL ITALY, A.D. 1250-1530. By OSCAR BROWNING, Fellow and Tutor of King's College, Cambridge. *Second Edition. In Two Volumes. Crown 8vo.* 5*s. each.*

VOL. I. 1250-1409.—Guelphs and Ghibellines.
VOL. II. 1409-1530.—The Age of the Condottieri.

'A vivid picture of mediæval Italy.'—*Standard.*
'Mr. Browning is to be congratulated on the production of a work of immense labour and learning.'—*Westminster Gazette.*

O'Grady. THE STORY OF IRELAND. By STANDISH O'GRADY, Author of 'Finn and his Companions.' *Cr. 8vo.* 2*s.* 6*d.*

'Most delightful, most stimulating. Its racy humour, its original imaginings, make it one of the freshest, breeziest volumes.'—*Methodist Times.*

Biography

S. Baring Gould. THE LIFE OF NAPOLEON BONAPARTE. By S. BARING GOULD. With over 450 Illustrations in the Text and 12 Photogravure Plates. *Large quarto. Gilt top.* 36*s.*

'The best biography of Napoleon in our tongue, nor have the French as good a biographer of their hero. A book very nearly as good as Southey's "Life of Nelson."'—*Manchester Guardian.*
'The main feature of this gorgeous volume is its great wealth of beautiful photogravures and finely-executed wood engravings, constituting a complete pictorial chronicle of Napoleon I.'s personal history from the days of his early childhood at Ajaccio to the date of his second interment under the dome of the Invalides in Paris.'—*Daily Telegraph.*
'The most elaborate account of Napoleon ever produced by an English writer.'—*Daily Chronicle.*
'A brilliant and attractive volume. Never before have so many pictures relating to Napoleon been brought within the limits of an English book.'—*Globe.*
'Particular notice is due to the vast collection of contemporary illustrations.'—*Guardian.*
'Nearly all the illustrations are real contributions to history.'—*Westminster Gazette.*
'The illustrations are of supreme interest.'—*Standard'.*

Morris Fuller. THE LIFE AND WRITINGS OF JOHN DAVENANT, D.D. (1571-1641), President of Queen's College, Lady Margaret Professor of Divinity, Bishop of Salisbury. By MORRIS FULLER, B.D. *Demy 8vo.* 10s. 6d.

'A valuable contribution to ecclesiastical history.'—*Birmingham Gazette.*

J. M. Rigg. ST. ANSELM OF CANTERBURY: A CHAPTER IN THE HISTORY OF RELIGION. By J. M. RIGG. *Demy 8vo.* 7s. 6d.

'Mr. Rigg has told the story of the great Primate's life with scholarly ability, and has thereby contributed an interesting chapter to the history of the Norman period.' —*Daily Chronicle.*

F. W. Joyce. THE LIFE OF SIR FREDERICK GORE OUSELEY. By F. W. JOYCE, M.A. With Portraits and Illustrations. *Crown 8vo.* 7s. 6d.

'This book has been undertaken in quite the right spirit, and written with sympathy insight, and considerable literary skill.'—*Times.*

W. G. Collingwood. THE LIFE OF JOHN RUSKIN. By W. G. COLLINGWOOD, M.A., Editor of Mr. Ruskin's Poems. With numerous Portraits, and 13 Drawings by Mr. Ruskin. *Second Edition.* 2 vols. 8vo. 32s.

'No more magnificent volumes have been published for a long time.'—*Times.*
'It is long since we had a biography with such delights of substance and of form. Such a book is a pleasure for the day, and a joy for ever.'—*Daily Chronicle.*

C. Waldstein. JOHN RUSKIN: a Study. By CHARLES WALDSTEIN, M.A., Fellow of King's College, Cambridge. With a Photogravure Portrait after Professor HERKOMER. *Post 8vo.* 5s.

'A thoughtful, impartial, well-written criticism of Ruskin's teaching, intended to separate what the author regards as valuable and permanent from what is transient and erroneous in the great master's writing.'—*Daily Chronicle.*

W. H. Hutton. THE LIFE OF SIR THOMAS MORE. By W. H. HUTTON, M.A., Author of 'William Laud.' *With Portraits.* *Crown 8vo.* 5s.

'The book lays good claim to high rank among our biographies. It is excellently, even lovingly, written.'—*Scotsman.*   'An excellent monograph.'—*Times.*

Clark Russell. THE LIFE OF ADMIRAL LORD COLLINGWOOD. By W. CLARK RUSSELL, Author of 'The Wreck of the Grosvenor.' With Illustrations by F. BRANGWYN. *Third Edition.* *Crown 8vo.* 6s.

'A book which we should like to see in the hands of every boy in the country.'— *St. James's Gazette.*   'A really good book.'—*Saturday Review.*

Southey. ENGLISH SEAMEN (Howard, Clifford, Hawkins, Drake, Cavendish). By ROBERT SOUTHEY. Edited, with an Introduction, by DAVID HANNAY. *Second Edition. Crown 8vo. 6s.*

'Admirable and well-told stories of our naval history.'—*Army and Navy Gazette.*
'A brave, inspiriting book.'—*Black and White.*

Travel, Adventure and Topography

R. S. S. Baden-Powell. THE DOWNFALL OF PREMPEH. A Diary of Life with the Native Levy in Ashanti, 1895. By Colonel BADEN-POWELL. With 21 Illustrations and a Map. *Demy 8vo.* 10s. 6d.

'A compact, faithful, most readable record of the campaign.'—*Daily News.*
'A bluff and vigorous narrative.'—*Glasgow Herald.*

R. S. S. Baden-Powell. THE MATEBELE CAMPAIGN 1896. By Colonel R. S. S. BADEN-POWELL. With nearly 100 Illustrations. *Second Edition. Demy 8vo.* 15s.

'Written in an unaffectedly light and humorous style.'—*The World.*
'A very racy and eminently readable book.'—*St. James's Gazette.*
'As a straightforward account of a great deal of plucky work unpretentiously done, this book is well worth reading. The simplicity of the narrative is all in its favour, and accords in a peculiarly English fashion with the nature of the subject.' *Times.*

Captain Hinde. THE FALL OF THE CONGO ARABS. By SIDNEY L. HINDE. With Portraits and Plans. *Demy 8vo.* 12s. 6d.

'The book is full of good things, and of sustained interest.'—*St. James's Gazette.*

A graphic sketch of one of the most exciting and important episodes in the struggle for supremacy in Central Africa between the Arabs and their European rivals. Apart from the story of the campaign, Captain Hinde's book is mainly remarkable for the fulness with which he discusses the question of cannibalism. It is, indeed, the only connected narrative—in English, at any rate—which has been published of this particular episode in African history.'—*Times.*
'Captain Hinde's book is one of the most interesting and valuable contributions yet made to the literature of modern Africa.'—*Daily News.*

W. Crooke. THE NORTH-WESTERN PROVINCES OF INDIA: THEIR ETHNOLOGY AND ADMINISTRATION. By W. CROOKE. With Maps and Illustrations. *Demy 8vo.* 10s. 6d.

'A carefully and well-written account of one of the most important provinces of the Empire. In seven chapters Mr. Crooke deals successively with the land in its physical aspect, the province under Hindoo and Mussulman rule, the province under British rule, the ethnology and sociology of the province, the religious and social life of the people, the land and its settlement, and the native peasant in his relation to the land. The illustrations are good and well selected, and the map is excellent.'—*Manchester Guardian.*

W. B. Worsfold. SOUTH AFRICA : Its History and its Future. By W. BASIL WORSFOLD, M.A. *With a Map. Second Edition. Crown 8vo. 6s.*

' An intensely interesting book.'—*Daily Chronicle.*

' A monumental work compressed into a very moderate compass.'—*World.*

General Literature

S. Baring Gould. OLD COUNTRY LIFE. By S. BARING GOULD, Author of ' Mehalah,' etc. With Sixty-seven Illustrations by W. PARKINSON, F. D. BEDFORD, and F. MASEY. *Large Crown 8vo.* 10s. 6d. *Fifth and Cheaper Edition.* 6s.

' " Old Country Life," as healthy wholesome reading, full of breezy life and movement, full of quaint stories vigorously told, will not be excelled by any book to be published throughout the year. Sound, hearty, and English to the core.'—*World.*

S. Baring Gould. HISTORIC ODDITIES AND STRANGE EVENTS. By S. BARING GOULD. *Third Edition. Crown 8vo. 6s.*

' A collection of exciting and entertaining chapters. The whole volume is delightful reading.'—*Times.*

S. Baring Gould. FREAKS OF FANATICISM. By S. BARING GOULD. *Third Edition. Crown 8vo. 6s.*

' Mr. Baring Gould has a keen eye for colour and effect, and the subjects he has chosen give ample scope to his descriptive and analytic faculties. A perfectly fascinating book.'—*Scottish Leader.*

S. Baring Gould. A GARLAND OF COUNTRY SONG : English Folk Songs with their Traditional Melodies. Collected and arranged by S. BARING GOULD and H. FLEETWOOD SHEPPARD. *Demy 4to. 6s.*

S. Baring Gould. SONGS OF THE WEST : Traditional Ballads and Songs of the West of England, with their Traditional Melodies. Collected by S. BARING GOULD, M.A., and H. FLEETWOOD SHEPPARD, M.A. Arranged for Voice and Piano. In 4 Parts (containing 25 Songs each), *Parts I., II., III.,* 3s. each. *Part IV.,* 5s. *In one Vol., French morocco,* 15s.

' A rich collection of humour, pathos, grace, and poetic fancy.'—*Saturday Review.*

S. Baring Gould. YORKSHIRE ODDITIES AND STRANGE EVENTS. *Fourth Edition. Crown 8vo. 6s.*

S. Baring Gould. STRANGE SURVIVALS AND SUPER-STITIONS. With Illustrations. By S. BARING GOULD. *Crown 8vo. Second Edition. 6s.*

'We have read Mr. Baring Gould's book from beginning to end. It is full of quaint and various information, and there is not a dull page in it.'—*Notes and Queries.*

S. Baring Gould. THE DESERTS OF SOUTHERN FRANCE. By S. BARING·GOULD. With numerous Illustrations by F. D. BEDFORD, S. HUTTON, etc. *2 vols. Demy 8vo. 32s.*

'His two richly-illustrated volumes are full of matter of interest to the geologist, the archæologist, and the student of history and manners.'--*Scotsman.*

G. W. Steevens. NAVAL POLICY: WITH A DESCRIP-TION OF ENGLISH AND FOREIGN NAVIES. By G. W. STEEVENS. *Demy 8vo. 6s.*

This book is a description of the British and other more important navies of the world, with a sketch of the lines on which our naval policy might possibly be developed. It describes our recent naval policy, and shows what our naval force really is. A detailed but non-technical account is given of the instruments of modern warfare—guns, armour, engines, and the like—with a view to determine how far we are abreast of modern invention and modern requirements. An ideal policy is then sketched for the building and manning of our fleet; and the last chapter is devoted to docks, coaling-stations, and especially colonial defence.

'An extremely able and interesting work.'—*Daily Chronicle.*

W. E. Gladstone. THE SPEECHES AND PUBLIC AD-DRESSES OF THE RT. HON. W. E. GLADSTONE, M.P. Edited by A. W. HUTTON, M.A., and H. J. COHEN, M.A. With Portraits. *8vo. Vols. IX. and X. 12s. 6d. each.*

J. Wells. OXFORD AND OXFORD LIFE. By Members of the University. Edited by J. WELLS, M.A., Fellow and Tutor of Wadham College. *Crown 8vo. 3s. 6d.*

'We congratulate Mr. Wells on the production of a readable and intelligent account of Oxford as it is at the present time, written by persons who are possessed of a close acquaintance with the system and life of the University.'—*Athenæum.*

L. Whibley. GREEK OLIGARCHIES: THEIR ORGANISA-TION AND CHARACTER. By L. WHIBLEY, M.A., Fellow of Pembroke College, Cambridge. *Crown 8vo. 6s.*

'An exceedingly useful handbook: a careful and well-arranged study of an obscure subject.'—*Times.*

'Mr. Whibley is never tedious or pedantic.'—*Pall Mall Gazette.*

L. L. Price. ECONOMIC SCIENCE AND PRACTICE. By L. L. PRICE, M.A., Fellow of Oriel College, Oxford. *Crown 8vo. 6s.*

'The book is well written, giving evidence of considerable literary ability, and clear mental grasp of the subject under consideration.'—*Western Morning News.*

C. F. Andrews. CHRISTIANITY AND THE LABOUR QUESTION. By C. F. ANDREWS, B.A. *Crown 8vo. 2s. 6d.*

'A bold and scholarly survey.'—*Speaker.*

J. S. Shedlock. THE PIANOFORTE SONATA: Its Origin and Development. By J. S. SHEDLOCK. *Crown 8vo. 5s.*

'This work should be in the possession of every musician and amateur, for it not only embodies a concise and lucid history of the origin of one of the most important forms of musical composition, but, by reason of the painstaking research and accuracy of the author's statements, it is a very valuable work for reference.' —*Athenæum.*

E. M. Bowden. THE EXAMPLE OF BUDDHA: Being Quotations from Buddhist Literature for each Day in the Year. Compiled by E. M. BOWDEN. With Preface by Sir EDWIN ARNOLD. *Third Edition.* 16mo. 2s. 6d.

Science

Freudenreich. DAIRY BACTERIOLOGY. A Short Manual for the Use of Students. By Dr. ED. VON FREUDENREICH. Translated from the German by J. R. AINSWORTH DAVIS, B.A., F.C.P. *Crown 8vo. 2s. 6d.*

Chalmers Mitchell. OUTLINES OF BIOLOGY. By P. CHALMERS MITCHELL, M.A., F.Z.S. *Fully Illustrated. Crown 8vo. 6s.*

A text-book designed to cover the new Schedule issued by the Royal College of Physicians and Surgeons.

G. Massee. A MONOGRAPH OF THE MYXOGASTRES. By GEORGE MASSEE. With 12 Coloured Plates. *Royal 8vo. 18s. net.*

'A work much in advance of any book in the language treating of this group of organisms. It is indispensable to every student of the Myxogastres. The coloured plates deserve high praise for their accuracy and execution.'—*Nature.*

Philosophy

L. T. Hobhouse. THE THEORY OF KNOWLEDGE. By L. T. HOBHOUSE, Fellow and Tutor of Corpus College, Oxford. *Demy 8vo.* 21*s*.

'The most important contribution to English philosophy since the publication of Mr. Bradley's "Appearance and Reality." Full of brilliant criticism and of positive theories which are models of lucid statement.'—*Glasgow Herald.*

'An elaborate and often brilliantly written volume. The treatment is one of great freshness, and the illustrations are particularly numerous and apt.'—*Times.*

W. H. Fairbrother. THE PHILOSOPHY OF T. H. GREEN. By W. H. FAIRBROTHER, M.A., Lecturer at Lincoln College, Oxford. *Crown 8vo.* 3*s*. 6*d*.

This volume is expository, not critical, and is intended for senior students at the Universities and others, as a statement of Green's teaching, and an introduction to the study of Idealist Philosophy.

'In every way an admirable book. As an introduction to the writings of perhaps the most remarkable speculative thinker whom England has produced in the present century, nothing could be better.'—*Glasgow Herald.*

F. W. Bussell. THE SCHOOL OF PLATO : its Origin and its Revival under the Roman Empire. By F. W. BUSSELL, M.A., Fellow and Tutor of Brasenose College, Oxford. *Demy 8vo.* 10*s*. 6*d*.

'A highly valuable contribution to the history of ancient thought.'—*Glasgow Herald.*
'A clever and stimulating book, provocative of thought and deserving careful reading.' —*Manchester Guardian.*

F. S. Granger. THE WORSHIP OF THE ROMANS. By F. S. GRANGER, M.A., Litt.D., Professor of Philosophy at University College, Nottingham. *Crown 8vo.* 6*s*.

'A scholarly analysis of the religious ceremonies, beliefs, and superstitions of ancient Rome, conducted in the new instructive light of comparative anthropology.'—*Times.*

Theology

E. C. S. Gibson. THE XXXIX. ARTICLES OF THE CHURCH OF ENGLAND. Edited with an Introduction by E. C. S. GIBSON, D.D., Vicar of Leeds, late Principal of Wells Theological College. *In Two Volumes. Demy 8vo.* 15*s*.

'The tone maintained throughout is not that of the partial advocate, but the faithful exponent.'—*Scotsman.*

'There are ample proofs of clearness of expression, sobriety of judgment, and breadth of view. . . . The book will be welcome to all students of the subject, and its sound, definite, and loyal theology ought to be of great service.'—*National Observer.*

'So far from repelling the general reader, its orderly arrangement, lucid treatment, and felicity of diction invite and encourage his attention.'—*Yorkshire Post.*

R. L. Ottley. THE DOCTRINE OF THE INCARNATION. By R. L. OTTLEY, M.A., late fellow of Magdalen College, Oxon., Principal of Pusey House. *In Two Volumes. Demy 8vo.* 15*s.*

'Learned and reverent : lucid and well arranged.'—*Record.*
'Accurate, well ordered, and judicious.'—*National Observer.*
'A clear and remarkably full account of the main currents of speculation. Scholarly precision . . . genuine tolerance . . . intense interest in his subject—are Mr. Ottley's merits.'—*Guardian.*

F. B. Jevons. AN INTRODUCTION TO THE HISTORY OF RELIGION. By F. B. JEVONS, M.A., Litt.D., Principal of Bishop Hatfield's Hall. *Demy 8vo.* 10*s.* 6*d.*

Mr. F. B. Jevons' 'Introduction to the History of Religion' treats of early religion, from the point of view of Anthropology and Folk-lore ; and is the first attempt that has been made in any language to weave together the results of recent investigations into such topics as Sympathetic Magic, Taboo, Totemism. Fetishism, etc., so as to present a systematic account of the growth of primitive religion and the development of early religious institutions.
'Dr. Jevons has written a notable work, and we can strongly recommend it to the serious attention of theologians, anthropologists, and classical scholars.'—*Manchester Guardian.*
'The merit of this book lies in the penetration, the singular acuteness and force of the author's judgment. He is at once critical and luminous, at once just and suggestive. It is but rarely that one meets with a book so comprehensive and so thorough as this, and it is more than an ordinary pleasure for the reviewer to welcome and recommend it. Dr. Jevons is something more than an historian of primitive belief—he is a philosophic thinker, who sees his subject clearly and sees it whole, whose mastery of detail is no less complete than his view of the broader aspects and issues of his subject is convincing.'—*Birmingham Post.*

S. R. Driver. SERMONS ON SUBJECTS CONNECTED WITH THE OLD TESTAMENT. By S. R. DRIVER, D.D., Canon of Christ Church, Regius Professor of Hebrew in the University of Oxford. *Crown 8vo.* 6*s.*

'A welcome companion to the author's famous 'Introduction.' No man can read these discourses without feeling that Dr. Driver is fully alive to the deeper teaching of the Old Testament.'—*Guardian.*

T. K. Cheyne. FOUNDERS OF OLD TESTAMENT CRITICISM : Biographical, Descriptive, and Critical Studies. By T. K. CHEYNE, D.D., Oriel Professor of the Interpretation of Holy Scripture at Oxford. *Large crown 8vo.* 7*s.* 6*d.*

This book is a historical sketch of O. T. Criticism in the form of biographical studies from the days of Eichhorn to those of Driver and Robertson Smith.
'A very learned and instructive work.'—*Times.*

C. H. Prior. CAMBRIDGE SERMONS. Edited by C. H. PRIOR, M.A., Fellow and Tutor of Pembroke College. *Crown 8vo.* 6*s.*

A volume of sermons preached before the University of Cambridge by various preachers, including the Archbishop of Canterbury and Bishop Westcott.
A representative collection. Bishop Westcott's is a noble sermon.'—*Guardian.*

E. B. Layard. RELIGION IN BOYHOOD. Notes on the Religious Training of Boys. With a Preface by J. R. ILLINGWORTH. By E. B. LAYARD, M.A. 18*mo.* 1*s.*

W. Yorke Faussett. THE *DE CATECHIZANDIS RUDIBUS* OF ST. AUGUSTINE. Edited, with Introduction, Notes, etc., by W. YORKE FAUSSETT, M.A., late Scholar of Balliol Coll. *Crown 8vo.* 3s. 6d.

An edition of a Treatise on the Essentials of Christian Doctrine, and the best methods of impressing them on candidates for baptism.

'Ably and judiciously edited on the same principle as the ordinary Greek and Latin texts.'—*Glasgow Herald.*

Devotional Books.

With Full-page Illustrations. Fcap. 8vo. Buckram. 3s. 6d.
Padded morocco, 5s.

THE IMITATION OF CHRIST. By THOMAS À KEMPIS. With an Introduction by DEAN FARRAR. Illustrated by C. M. GERE, and printed in black and red. *Second Edition.*

'Amongst all the innumerable English editions of the "Imitation," there can have been few which were prettier than this one, printed in strong and handsome type, with all the glory of red initials.'—*Glasgow Herald.*

THE CHRISTIAN YEAR. By JOHN KEBLE. With an Introduction and Notes by W. LOCK, D.D., Warden of Keble College, Ireland, Professor at Oxford. Illustrated by R. ANNING BELL.

'The present edition is annotated with all the care and insight to be expected from Mr. Lock. The progress and circumstances of its composition are detailed in the Introduction. There is an interesting Appendix on the MSS. of the "Christian Year," and another giving the order in which the poems were written. A "Short Analysis of the Thought" is prefixed to each, and any difficulty in the text is explained in a note.'—*Guardian.*

'The most acceptable edition of this ever-popular work.'—*Globe.*

Leaders of Religion

Edited by H. C. BEECHING, M.A. *With Portraits, crown 8vo.*

A series of short biographies of the most prominent leaders of religious life and thought of all ages and countries.

The following are ready—

3/6

CARDINAL NEWMAN. By R. H. HUTTON.

JOHN WESLEY. By J. H. OVERTON, M.A.

BISHOP WILBERFORCE. By G. W. DANIEL, M.A.

CARDINAL MANNING. By A. W. HUTTON, M.A.

CHARLES SIMEON. By H. C. G. MOULE, M.A.

JOHN KEBLE. By WALTER LOCK, D.D.

THOMAS CHALMERS. By Mrs. OLIPHANT.

LANCELOT ANDREWES. By R. L. OTTLEY, M.A.

AUGUSTINE OF CANTERBURY. By E. L. CUTTS, D.D.

WILLIAM LAUD. By W. H. HUTTON, B.D.

JOHN KNOX. By F. M'Cunn.
JOHN HOWE. By R. F. Horton, D.D.
BISHOP KEN. By F. A. Clarke, M.A.
GEORGE FOX, THE QUAKER. By T. Hodgkin, D.C.L.
Other volumes will be announced in due course.

Fiction

SIX SHILLING NOVELS

Marie Corelli's Novels

Crown 8vo. 6s. each.

A ROMANCE OF TWO WORLDS. *Sixteenth Edition.*

VENDETTA. *Thirteenth Edition.*

THELMA. *Seventeenth Edition.*

ARDATH. *Eleventh Edition.*

THE SOUL OF LILITH *Ninth Edition.*

WORMWOOD. *Eighth Edition.*

BARABBAS: A DREAM OF THE WORLD'S TRAGEDY.
Thirty-first Edition.

'The tender reverence of the treatment and the imaginative beauty of the writing
have reconciled us to the daring of the conception, and the conviction is forced on
us that even so exalted a subject cannot be made too familiar to us, provided it be
presented in the true spirit of Christian faith. The amplifications of the Scripture
narrative are often conceived with high poetic insight, and this "Dream of the
World's Tragedy" is, despite some trifling incongruities, a lofty and not inade-
quate paraphrase of the supreme climax of the inspired narrative.'—*Dublin
Review.*

THE SORROWS OF SATAN. *Thirty-sixth Edition.*

'A very powerful piece of work. . . . The conception is magnificent, and is likely
to win an abiding place within the memory of man. . . . The author has immense
command of language, and a limitless audacity. . . . This interesting and remarkable romance will live long after much of the ephemeral literature of the day
is forgotten. . . . A literary phenomenon . . . novel, and even sublime.'—W. T.
Stead in the *Review of Reviews.*

Anthony Hope's Novels

Crown 8vo. 6s. each.

THE GOD IN THE CAR. *Seventh Edition.*

'A very remarkable book, deserving of critical analysis impossible within our limit ;
brilliant, but not superficial ; well considered, but not elaborated ; constructed
with the proverbial art that conceals, but yet allows itself to be enjoyed by readers
to whom fine literary method is a keen pleasure.'—*The World.*

A CHANGE OF AIR. *Fourth Edition.*

'A graceful, vivacious comedy, true to human nature. The characters are traced
with a masterly hand.'—*Times.*

A MAN OF MARK. *Fourth Edition.*

'Of all Mr. Hope's books, "A Man of Mark" is the one which best compares with
"The Prisoner of Zenda."'—*National Observer.*

THE CHRONICLES OF COUNT ANTONIO. *Third Edition.*
'It is a perfectly enchanting story of love and chivalry, and pure romance. The outlawed Count is the most constant, desperate, and withal modest and tender of lovers, a peerless gentleman, an intrepid fighter, a very faithful friend, and a most magnanimous foe.'—*Guardian.*

PHROSO. Illustrated by H. R. MILLAR. *Third Edition.*
'The tale is thoroughly fresh, quick with vitality, stirring the blood, and humorously, dashingly told.'—*St. James's Gazette.*
'A story of adventure, every page of which is palpitating with action and excitement.' —*Speaker.*
'From cover to cover "Phroso" not only engages the attention, but carries the reader in little whirls of delight from adventure to adventure.'—*Academy.*

S. Baring Gould's Novels
Crown 8vo.   6s. each.
'To say that a book is by the author of "Mehalah" is to imply that it contains a story cast on strong lines, containing dramatic possibilities, vivid and sympathetic descriptions of Nature, and a wealth of ingenious imagery.'—*Speaker.*
'That whatever Mr. Baring Gould writes is well worth reading, is a conclusion that may be very generally accepted. His views of life are fresh and vigorous, his language pointed and characteristic, the incidents of which he makes use are striking and original, his characters are life-like, and though somewhat exceptional people, are drawn and coloured with artistic force. Add to this that his descriptions of scenes and scenery are painted with the loving eyes and skilled hands of a master of his art, that he is always fresh and never dull, and under such conditions it is no wonder that readers have gained confidence both in his power of amusing and satisfying them, and that year by year his popularity widens.'—*Court Circular.*

ARMINELL : A Social Romance. *Fourth Edition.*

URITH : A Story of Dartmoor. *Fifth Edition.*
'The author is at his best.'—*Times.*

IN THE ROAR OF THE SEA. *Sixth Edition.*
'One of the best imagined and most enthralling stories the author has produced. —*Saturday Review.*

MRS. CURGENVEN OF CURGENVEN. *Fourth Edition.*
'The swing of the narrative is splendid.'—*Sussex Daily News.*

CHEAP JACK ZITA. *Fourth Edition.*
'A powerful drama of human passion.'—*Westminster Gazette.*
'A story worthy the author.'—*National Observer.*

THE QUEEN OF LOVE. *Fourth Edition.*
'You cannot put it down until you have finished it.'—*Punch.*
'Can be heartily recommended to all who care for cleanly, energetic, and interesting fiction.'—*Sussex Daily News.*

KITTY ALONE. *Fourth Edition.*
'A strong and original story, teeming with graphic description, stirring incident, and, above all, with vivid and enthralling human interest.'—*Daily Telegraph.*

NOÉMI : A Romance of the Cave-Dwellers. Illustrated by R. CATON WOODVILLE. *Third Edition.*
'"Noémi" is as excellent a tale of fighting and adventure as one may wish to meet. The narrative also runs clear and sharp as the Loire itself.'—*Pall Mall Gazette.*
'Mr. Baring Gould's powerful story is full of the strong lights and shadows and vivid colouring to which he has accustomed us.'—*Standard.*

THE BROOM-SQUIRE. Illustrated by FRANK DADD.
Fourth Edition.
'A strain of tenderness is woven through the web of his tragic tale, and its atmosphere is sweetened by the nobility and sweetness of the heroine's character.'—*Daily News.*
'A story of exceptional interest that seems to us to be better than anything he has written of late.'—*Speaker.*

THE PENNYCOMEQUICKS. *Third Edition.*

DARTMOOR IDYLLS.
'A book to read, and keep and read again; for the genuine fun and pathos of it will not early lose their effect.'—*Vanity Fair.*

GUAVAS THE TINNER. Illustrated by Frank Dadd. *Second Edition.*
'Mr. Baring Gould is a wizard who transports us into a region of visions, often lurid and disquieting, but always full of interest and enchantment.'—*Spectator.*
'In the weirdness of the story, in the faithfulness with which the characters are depicted, and in force of style, it closely resembles "Mehalah."'—*Daily Telegraph.*
'There is a kind of flavour about this book which alone elevates it above the ordinary novel. The story itself has a grandeur in harmony with the wild and rugged scenery which is its setting.'—*Athenæum.*

Gilbert Parker's Novels

Crown 8vo. 6s. each.

PIERRE AND HIS PEOPLE. *Fourth Edition.*
'Stories happily conceived and finely executed. There is strength and genius in Mr. Parker's style.'—*Daily Telegraph.*

MRS. FALCHION. *Fourth Edition.*
'A splendid study of character.'—*Athenæum.*
'But little behind anything that has been done by any writer of our time.'—*Pall Mall Gazette.* 'A very striking and admirable novel.'—*St. James's Gazette.*

THE TRANSLATION OF A SAVAGE.
'The plot is original and one difficult to work out; but Mr. Parker has done it with great skill and delicacy. The reader who is not interested in this original, fresh, and well-told tale must be a dull person indeed.'—*Daily Chronicle.*

THE TRAIL OF THE SWORD. *Fifth Edition.*
'Everybody with a soul for romance will thoroughly enjoy "The Trail of the Sword."'—*St. James's Gazette.*
'A rousing and dramatic tale. A book like this, in which swords flash, great surprises are undertaken, and daring deeds done, in which men and women live and love in the old straightforward passionate way, is a joy inexpressible to the reviewer.'—*Daily Chronicle.*

WHEN VALMOND CAME TO PONTIAC: The Story of a Lost Napoleon. *Fourth Edition.*
'Here we find romance—real, breathing, living romance, but it runs flush with our own times, level with our own feelings. The character of Valmond is drawn unerringly; his career, brief as it is, is placed before us as convincingly as history itself. The book must be read, we may say re-read, for any one thoroughly to appreciate Mr. Parker's delicate touch and innate sympathy with humanity.'—*Pall Mall Gazette.*
'The one work of genius which 1895 has as yet produced.'—*New Age.*

AN ADVENTURER OF THE NORTH: The Last Adventures of 'Pretty Pierre.' *Second Edition.*
'The present book is full of fine and moving stories of the great North, and it will add to Mr. Parker's already high reputation.'—*Glasgow Herald.*

THE SEATS OF THE MIGHTY. *Illustrated. Eighth Edition.*
'The best thing he has done; one of the best things that any one has done lately.'—
St. James's Gazette.
'Mr. Parker seems to become stronger and easier with every serious novel that he
attempts. . . . In "The Seats of the Mighty" he shows the matured power which
his former novels have led us to expect, and has produced a really fine historical
novel. . . . Most sincerely is Mr. Parker to be congratulated on the finest
novel he has yet written.'—*Athenæum.*
'Mr. Parker's latest book places him in the front rank of living novelists. "The
Seats of the Mighty" is a great book.'—*Black and White.*
'One of the strongest stories of historical interest and adventure that we have read
for many a day. . . . A notable and successful book.'—*Speaker.*

Conan Doyle. ROUND THE RED LAMP. By A. CONAN
DOYLE, Author of 'The White Company,' 'The Adventures of
Sherlock Holmes,' etc. *Fifth Edition. Crown 8vo. 6s.*
'The book is, indeed, composed of leaves from life, and is far and away the best view
that has been vouchsafed us behind the scenes of the consulting-room. It is very
superior to "The Diary of a late Physician."'—*Illustrated London News.*

Stanley Weyman. UNDER THE RED ROBE. By STANLEY
WEYMAN, Author of 'A Gentleman of France.' With Twelve Illustrations by R. Caton Woodville. *Twelfth Edition. Crown 8vo. 6s.*
'A book of which we have read every word for the sheer pleasure of reading, and
which we put down with a pang that we cannot forget it all and start again.'—
Westminster Gazette.
'Every one who reads books at all must read this thrilling romance, from the first
page of which to the last the breathless reader is haled along. An inspiration of
"manliness and courage."'—*Daily Chronicle.*

Lucas Malet. THE WAGES OF SIN. By LUCAS
MALET. *Thirteenth Edition. Crown 8vo. 6s.*

Lucas Malet. THE CARISSIMA. By LUCAS MALET,
Author of 'The Wages of Sin,' etc. *Third Edition. Crown 8vo. 6s.*

Arthur Morrison. TALES OF MEAN STREETS. By ARTHUR
MORRISON. *Fourth Edition. Crown 8vo. 6s.*
'Told with consummate art and extraordinary detail. He tells a plain, unvarnished
tale, and the very truth of it makes for beauty. In the true humanity of the book
lies its justification, the permanence of its interest, and its indubitable triumph.'—
Athenæum.
'A great book. The author's method is amazingly effective, and produces a thrilling
sense of reality. The writer lays upon us a master hand. The book is simply
appalling and irresistible in its interest. It is humorous also; without humour
it would not make the mark it is certain to make.'—*World.*

Arthur Morrison. A CHILD OF THE JAGO. By ARTHUR
MORRISON. *Third Edition. Crown 8vo. 6s.*
This, the first long story which Mr. Morrison has written, is like his remarkable
'Tales of Mean Streets,' a realistic study of East End life.
'The book is a masterpiece.'—*Pall Mall Gazette.*
'Told with great vigour and powerful simplicity.'—*Athenæum.*

Mrs. Clifford. A FLASH OF SUMMER. By Mrs. W. K. CLIF-
FORD, Author of 'Aunt Anne,' etc. *Second Edition. Crown 8vo. 6s.*
'The story is a very sad and a very beautiful one, exquisitely told, and enriched with
many subtle touches of wise and tender insight. It will, undoubtedly, add to its
author's reputation—already high—in the ranks of novelists.'—*Speaker.*

Emily Lawless. HURRISH. By the Honble. EMILY LAW-
LESS, Author of 'Maelcho,' etc. *Fifth Edition. Crown 8vo. 6s.*
A reissue of Miss Lawless' most popular novel, uniform with 'Maelcho.'

Emily Lawless. MAELCHO : a Sixteenth Century Romance.
By the Honble. EMILY LAWLESS. *Second Edition. Crown 8vo. 6s.*
'A really great book.'—*Spectator.*
'There is no keener pleasure in life than the recognition of genius. Good work is
commoner than it used to be, but the best is as rare as ever. All the more
gladly, therefore, do we welcome in "Maelcho" a piece of work of the first order,
which we do not hesitate to describe as one of the most remarkable literary
achievements of this generation. Miss Lawless is possessed of the very essence
of historical genius.'—*Manchester Guardian.*

J. H. Findlater. THE GREEN GRAVES OF BALGOWRIE.
By JANE H. FINDLATER. *Fourth Edition. Crown 8vo. 6s.*
'A powerful and vivid story.'—*Standard.*
'A beautiful story, sad and strange as truth itself.'—*Vanity Fair.*
'A work of remarkable interest and originality.'—*National Observer.*
'A very charming and pathetic tale.'—*Pall Mall Gazette.*
'A singularly original, clever, and beautiful story.'—*Guardian.*
'"The Green Graves of Balgowrie" reveals to us a new Scotch writer of undoubted
faculty and reserve force.'—*Spectator.*
'An exquisite idyll, delicate, affecting, and beautiful.'—*Black and White.*

H. G. Wells. THE STOLEN BACILLUS, and other Stories.
By H. G. WELLS, Author of 'The Time Machine.' *Second Edition.
Crown 8vo. 6s.*
'The ordinary reader of fiction may be glad to know that these stories are eminently
readable from one cover to the other, but they are more than that ; they are the
impressions of a very striking imagination, which, it would seem, has a great deal
within its reach.'—*Saturday Review.*

H. G. Wells. THE PLATTNER STORY AND OTHERS. By H.
G. WELLS. *Second Edition. Crown 8vo. 6s.*
'Weird and mysterious, they seem to hold the reader as by a magic spell.'—*Scotsman.*
'Such is the fascination of this writer's skill that you unhesitatingly prophesy that
none of the many readers, however his flesh do creep, will relinquish the volume
ere he has read from first word to last.'—*Black and White.*
'No volume has appeared for a long time so likely to give equal pleasure to the
simplest reader and to the most fastidious critic.'—*Academy.*
'Mr. Wells is a magician skilled in wielding that most potent of all spells—the fear
of the unknown.'—*Daily Telegraph.*

E. F. Benson. DODO : A DETAIL OF THE DAY. By E. F.
BENSON. *Sixteenth Edition. Crown 8vo. 6s.*
'A delightfully witty sketch of society.'—*Spectator.*
'A perpetual feast of epigram and paradox.'—*Speaker.*

E. F. Benson. THE RUBICON. By E. F. BENSON, Author of
'Dodo.' *Fifth Edition. Crown 8vo. 6s.*
'An exceptional achievement ; a notable advance on his previous work.'—*National
Observer.*

Mrs. Oliphant. SIR ROBERT'S FORTUNE. By MRS.
OLIPHANT. *Crown 8vo. 6s.*
'Full of her own peculiar charm of style and simple, subtle character-painting comes
her new gift, the delightful story before us. The scene mostly lies in the moors,
and at the touch of the authoress a Scotch moor becomes a living thing, strong,
tender, beautiful, and changeful.'—*Pall Mall Gazette.*

Mrs. Oliphant. THE TWO MARYS. By MRS. OLIPHANT. *Second Edition. Crown 8vo. 6s.*

W. E. Norris. MATTHEW AUSTIN. By W. E. NORRIS, Author of ' Mademoiselle de Mersac,' etc. *Fourth Edition. Crown 8vo. 6s.*

"Matthew Austin" may safely be pronounced one of the most intellectually satisfactory and morally bracing novels of the current year.'—*Daily Telegraph.*

W. E. Norris. HIS GRACE. By W. E. NORRIS. *Third Edition. Crown 8vo. 6s.*

' Mr. Norris has drawn a really fine character in the Duke of Hurstbourne, at once unconventional and very true to the conventionalities of life.'—*Athenæum.*

W. E. Norris. THE DESPOTIC LADY AND OTHERS. By W. E. NORRIS. *Crown 8vo. 6s.*

' A budget of good fiction of which no one will tire.'—*Scotsman.*

W. E. Norris. CLARISSA FURIOSA. By W. E. NORRIS, Author of ' The Rogue,' etc. *Crown 8vo. 6s.*

' One of Mr. Norris's very best novels. As a story it is admirable, as a *jeu d'esprit* it is capital, as a lay sermon studded with gems of wit and wisdom it is a model which will not, we imagine, find an efficient imitator.'—*The World.*
' The best novel he has written for some time: a story which is full of admirable character-drawing.'—*The Standard.*

Robert Barr. IN THE MIDST OF ALARMS. By ROBERT BARR. *Third Edition. Crown 8vo. 6s.*

' A book which has abundantly satisfied us by its capital humour.'—*Daily Chronicle.*
' Mr. Barr has achieved a triumph whereof he has every reason to be proud.'—*Pall Mall Gazette.*

J. Maclaren Cobban. THE KING OF ANDAMAN : A Saviour of Society. By J. MACLAREN COBBAN. *Crown 8vo. 6s.*

' An unquestionably interesting book. It would not surprise us if it turns out to be the most interesting novel of the season, for it contains one character, at least, who has in him the root of immortality, and the book itself is ever exhaling the sweet savour of the unexpected. . . . Plot is forgotten and incident fades, and only the really human endures, and throughout this book there stands out in bold and beautiful relief its high-souled and chivalric protagonist, James the Master of Hutcheon, the King of Andaman himself.'—*Pall Mall Gazette.*

J. Maclaren Cobban. WILT THOU HAVE THIS WOMAN ? By J. M. COBBAN, Author of ' The King of Andaman.' *Crown 8vo. 6s.*

' Mr. Cobban has the true story-teller's art. He arrests attention at the outset, and he retains it to the end.'—*Birmingham Post.*

H. Morrah. A SERIOUS COMEDY. By HERBERT MORRAH. *Crown 8vo. 6s.*

' This volume is well worthy of its title. The theme has seldom been presented with more freshness or more force.'—*Scotsman.*

H. Morrah. THE FAITHFUL CITY. By HERBERT MORRAH, Author of 'A Serious Comedy.' *Crown 8vo. 6s.*

'Conveys a suggestion of weirdness and horror, until finally he convinces and enthrals the reader with his mysterious savages, his gigantic tower, and his uncompromising men and women. This is a haunting, mysterious book, not without an element of stupendous grandeur.'—*Athenæum.*

L. B. Walford. SUCCESSORS TO THE TITLE. By MRS. WALFORD, Author of 'Mr. Smith,' etc. *Second Edition. Crown 8vo. 6s.*

'The story is fresh and healthy from beginning to finish; and our liking for the two simple people who are the successors to the title mounts steadily, and ends almost in respect.'—*Scotsman.*

T. L. Paton. A HOME IN INVERESK. By T. L. PATON. *Crown 8vo. 6s.*

'A pleasant and well-written story.'—*Daily Chronicle.*

John Davidson. MISS ARMSTRONG'S AND OTHER CIRCUMSTANCES. By JOHN DAVIDSON. *Crown 8vo. 6s.*

'Throughout the volume there is a strong vein of originality, and a knowledge of human nature that are worthy of the highest praise.'—*Scotsman.*

M. M. Dowie. GALLIA. By MÉNIE MURIEL DOWIE, Author of 'A Girl in the Carpathians.' *Third Edition. Crown 8vo. 6s.*

'The style is generally admirable, the dialogue not seldom brilliant, the situations surprising in their freshness and originality, while the subsidiary as well as the principal characters live and move, and the story itself is readable from title-page to colophon.'—*Saturday Review.*

J. A. Barry. IN THE GREAT DEEP : TALES OF THE SEA. By J. A. BARRY. Author of 'Steve Brown's Bunyip.' *Crown 8vo. 6s.*

'A collection of really admirable short stories of the sea, very simply told, and placed before the reader in pithy and telling English.'—*Westminster Gazette.*

J. B. Burton. IN THE DAY OF ADVERSITY. By J. BLOUNDELLE BURTON.' *Second Edition. Crown 8vo. 6s.*

'Unusually interesting and full of highly dramatic situations.'—*Guardian.*

J. B. Burton. DENOUNCED. By J. BLOUNDELLE BURTON. *Second Edition. Crown 8vo. 6s.*

The plot is an original one, and the local colouring is laid on with a delicacy and an accuracy of detail which denote the true artist.'—*Broad Arrow.*

W. C. Scully. THE WHITE HECATOMB. By W. C. SCULLY, Author of 'Kafir Stories.' *Crown 8vo. 6s.*

'The author is so steeped in Kaffir lore and legend, and so thoroughly well acquainted with native sagas and traditional ceremonial that he is able to attract the reader by the easy familiarity with which he handles his characters.'—*South Africa.*

'It reveals a marvellously intimate understanding of the Kaffir mind, allied with literary gifts of no mean order.'—*African Critic.*

H. Johnston. DR. CONGALTON'S LEGACY. By HENRY JOHNSTON. *Crown 8vo. 6s.*

'A worthy and permanent contribution to Scottish literature.'—*Glasgow Herald.*

J. F. Brewer. THE SPECULATORS. By J. F. BREWER. *Second Edition. Crown 8vo. 6s.*
'A pretty bit of comedy. . . . It is undeniably a clever booκ.'—*Academy.*
'A clever and amusing story. It makes capital out of the comic aspects of culture, and will be read with amusement by every intellectual reader.'—*Scotsman.*
'A remarkably clever study.'—*Vanity Fair.*

Julian Corbett. A BUSINESS IN GREAT WATERS. By JULIAN CORBETT. *Crown 8vo. 6s.*
'Mr. Corbett writes with immense spirit, and the book is a thoroughly enjoyable one in all respects. The salt of the ocean is in it, and the right heroic ring resounds through its gallant adventures.'—*Speaker.*

L. Cope Cornford. CAPTAIN JACOBUS: A ROMANCE OF THE ROAD. By L. COPE CORNFORD. Illustrated. *Crown 8vo. 6s.*
'An exceptionally good story of adventure and character.'—*World.*

C. P. Wolley. THE QUEENSBERRY CUP. A Tale of Adventure. By CLIVE PHILLIPS WOLLEY. *Illustrated. Crown 8vo. 6s.*
'A book which will delight boys: a book which upholds the healthy schoolboy code of morality.'—*Scotsman.*

L. Daintrey. THE KING OF ALBERIA. A Romance of the Balkans. By LAURA DAINTREY. *Crown 8vo. 6s.*
'Miss Daintrey seems to have an intimate acquaintance with the people and politics of the Balkan countries in which the scene of her lively and picturesque romance is laid.'—*Glasgow Herald.*

M. A. Owen. THE DAUGHTER OF ALOUETTE. By MARY A. OWEN. *Crown 8vo. 6s.*
A story of life among the American Indians.
'A fascinating story.'—*Literary World.*

Mrs. Pinsent. CHILDREN OF THIS WORLD. By ELLEN F. PINSENT, Author of 'Jenny's Case.' *Crown 8vo. 6s.*
'Mrs. Pinsent's new novel has plenty of vigour, variety, and good writing. There are certainty of purpose, strength of touch, and clearness of vision.'—*Athenæum.*

Clark Russell. MY DANISH SWEETHEART. By W. CLARK RUSSELL, Author of 'The Wreck of the Grosvenor,' etc. *Illustrated. Fourth Edition. Crown 8vo. 6s.*

G. Manville Fenn. AN ELECTRIC SPARK. By G. MANVILLE FENN, Author of 'The Vicar's Wife,' 'A Double Knot,' etc. *Second Edition. Crown 8vo. 6s.*

L. S. McChesney. UNDER SHADOW OF THE MISSION. By L. S. McCHESNEY. *Crown 8vo. 6s.*
'Those whose minds are open to the finer issues of life, who can appreciate graceful thought and refined expression of it, from them this volume will receive a welcome as enthusiastic as it will be based on critical knowledge.'—*Church Times.*

Ronald Ross. THE SPIRIT OF STORM. By RONALD ROSS, Author of 'The Child of Ocean.' *Crown 8vo. 6s.*
A romance of the Sea.   'Weird, powerful, and impressive.'—*Black and White.*

R. Pryce. TIME AND THE WOMAN. By RICHARD PRYCE. *Second Edition. Crown 8vo. 6s.*

Mrs. Watson. THIS MAN'S DOMINION. By the Author of ' A High Little World.' *Second Edition. Crown 8vo. 6s.*

Marriott Watson. DIOGENES OF LONDON. By H. B. MARRIOTT WATSON. *Crown 8vo. Buckram. 6s.*

M. Gilchrist. THE STONE DRAGON. By MURRAY GIL-CHRIST. *Crown 8vo. Buckram. 6s.*

'The author's faults are atoned for by certain positive and admirable merits. The romances have not their counterpart in modern literature, and to read them is a unique experience.'—*National Observer.*

E. Dickinson. A VICAR'S WIFE. By EVELYN DICKINSON. *Crown 8vo. 6s.*

E. M. Gray. ELSA. By E. M'QUEEN GRAY. *Crown 8vo. 6s.*

THREE-AND-SIXPENNY NOVELS 3/6
Crown 8vo.

DERRICK VAUGHAN, NOVELIST. By EDNA LYALL.

MARGERY OF QUETHER. By S. BARING GOULD.

JACQUETTA. By S. BARING GOULD.

SUBJECT TO VANITY. By MARGARET BENSON.

THE SIGN OF THE SPIDER. By BERTRAM MITFORD.

THE MOVING FINGER. By MARY GAUNT.

JACO TRELOAR. By J. H. PEARCE.

THE DANCE OF THE HOURS. By 'VERA.'

A WOMAN OF FORTY. By ESMÉ STUART.

A CUMBERER OF THE GROUND. By CONSTANCE SMITH.

THE SIN OF ANGELS. By EVELYN DICKINSON.

AUT DIABOLUS AUT NIHIL. By X. L.

THE COMING OF CUCULAIN. By STANDISH O'GRADY.

THE GODS GIVE MY DONKEY WINGS. By ANGUS EVAN ABBOTT.

THE STAR GAZERS. By G. MANVILLE FENN.

THE POISON OF ASPS. By R. ORTON PROWSE.

THE QUIET MRS. FLEMING. By R. PRYCE.

DISENCHANTMENT. By F. MABEL ROBINSON.

THE SQUIRE OF WANDALES. By A. SHIELD.

A REVEREND GENTLEMAN. By J. M. COBBAN.

A DEPLORABLE AFFAIR. By W. E. NORRIS.
A CAVALIER'S LADYE. By Mrs. DICKER.
THE PRODIGALS. By Mrs. OLIPHANT.
THE SUPPLANTER. By P. NEUMANN.
A MAN WITH BLACK EYELASHES. By H. A. KENNEDY.
A HANDFUL OF EXOTICS. By S. GORDON.
AN ODD EXPERIMENT. By HANNAH LYNCH.

HALF-CROWN NOVELS   2/6
A Series of Novels by popular Authors.

1. HOVENDEN, V.C. By F. MABEL ROBINSON.
2. ELI'S CHILDREN. By G. MANVILLE FENN.
3. A DOUBLE KNOT. By G. MANVILLE FENN.
4. DISARMED. By M. BETHAM EDWARDS.
5. A MARRIAGE AT SEA. By W. CLARK RUSSELL.
6. IN TENT AND BUNGALOW. By the Author of 'Indian Idylls.'
7. MY STEWARDSHIP. By E. M'QUEEN GRAY.
8. JACK'S FATHER. By W. E. NORRIS.
9. JIM B.
10. THE PLAN OF CAMPAIGN. By F. MABEL ROBINSON.
11. MR. BUTLER'S WARD. By F. MABEL ROBINSON.
12. A LOST ILLUSION. By LESLIE KEITH.

Lynn Linton. THE TRUE HISTORY OF JOSHUA DAVID-
SON, Christian and Communist. By E. LYNN LINTON. *Eleventh
Edition. Post 8vo.* 1s.

Books for Boys and Girls   3/6
A Series of Books by well-known Authors, well illustrated.

1. THE ICELANDER'S SWORD. By S. BARING GOULD.
2. TWO LITTLE CHILDREN AND CHING. By EDITH E. CUTHELL.
3. TODDLEBEN'S HERO. By M. M. BLAKE.
4. ONLY A GUARD-ROOM DOG. By EDITH E. CUTHELL.
5. THE DOCTOR OF THE JULIET. By HARRY COLLING-WOOD.
6. MASTER ROCKAFELLAR'S VOYAGE. By W. CLARK RUSSELL.
7. SYD BELTON : Or, The Boy who would not go to Sea. By G. MANVILLE FENN.

The Peacock Library

A Series of Books for Girls by well-known Authors, handsomely bound in blue and silver, and well illustrated. **3/6**

1. A PINCH OF EXPERIENCE. By L. B. WALFORD.
2. THE RED GRANGE. By Mrs. MOLESWORTH.
3. THE SECRET OF MADAME DE MONLUC. By the Author of 'Mdle Mori.'
4. DUMPS. By Mrs. PARR, Author of 'Adam and Eve.'
5. OUT OF THE FASHION. By L. T. MEADE.
6. A GIRL OF THE PEOPLE. By L. T. MEADE.
7. HEPSY GIPSY. By L. T. MEADE. *2s. 6d.*
8. THE HONOURABLE MISS. By L. T. MEADE.
9. MY LAND OF BEULAH. By Mrs. LEITH ADAMS.

University Extension Series

A series of books on historical, literary, and scientific subjects, suitable for extension students and home-reading circles. Each volume is complete in itself, and the subjects are treated by competent writers in a broad and philosophic spirit.

Edited by J. E. SYMES, M.A.,
Principal of University College, Nottingham.

Crown 8vo. Price (with some exceptions) 2s. 6d.

The following volumes are ready :—

THE INDUSTRIAL HISTORY OF ENGLAND. By H. DE B. GIBBINS, D.Litt., M.A., late Scholar of Wadham College, Oxon., Cobden Prizeman. *Fifth Edition, Revised. With Maps and Plans. 3s.*

'A compact and clear story of our industrial development. A study of this concise but luminous book cannot fail to give the reader a clear insight into the principal phenomena of our industrial history. The editor and publishers are to be congratulated on this first volume of their venture, and we shall look with expectant interest for the succeeding volumes of the series.'—*University Extension Journal.*

A HISTORY OF ENGLISH POLITICAL ECONOMY. By L. L. PRICE, M.A., Fellow of Oriel College, Oxon. *Second Edition.*

PROBLEMS OF POVERTY: An Inquiry into the Industrial Conditions of the Poor. By J. A. HOBSON, M.A. *Third Edition.*

VICTORIAN POETS. By A. SHARP.

THE FRENCH REVOLUTION. By J. E. SYMES, M.A.

PSYCHOLOGY. By F. S. GRANGER, M.A.

THE EVOLUTION OF PLANT LIFE: Lower Forms.   By G. MASSEE.
With Illustrations.

AIR AND WATER.   Professor V. B. LEWES, M.A.   *Illustrated.*

THE CHEMISTRY OF LIFE AND HEALTH.   By C. W. KIMMINS,
M.A.   *Illustrated.*

THE MECHANICS OF DAILY LIFE.   By V. P. SELLS, M.A.   *Illustrated.*

ENGLISH SOCIAL REFORMERS.   H. DE B. GIBBINS, D.Litt., M.A.

ENGLISH TRADE AND FINANCE IN THE SEVENTEENTH
CENTURY.   By W. A. S. HEWINS, B.A.

THE CHEMISTRY OF FIRE.   The Elementary Principles of Chemistry.
By M. M. PATTISON MUIR, M.A.   *Illustrated.*

A TEXT-BOOK OF AGRICULTURAL BOTANY.   By M. C. POTTER,
M.A.. F.L.S.   *Illustrated.*   3s. 6d.

THE VAULT OF HEAVEN.   A Popular Introduction to Astronomy.
By R. A. GREGORY.   *With numerous Illustrations.*

METEOROLOGY.   The Elements of Weather and Climate.   By H. N.
DICKSON, F.R.S.E., F.R. Met. Soc.   *Illustrated.*

A MANUAL OF ELECTRICAL SCIENCE.   By GEORGE J. BURCH,
M.A.   *With numerous Illustrations.*   3s.

THE EARTH.   An Introduction to Physiography.   By EVAN SMALL, M.A.
Illustrated.

INSECT LIFE.   By F. W. THEOBALD, M.A.   *Illustrated.*

ENGLISH POETRY FROM BLAKE TO BROWNING.   By W. M.
DIXON, M.A.

ENGLISH LOCAL GOVERNMENT.   By E. JENKS, M.A., Professor of
Law at University College, Liverpool.

THE GREEK VIEW OF LIFE.   By G. L. DICKINSON, Fellow of King's
College, Cambridge.   *Second Edition.*

Social Questions of To-day

Edited by H. DE B. GIBBINS, D.Litt., M.A.
Crown 8vo.   2s. 6d.

2/6

A series of volumes upon those topics of social, economic,
and industrial interest that are at the present moment fore-
most in the public mind.   Each volume of the series is written by an
author who is an acknowledged authority upon the subject with which
he deals.

The following Volumes of the Series are ready :—

TRADE UNIONISM—NEW AND OLD.   By G. HOWELL, Author of
' The Conflicts of Capital and Labour.'   *Second Edition.*

THE CO-OPERATIVE MOVEMENT TO-DAY.   By G. J. HOLYOAKE,
Author of 'The History of Co-Operation.'   *Second Edition.*

MUTUAL THRIFT.   By Rev. J. FROME WILKINSON, M.A., Author of
' The Friendly Society Movement.'

PROBLEMS OF POVERTY : An Inquiry into the Industrial Conditions of the Poor. By J. A. HOBSON, M.A. *Third Edition.*

THE COMMERCE OF NATIONS. By C. F. BASTAPLE, M.A., Professor of Economics at Trinity College, Dublin.

THE ALIEN INVASION. By W. H. WILKINS, B.A., Secretary to the Society for Preventing the Immigration of Destitute Aliens.

THE RURAL EXODUS. By P. ANDERSON GRAHAM.

LAND NATIONALIZATION. By HAROLD COX, B.A.

A SHORTER WORKING DAY. By H. DE B. GIBBINS, D.Litt., M.A., and R. A. HADFIELD, of the Hecla Works, Sheffield.

BACK TO THE LAND : An Inquiry into the Cure for Rural Depopulation. By H. E. MOORE.

TRUSTS, POOLS AND CORNERS: As affecting Commerce and Industry. By J. STEPHEN JEANS, M.R.I., F.S.S.

THE FACTORY SYSTEM. By R. COOKE TAYLOR.

THE STATE AND ITS CHILDREN. By GERTRUDE TUCKWELL.

WOMEN'S WORK. By LADY DILKE, Miss BULLEY, and Miss WHITLEY.

MUNICIPALITIES AT WORK. The Municipal Policy of Six Great Towns, and its Influence on their Social Welfare. By FREDERICK DOLMAN.

SOCIALISM AND MODERN THOUGHT. By M. KAUFMANN.

THE HOUSING OF THE WORKING CLASSES. By R. F. BOWMAKER.

MODERN CIVILIZATION IN SOME OF ITS ECONOMIC ASPECTS. By W. CUNNINGHAM, D.D., Fellow of Trinity College, Cambridge.

THE PROBLEM OF THE UNEMPLOYED. By J. A. HOBSON, B.A., Author of ' The Problems of Poverty.'

LIFE IN WEST LONDON. By ARTHUR SHERWELL, M.A. *Second Edition.*

Classical Translations

Edited by H. F. FOX, M.A., Fellow and Tutor of Brasenose College, Oxford.

Messrs. Methuen are issuing a New Series of Translations from the Greek and Latin Classics.   They have enlisted the services of some of the best Oxford and Cambridge Scholars, and it is their intention that the Series shall be distinguished by literary excellence as well as by scholarly accuracy.

ÆSCHYLUS—Agamemnon, Chöephoroe, Eumenides. Translated by LEWIS CAMPBELL, LL.D., late Professor of Greek at St. Andrews, 5*s.*

CICERO—De Oratore I.   Translated by E. N. P. MOOR, M.A. 3*s.* 6*d.*

CICERO — Select Orations (Pro Milone, Pro Murena, Philippic II., In Catilinam). Translated by H. E. D. BLAKISTON, M.A., Fellow and Tutor of Trinity College, Oxford. 5*s.*

CICERO—De Natura Deorum. Translated by F. BROOKS, M.A., late Scholar of Balliol College, Oxford. 3s. 6d.

LUCIAN—Six Dialogues (Nigrinus, Icaro-Menippus, The Cock, The Ship, The Parasite, The Lover of Falsehood). Translated by S. T. IRWIN, M.A., Assistant Master at Clifton; late Scholar of Exeter College, Oxford. 3s. 6d.

SOPHOCLES—Electra and Ajax. Translated by E. D. A. MORSHEAD, M.A., Assistant Master at Winchester. 2s. 6d.

TACITUS—Agricola and Germania. Translated by R. B. TOWNSHEND, late Scholar of Trinity College, Cambridge. 2s. 6d.

Educational Books

CLASSICAL

PLAUTI BACCHIDES. Edited with Introduction, Commentary, and Critical Notes by J. M'COSH, M.A. *Fcap. 4to.* 12s. 6d.
'The notes are copious, and contain a great deal of information that is good and useful.'—*Classical Review.*

TACITI AGRICOLI. With Introduction, Notes, Map, etc. By R. F. DAVIS, M.A., Assistant Master at Weymouth College. *Crown 8vo.* 2s.

TACITI GERMANIA. By the same Editor. *Crown 8vo.* 2s.

HERODOTUS: EASY SELECTIONS. With Vocabulary. By A. C. LIDDELL, M.A., Assistant Master at Nottingham High School. *Fcap. 8vo.* 1s. 6d.

SELECTIONS FROM THE ODYSSEY. By E. D. STONE, M.A., late Assistant Master at Eton. *Fcap. 8vo.* 1s. 6d.

PLAUTUS: THE CAPTIVI. Adapted for Lower Forms by J. H. FRESSE, M.A., late Fellow of St. John's, Cambridge. 1s. 6d.

DEMOSTHENES AGAINST CONON AND CALLICLES. Edited with Notes and Vocabulary, by F. DARWIN SWIFT, M.A., formerly Scholar of Queen's College, Oxford; Assistant Master at Denstone College. *Fcap. 8vo.* 2s.

GERMAN

A COMPANION GERMAN GRAMMAR. By H. DE B. GIBBINS, D.Litt., M.A., Assistant Master at Nottingham High School. *Crown 8vo.* 1s. 6d.

GERMAN PASSAGES FOR UNSEEN TRANSLATION. By E. M'QUEEN GRAY. *Crown 8vo.* 2s. 6d.

SCIENCE

THE WORLD OF SCIENCE. Including Chemistry, Heat, Light, Sound, Magnetism, Electricity, Botany, Zoology, Physiology, Astronomy, and Geology. By R. ELLIOTT STEEL, M.A., F.C.S. 147 Illustrations. *Second Edition. Crown 8vo.* 2s. 6d.
'If Mr. Steel is to be placed second to any for this quality of lucidity, it is only to Huxley himself; and to be named in the same breath with this master of the craft of teaching is to be accredited with the clearness of style and simplicity of arrangement that belong to thorough mastery of a subject.'—*Parents' Review.*

ELEMENTARY LIGHT. By R. E. STEEL. With numerous Illustrations. *Crown 8vo.* 4s. 6d.

ENGLISH

ENGLISH RECORDS. A Companion to the History of England. By
H. E. MALDEN, M.A. *Crown 8vo.* 3s. 6d.

A book which aims at concentrating information upon dates, genealogy, officials, con-
stitutional documents, etc., which is usually found scattered in different volumes.

THE ENGLISH CITIZEN: HIS RIGHTS AND DUTIES. By H. E.
MALDEN, M.A. 1s. 6d.

'The book goes over the same ground as is traversed in the school books on this
subject written to satisfy the requirements of the Education Code. It would
serve admirably the purposes of a text-book, as it is well based in historical
facts, and keeps quite clear of party matters.'—*Scotsman.*

METHUEN'S COMMERCIAL SERIES

Edited by H. DE B. GIBBINS, D.Litt., M.A.

BRITISH COMMERCE AND COLONIES FROM ELIZABETH TO
VICTORIA. By H. DE B. GIBBINS, D.Litt., M.A., Author of 'The
Industrial History of England,' etc., etc., 2s.

COMMERCIAL EXAMINATION PAPERS. By H. DE B. GIBBINS,
D.Litt., M.A., 1s. 6d.

THE ECONOMICS OF COMMERCE. By H. DE B. GIBBINS, D.Litt.,
M.A. 1s. 6d.

A MANUAL OF FRENCH COMMERCIAL CORRESPONDENCE.
By S. E. BALLY, Modern Language Master at the Manchester Grammar
School. 2s.

GERMAN COMMERCIAL CORRESPONDENCE. By S. E. BALLY,
Assistant Master at the Manchester Grammar School. *Crown 8vo.* 2s. 6d.

A FRENCH COMMERCIAL READER. By S. E. BALLY. 2s.

COMMERCIAL GEOGRAPHY, with special reference to Trade Routes,
New Markets, and Manufacturing Districts. By L. W. LYDE, M.A., of
the Academy, Glasgow. 2s.

A PRIMER OF BUSINESS. By S. JACKSON, M.A. 1s. 6d.

COMMERCIAL ARITHMETIC. By F. G. TAYLOR, M.A. 1s. 6d.

PRÉCIS WRITING AND OFFICE CORRESPONDENCE. By E. E.
WHITFIELD, M.A.

WORKS BY A. M. M. STEDMAN, M.A.

INITIA LATINA: Easy Lessons on Elementary Accidence. *Second Edition.*
Fcap. 8vo. 1s.

FIRST LATIN LESSONS. *Fourth Edition. Crown 8vo.* 2s.

FIRST LATIN READER. With Notes adapted to the Shorter Latin
Primer and Vocabulary. *Third Edition.* 18mo. 1s. 6d.

EASY SELECTIONS FROM CAESAR. Part I. The Helvetian War.
18mo. 1s.

EASY SELECTIONS FROM LIVY. Part I. The Kings of Rome. 18mo.
1s. 6d.

EASY LATIN PASSAGES FOR UNSEEN TRANSLATION. *Fifth
Edition. Fcap. 8vo.* 1s. 6d.

EXEMPLA LATINA. First Lessons in Latin Accidence. With Vocabulary.
Crown 8vo. 1s.

EASY LATIN EXERCISES ON THE SYNTAX OF THE SHORTER
AND REVISED LATIN PRIMER. With Vocabulary. *Sixth
Edition. Crown 8vo.* 2s. 6d. Issued with the consent of Dr. Kennedy.

THE LATIN COMPOUND SENTENCE : Rules and Exercises. *Crown 8vo. 1s. 6d.* With Vocabulary. *2s.*

NOTANDA QUAEDAM : Miscellaneous Latin Exercises on Common Rules and Idioms. *Third Edition. Fcap. 8vo. 1s. 6d.* With Vocabulary. *2s.*

LATIN VOCABULARIES FOR REPETITION : Arranged according to Subjects. *Sixth Edition. Fcap. 8vo. 1s. 6d.*

A VOCABULARY OF LATIN IDIOMS AND PHRASES. *18mo. 1s.*

STEPS TO GREEK. *18mo. 1s.*

EASY GREEK PASSAGES FOR UNSEEN TRANSLATION. *Second Edition. Fcap. 8vo. 1s. 6d.*

GREEK VOCABULARIES FOR REPETITION. Arranged according to Subjects. *Second Edition. Fcap. 8vo. 1s. 6d.*

GREEK TESTAMENT SELECTIONS. For the use of Schools. *Third Edition.* With Introduction, Notes, and Vocabulary. *Fcap. 8vo. 2s. 6d.*

STEPS TO FRENCH. *Second Edition. 18mo. 8d.*

FIRST FRENCH LESSONS. *Second Edition. Crown 8vo. 1s.*

EASY FRENCH PASSAGES FOR UNSEEN TRANSLATION. *Second Edition. Fcap. 8vo. 1s. 6d.*

EASY FRENCH EXERCISES ON ELEMENTARY SYNTAX. With Vocabulary. *Crown 8vo. 2s. 6d.*

FRENCH VOCABULARIES FOR REPETITION : Arranged according to Subjects. *Fifth Edition. Fcap. 8vo. 1s.*

SCHOOL EXAMINATION SERIES

EDITED BY A. M. M. STEDMAN, M.A. *Crown 8vo. 2s. 6d.*

FRENCH EXAMINATION PAPERS IN MISCELLANEOUS GRAMMAR AND IDIOMS. By A. M. M. STEDMAN, M.A. *Ninth Edition.* A KEY, issued to Tutors and Private Students only, to be had on application to the Publishers. *Fourth Edition. Crown 8vo. 6s. net.*

LATIN EXAMINATION PAPERS IN MISCELLANEOUS GRAMMAR AND IDIOMS. By A. M. M. STEDMAN, M.A. *Seventh Edition.* KEY issued as above. *6s. net.*

GREEK EXAMINATION PAPERS IN MISCELLANEOUS GRAMMAR AND IDIOMS. By A. M. M. STEDMAN, M.A. *Fifth Edition.* KEY issued as above. *6s. net.*

GERMAN EXAMINATION PAPERS IN MISCELLANEOUS GRAMMAR AND IDIOMS. By R. J. MORICH, Manchester. *Fifth Edition.* KEY issued as above. *6s. net.*

HISTORY AND GEOGRAPHY EXAMINATION PAPERS. By C. H. SPENCE, M.A., Clifton College.

SCIENCE EXAMINATION PAPERS. By R. E. STEEL, M.A., F.C.S., Chief Natural Science Master, Bradford Grammar School. *In two vols.* Part I. Chemistry ; Part II. Physics.

GENERAL KNOWLEDGE EXAMINATION PAPERS. By A. M. M. STEDMAN, M.A. *Third Edition.* KEY issued as above. *7s. net.*

Printed by T. and A. CONSTABLE, Printers to Her Majesty
at the Edinburgh University Press

Printed in Great Britain
by Amazon